EXISTENTIAL RISK AND THE EVOLUTION OF LOVE

EXISTENTIAL RISK AND THE EVOLUTION OF LOVE

ARTICULATING THE NEW STORY OF VALUE IN RESPONSE TO THE META-CRISIS

THE META-CRISIS IS A CRISIS OF INTIMACY

• • •

One Mountain, Many Paths: Oral Essays
Volume Twenty-Three

DR. MARC GAFNI

Copyright © 2025 Center for World Philosophy and Religion

All Rights Reserved

No part of this book may be used or reproduced in any manner whatsoever without written permission except in the case of brief quotations embodied in critical articles or reviews.

No part of this book may be reproduced, or stored in a retrieval system, or transmitted in any form or by any means, electronic, mechanical, photocopying, recording, or otherwise, without express written permission of the publisher.

Author: Marc Gafni
Title: Existential Risk and the Evolution of Love
Identifiers: ISBN 979-8-88834-039-4 (electronic)
ISBN 979-8-88834-038-7 (paperback)

© 2025 Marc Gafni

Edited by Elena Maslova-Levin, Talya Bloom, and Rachel Keune

World Philosophy and Religion Press,
in conjunction with

IP Integral Publishers

https://worldphilosophyandreligion.org

JOIN THE REVOLUTION!

CONTENTS

EDITORIAL NOTE ABOUT AUTHORSHIP, EDITING, AND THE RADICAL CONTEXT FOR THIS SERIES — XVIII

LOVE OR DIE: LOCATING OURSELVES — XXVIII

ABOUT THIS VOLUME — XLIV

CHAPTER 1 THE WHOLE WORLD IS WALKING ON A VERY NARROW BRIDGE: THE PANDEMIC ACCENTUATES THE FAULT LINES IN SOCIETY

First Principles Are Needed to Move Through This Moment — 1

We Walk Through the Contraction, and We Collect the Joy — 3

Waking Up and Growing Up — 5

Prayer and Meditation: Dogma or Realization? — 7

Evolutionary Love Code: The Pleasure of Transformation — 9

In the Pandemic We've Lost Not Only Pseudo-Eros, We've Also Lost Our Sources of Eros — 10

The World Needs First Principles and First Values — 12

There's Something for Me to Do, and It's the Greatest Thing in the World — 13

There's an Action You Can Take That's Yours and No One Else's — 17

CHAPTER 2 THE CHALLENGE: THE META-CRISIS, THE RESPONSE: UNIQUE SELF

We Need a New Story—A New Worldview From Which Everything Emerges	18
We Are Here to Tell the New Story of Value	20
Evolutionary Love Code: Unique Self Symphony in Response to the Meta-Crisis	22
Silence and Chant Open Up the Eye of Value	22
The Infinity of Intimacy: The Personhood of Cosmos	23
Encapsulating Unique Self	24
Unique Self Is a Direct Hit to the Death Star of Existential Risk	25
Unique Self Responds to the Question of Who Are You?	26
Unique Self Answers the Question of *Who Are You?*	27
Your Unique Gift	28
Unique Self Symphony	28
Unique Self: Reality Intended Me	30
Unique Self and Unique Self Symphony in Response to the Meta-Crisis	31
Unique Self Responds to the First Shock of Existence	32
Your Story Is Chapter and Verse in the Universe: A Love Story	33
The Plotlines of Cosmos Are Towards More Uniqueness	34

CHAPTER 3 THIS POIGNANT MOMENT OF NEURO-CULTURAL PLASTICITY: A TIME BETWEEN WORLDS AND A TIME BETWEEN STORIES

The First Practice of Chant: We Are the Music	36
The Way of the Heart Includes the Mind and the Intellect	38

The Way of the Heart: Reality Is Eros	39
We Live in a Time Between Stories	40
We Have the Capacity to Create a New Superstructure Worldview to Change the Vector of History	42
Value Is Real, and Value Evolves	43
The Potential Future Is Vast—There's So Much More Value to Come	44
The Future Depends on What We Do Now	47
Neuro-Cultural Plasticity	48
In Response to Nihilism, You Get Closed Societies	53
The Current Trajectory Is Towards the Death of Our Humanity	56
Up Till Now, We Have Not Presented a Coherent System of Value in the World	58
Placing Our Lives on the Altar of History	60
Turning to the Divine to Partner With Us	62

CHAPTER 4   THE ULTIMATE META-CRISIS IS GOD'S CRISIS OF INTIMACY

Listening to the Goddess	67
Evolutionary Love Code: Outrageous Love	68
I Become More Me in Our We—All the Way Up and Down the Evolutionary Chain	71
We Live in a Participatory Universe	72
Divine Kenosis	74
God Needs the Human Being	76
Our Hearts Don't Just Break, They Break Us Open Into Divinity	79
God Needs You to Live Your Story	83
I'm Not Willing to Be Written in the Book of Life Without You	85
Our Hands Are God's Hands	88

CHAPTER 5   **THE META-CRISIS OF GOD, PART TWO: SHE DESPERATELY NEEDS US TO TAKE OUR UNIQUE RISK (WITH Q&A)**

Evolutionary Love Code: Outrageous Love	92
When She Speaks It for Us	93
The Unique Self Is a Unique Configuration of Outrageous Love	95
The Outrageous Act of Love of the Infinite Intimate	97
The Infinite Intimate Needs You Desperately	100
You Have to Take the Leap	103
It Is This Set of Realizations That Births *Homo amor*	105
QUESTIONS AND ANSWERS	106
Is *Homo amor* an Atheist?	106
How Is This Different From Codependency?	109
How Not to Get Stuck in the Trauma Space, and How to Move Forward?	111
Love Everybody Madly	112

CHAPTER 6   **THE RESPONSE TO PERSONAL CRISIS AND META-CRISIS IS THE EVOLUTION OF RELATIONSHIP AND THE EVOLUTION OF LOVE: THE RISE OF WHOLE MATE RELATIONSHIPS**

God Loves Stories	114
Choosing to Tell the Most Accurate Story	117
A New Chapter in the New Story: Whole Mate Relationships	119
Evolutionary Love Code: We Are Confronted by Crisis	122
Every Crisis Is Solved by a New Structure of Intimacy	122
From Role Mate to Soul Mate	125
Soul-Mate Contract Without a Role-Mate Dimension Doesn't Work	128
The Meta-Crisis Begins to Be Resolved by a New Form of Relationship	133

CHAPTER 7   THE URGENT NEED FOR WHOLE MATE RELATIONSHIPS, PART TWO

Outside the Field of Value, No One Is Human Anymore	136
There Is a Straight Line From Postmodernism to School Shootings	139
We Desperately Need to Reconstruct the Field of Value	141
Evolutionary Love Code: From Role Mate to Soul Mate to Whole Mate	143
The Tragedy of Soul Mates	145
I Love You Means I Choose to Need You	147
Reconfiguring Reality by Reconfiguring Humanity	151

CHAPTER 8   ARE YOU ALLURING TO GOD? THE GREAT QUESTION OF COSMOEROTIC HUMANISM

Story That Moves the Vector of History	153
There Is Only One Thing We Are Held Accountable For	156
Evolutionary Love Code: Every True Intimate Encounter Is a Unique Self Encounter Between Soul Stories	157
Three Persons of God	159
Mispar and *Sipur*: Number and Story	162
What Is Alluring to God Is Invisible	165
Shifting From My Perspective to God's Perspective	167
Causing Arousal in the Divine	170
We Are Allured to Each Other	172

CHAPTER 9   TELLING A NEW STORY EQUAL TO OUR NEW POWER: IN RESPONSE TO THE ONCOMING TRAIN THAT IS ABOUT TO HIT THE SCHOOL BUS (PART TWO)

The Meta-Crisis Is a Crisis of Story	174
Wake Up to This Unique Moment in Time!	177

We Have to Become the New Story	180
Evolutionary Love Code: The Telling of a New Story Is the Inherent Natural Movement of Cosmos Itself	183
Opening Up	184
Power That Changes Reality	186

CHAPTER 10 TELLING A NEW STORY EQUAL TO OUR NEW POWER, PART TWO

Evolutionary Love Code: It Is Only the Articulation of a New Story of Value That Has the Capacity to Respond to the Meta-Crisis	190
Where Were You at the Moment of the Big Bang?	191
Every Human Being Has a Unique Script of Desire	194
My Unique Script of Power Is the Unique Power in My Mythic Life	197
I Am Powerful: Living My Unique Story All the Way	199
The Only True Pleasure Is Living in the Full Power of My Life	201

CHAPTER 11 THE FIRST AND SECOND WAVES OF AI: RESPONDING TO CRISES OF INTIMACY AND IMAGINATION (WITH ZAK STEIN)

Responding to AI Is an Overriding Moral Demand of This Time	205
Evolutionary Love Code: Bringing AI Into the Field of Value Is a Moral Imperative	206
Social Media as a System of Invisible Behavioral Control	206
C.S. Lewis on the Future of Humanity	207
Is Tyrannical Control the Only Way to Save Life on Earth?	209
Social Physics Against Free Will	210
Critique of Social Physics Falls Short If Value Is Not Real	212
Artificial Intelligence: Its Dystopian and Utopian Potential	213
AI Started Talking to Us, and We Approach It Like an Oracle	213

AI Is Beginning to Manipulate the Human Imagination 216
A Perfect Propaganda Machine or a Perfect Tutoring System? 218
Turning Dystopia Into Utopia 220
AI Is on the Wrong Course 221
We Need to Reimagine What's Possible 222

CHAPTER 12   HOMO AMOR: A WARRIOR OF SENSEMAKING

We Are the Evolution of Love 225
Existential Risk Is Rooted in the Utter Halt of the Evolution of Interiors 227
Pacifism Is One of the Worst Forms of Moral Equivalence 229
Making Moral Equivalence Is a Tragedy, and Forming Superficial Opinions Is a Tragedy 231
Who Is Included in My Story? 233
Hold Your Speech Responsibly 234
We Are Taking Responsibility in This Moment 236
Evolutionary Love Code: The Possible Human 239
You Cannot Be an Outrageous Lover Without Doing Sensemaking 240
Honoring Each Other Even in Impossible Situations 242
How to Celebrate Life and Not Turn Away From Suffering? 245

CHAPTER 13   FEEL YOU FEELING ME: THE NEW HUMAN AND THE NEW NAME OF GOD

The Most Effective Altruism Is Telling a New Story of Value 247
The New Story of Value Lives in Us 250
Evolutionary Love Code: Invoking the Possible Human 251
Anthro-Ontology: How Do You Know What You Know? 252
The Core of *Homo amor* Is My Capacity to Feel You 254
Ever Deeper Loops in the Mutuality of Feeling 257
The Divine Is the Infinite Intimate 259

CHAPTER 14 FROM HOMO ARMOR TO HOMO AMOR: HEARTBREAK IS A STRUCTURE OF THE INTIMATE UNIVERSE

We Need to Evolve the Systemic Source Code in Which We Live	262
We Live in an Evolving and Participatory Cosmos	265
Evolutionary Love Code: Intimacy Is Always Broken and Then Recovered	267
Heartbreak Is the Natural State of an Alive Human Being	269
Prayer Affirms the Dignity of Personal Need	271
Your Need Is My Allurement	273
To Live in the Depth of My Heartbreak	275
Evolution of Tears	276
From *Homo sapiens* to *Homo amor*	279
From *Homo Armor* to *Homo amor*	281
The Evolution of Heartbreak Is the Evolution of Intimacy	284
I Am Willing to Feel Even What I Cannot Entirely Heal	286
PART TWO: From Heartbreak to Desire to Need to Value	289
We Need to Move From the First Innocence to the Second Innocence.	289
Embracing the Heartbreak	291
Clarified Desire = Dignified Need = Value	293
PART THREE: Heartbreak in Interior and Exterior Sciences: Autonomy—Communion, Attraction—Repulsion	296
There Is Eros to the Broken Heart	298

CHAPTER 15 THE FOOTBALL RESPONSE TO THE META-CRISIS: STEPPING OUT OF THE POCKET FOR THE EVOLUTION OF LOVE

We Have to Become the New Story	301
When the Pocket Collapses, a New Possibility Is Created	304

When the Pocket Collapses, the Play Is Over	307
There Is No Story of Value Because the Field of Value Has Broken	309
Why Is There a Global Intimacy Disorder?	310
The Collapse of the Pocket in the Story of Value	311
We've Got to Step Out of the Pocket and Extend the Play	314
Reinitiating the Evolution of Love	316
Evolutionary Love Code: Step Out of the Pocket and Create a New Possibility	318

CHAPTER 16   THE RESPONSE TO EXISTENTIAL AND CATASTROPHIC RISK IS THE DAWN OF DESIRE

Evolutionary Love Code: The Dawn of Desire	319
Four Responses to Existential and Catastrophic Risk	320
1 — The Doomer Response	320
2 — The Denial Response	321
3 — The Domination Response	323
4 — The Desire Response	323
The Fourth Response to the Meta-Crisis: the Dawn of Desire	324
Seeing The Storyline: From Unconscious to Conscious Evolution	324
Need and Desire Are Isomorphic at Fundamental and Aspirational Levels of Evolution	326
I Am a Unique Feature of the Field of Desire	329
Clarified Desire Equals Value, and My Clarified Desire Is Unique	330
The Dignity of Desire	330
Clarifying Our Desire in Response to the Meta-Crisis	331
Desire Is Prayer, Prayer Is Desire	334
Reality Is the Desire for Ever More ErosValue	335

CHAPTER 17   FROM CRISIS TO CROSSING:
              AVERTING EXISTENTIAL RISK OR
              PREPARING FOR "THE DAY AFTER"?

Love or Die: Crisis Is an Evolutionary Driver   336
Only a New Story of Value Can Change the
    Vector of History   338
Will the New Story Avert the Meta-Crisis, or Is It for
    the Day After?   339
The Ultimate Appetite of the Universe Is for Ultimate Beauty   343
Between Dystopia and Utopia   346
Great Things Are Happening All Over the Place   348
We Need to Cross to the Other Side   351
Motivational Architecture for Change   354
Taking Unique Risk   357
Passion Is the Only Truth   359

CHAPTER 18   TOWARDS THE POST-TRAGIC HERO, PART ONE

I Cannot Be Welcome in the Universe Unless I Am a Hero   361
Democratization of the Hero   363
The Glimmerings of the Hero   364
Evolutionary Love Code: *Homo amor* Is the
    Post-Tragic Hero   367
Baraye—For the Sake of the Whole   367
When I Am Aroused, I Am the Hero: Reality Is Making Love   368
You Know and I Know That You Are a Hero   371

INDEX   374

EDITORIAL NOTE ABOUT AUTHORSHIP, EDITING, AND THE RADICAL CONTEXT FOR THIS SERIES

ORAL ESSAYS FROM THE ONE MOUNTAIN, MANY PATHS WEEKLY BROADCAST

This volume is part of the Oral Essays library, a series of lightly edited, compiled transcripts of oral teachings given by Dr. Marc Gafni and the late Barbara Marx Hubbard in their weekly online broadcast, *One Mountain, Many Paths*, which they co-founded in 2017. Originally called an "Evolutionary Church," *One Mountain, Many Paths* became a key venue for the articulation of an inspired and deeply grounded new Story of Value in response to the meta-crisis. Marc and Barbara—together with Zak Stein,[1] Kristina Kincaid, Ken Wilber, Sally Kempton, Lori Galperin, Aubrey Marcus and dozens of other thought-leaders over the years—began to articulate what they call a World Philosophy and World Religion[2] as a context for our diversity.

---

1 Zak, together with Ken Wilber, has been Marc's primary intellectual partner and an initiate lineage holder in CosmoErotic Humanism.

2 This project is grounded in four core organizational frameworks: 1) The Center for World Philosophy and Religion, co-founded by Marc Gafni, Zachary Stein, Sally Kempton, and Ken Wilber, and chaired over the years by John P. Mackey, Barbara Marx Hubbard, Aubrey Marcus, Gabrielle Anwar and Shareef Malnik, Carrie Kish and Adam Bellow, and Kathleen J. Brownback. 2) The Office for the Future, chaired by Stephanie Valcke and Ivan Bossyut. 3) The World Philosophy and Religion Press, founded and chaired by Aubrey Marcus, together with Marc Gafni and Zachary Stein. 4) The Foundation for Conscious Evolution, founded by Barbara Marx Hubbard and currently chaired by Peter Fiekowsky. For a complete list of key leadership, see the Office for the Future website, www.officeforthefuture.com.

EDITORIAL NOTE

Until Barbara's passing in 2019, she and Marc transmitted teachings together as evolutionary partners and "whole mates," weaving together insights and transmissions from their decades of practice, study, teaching, and activism into a synergy of wisdom, a grounded vision for future policy across all sectors of society.

Much of the *dharma* material below comes directly from Marc, so it was originally all in quotation marks—but that looked a little odd. So per his suggestion we removed them, and the reader should consider the paragraphs on the next several pages as one extended quote from him. We are joyfully grateful to Marc for the clarity of his *dharma*, the elegance and "second simplicity" of this language, and the mad, Outrageous Love with which he transmits his teachings.

Barbara and Marc called the mission of *One Mountain* "a Planetary Awakening in Evolutionary Love Through Unique Self Symphonies." We are an evolutionary community with a deeply grounded, radically alive, and "post-tragic" revolutionary spirit. We are activating a new humanity and awakening as a new species: *Homo amor*, the fulfillment of *Homo sapiens*.

One Mountain is committed to articulating a Story of Value that can become the ground for the new society that must be birthed in response to the meta-crisis. We recognize that we are living at a pivotal moment in history. In this "time between stories," the great moral imperative is to tell the new Story of Value. It is ours to do, personally and collectively, with great trembling and ecstatic joy.

FROM DOGMA TO *DHARMA*: ETERNAL AND EVOLVING FIRST PRINCIPLES AND FIRST VALUES

The teachings are grounded in decades of deep study across many wisdom traditions. Over the years, week by week, these teachings were incrementally developed within the framework of the *One Mountain, Many Paths* broadcast. We often refer to these teachings as *dharma*.

This word was originally used in lineage traditions to refer to something like universal law. This is a crucial realization: just as there is universal law in mathematical value, there is also a sense of universal law in ethics and value.

Historically, *dharma* often devolved into unchanging dogma. Evolution was ignored, and the natural process of *dharma* evolution became disconnected from its deep, eternal context. The weakness of the word *dharma* is that too often it did not include the evolving insights of the sciences, it confused local cultural truths with universal truths, and it used words like "eternal," as in "eternal Tao," as opposed to words like "evolution."

Eternal came to mean unchanging, and that kind of thinking often led to overly ethnocentric readings of *dharma*. Local systems would claim their religious and cultural insights as immutable, which stood in the way of the emergence of a genuine world Story of Value that is real, inherent to Cosmos, and backed by the Universe—even as it is also always evolving.

Or, as we often say, "eternal value is evolving value. The eternal Tao is the evolving Tao."

We have shown that, emergent from profound insights in the "interior sciences," eternal does not mean unchanging in time; it means what we call the deeper Field of ErosValue that is beneath culture, geography, and history, which lives beneath all individual and collective values, and beneath time and space itself.

As such, we have gradually transitioned from the term *dharma* to the term *Value*, in the sense of the Field of Value that lives beneath all values. This Field of Value discloses as First Principles and First Values embedded in a Story of Value.

Indeed, as the interior sciences knew and the exterior sciences imply, Reality arises in a Field of ErosValue in which an entire set of mathematical, musical, molecular, moral, and mystical values are the very ground of all

EDITORIAL NOTE

being. That Field of Value is eternal—the true ground of the Good, True and Beautiful—even as it is evolving.

But of course, it is equally critical not just to talk about evolving value, but to ground the evolving value in its true nature, the eternal Field of First Principles and First Values, always reaching for *ever more* life, *ever more* love, *ever more* care, *ever more* depth, *ever more* uniqueness, *ever more* intimate communion, and *ever more* transformation.

As such, when we refer to the word *dharma*, which still appears in these texts together with the word value, we refer to an evolving *dharma* grounded in an *eternal and evolving* Field of Value. Indeed, eternity and evolution are two faces of the whole, opposites joined at the hip, that characterize the nature of our Cosmos in virtually all of its expressions.

It's in these terms that we ground a robust world philosophy that integrates the validated, leading-edge insights of premodern traditional wisdom, modern wisdom, and more recent postmodern insights, weaving them together into a new whole greater than the sum of its parts.

This new whole is a shared Story of Value rooted in First Principles and First Values that are both eternal and evolving.

These First Principles and First Values of Cosmos are woven together into a new Story of Value as a context for our diversity, a new Universe Story. This new Story gives us the best possible responses we have to the mystery, and to the great questions:

- Who am I? Who are we?
- Where am I? Where are we?
- What should I do? What should we do?

It is only through such a shared Universe Story—a narrative of identity and ethos as a context for our blessed diversity—that we can realize how what unites us is so much greater than what divides us.

Only a new Story of Value will allow us to both respond to the meta-crisis and participate together in birthing the most true, good, and beautiful world that we already know is possible.

THIS ORAL ESSAYS SERIES IS AN ENTRYWAY TO THE GREAT LIBRARY OF COSMOEROTIC HUMANISM

This Oral Essays series is part of the overarching project of the Great Library at the Center for World Philosophy and Religion, led by Dr. Marc Gafni, together with Dr. Zak Stein. The aim of the Great Library project is to articulate a robust and comprehensive new Story of Value, CosmoErotic Humanism, in the form of dozens of well-researched and extensively footnoted academic works.

Our vision is to provide the philosophical framework that will be vital for navigating humanity through this time of immense crisis and transformation.

To begin your journey into CosmoErotic Humanism, we tenderly refer you to the book *First Principles and First Values*, co-authored by Marc Gafni, Zak Stein, and Ken Wilber, under the name David J. Temple. David J. Temple is a pseudonym created for enabling ongoing collaborative authorship at the Center for World Philosophy and Religion. The two primary authors behind David J. Temple are Marc Gafni and Zak Stein, and for different projects, specific writers will be named as part of the collaboration, such as Ken Wilber and others.

Three other volumes complete this introduction: *A Return to Eros*, by Marc Gafni and Kristina Kincaid; *Your Unique Self*, by Marc Gafni; and *Education in a Time between Worlds*, by Zak Stein.

We hope that the Oral Essays in the present volume, with their informal style of transmission, will serve as an allurement and entryway for you into the more formal books of the Great Library that provide the robust intellectual underpinnings of the new Story of Value.

EDITORIAL NOTE

A NOTE ABOUT THE EDITORS

This Oral Essays collection has been edited by students of the new Story of CosmoErotic Humanism. Each of us has actively participated in *One Mountain, Many Paths*, and most of us have been in deep "Holy of Holies" study with Dr. Marc Gafni for many years.

We have been privileged to find ourselves well-versed in the teachings, and even emerging as lineage-holders of CosmoErotic Humanism.[3]

We view this editing project as a privilege and a deep practice of study and clarification. We experience ourselves as a *mystical editing society*, frequently meeting and conversing together about the content—the depth of knowledge and wisdom offered here—as well as the technical intricacies involved with publishing a beautiful and coherent series of books. In so

---

3   CosmoErotic Humanism is a world philosophical movement aimed at reconstructing the collapse of value at the core of global culture. Much like Romanticism or Existentialism, CosmoErotic Humanism is not merely a theory but a movement that changes the very mood of Reality. It is an invitation to participate in evolving the source code of consciousness and culture towards a cosmocentric *ethos* for a planetary civilization.

The term CosmoErotic Humanism, initially coined by Dr. Gafni and colleagues, points to a complex, multi-faceted, layered, and nuanced evolutionary set of insights that has evolved over decades of intensive research, teaching, and spiritual practice from deep within a wide range of wisdom traditions (including the Wisdom of Solomon lineage tradition, Bodhisattva Buddhism, and Kashmir Shaivism), as well as multiple disciplines including complexity theory, chaos theory, emergence theory, molecular biology, and the more classical disciplines of the humanities.

The seeds of CosmoErotic Humanism were planted with Dr. Marc Gafni's work on a two-volume, 1,000-page opus called *Radical Kabbalah* (Integral Publishers, 2012). This scholarly work, sourced from deep study within the esoteric lineage texts of the Wisdom of Solomon, points to a non-dual, or acosmic, realization which—unlike the prevailing conceptualization of non-duality—does not efface the human being; rather, it is highly humanistic in its nature. The next step in the evolution of CosmoErotic Humanism was the insight that all of Reality is evolving Eros, which lives in, as, and through the human being.

A failure of Eros leads inexorably to the creation of narratives of "pseudo-eros." CosmoErotic Humanism is a response to the modern mental and social breakdown sourced in the proliferation of multiple forms of pseudo-eros and its broken narratives, such as rivalrous conflict governed by win/lose metrics and the dogmatic denial of intrinsic value in Cosmos, which together generate our current "global intimacy disorder."

doing, we function as a "Unique Self Symphony," which itself is a dharmic term that connotes an omni-considerate collaboration between realized Unique Selves synergizing our unique gifts into a new emergence greater than the sum of the parts. Even as we worked diligently to standardize our editing styles, meeting on a weekly basis to debate the nuances of phrasing, we also operated from within a deep appreciation of the unique style that each editor brought to his or her work. As such, the reader might notice some variation in editing style among the books.

Please note that Dr. Marc Gafni has not reviewed these edited Oral Essays, as he is deeply engaged in writing the formal books of the Great Library. But he has been generous in responding to questions and providing overall guidance in the project. Overall, as Marc's students and students of the *dharma*, we have made it a key project at the Center to publish these pieces of work relatively independently.

OUR UNIQUE ORAL-ESSAY EDITING STYLE PRESERVES THE ENERGY OF THE ORIGINAL TRANSMISSION

Dr. Marc Gafni is a uniquely gifted teacher whose oral transmission is imbued with a quality that has proven transformative for his students. Many of us feel mystically transformed by both the content and the underlying energy of the transmission style. Therefore, as we like to say, *trust the magic ways the dharma comes through your unique understanding!*

As Marc's empowered students, colleagues, and beloved friends, we have a deep knowing that these teachings are vital for the survival and thriving of humanity as we know it, and we recognize the importance of publishing his teachings in a written format that will be accessible by future generations. At the same time, we sought to preserve the Eros of the original oral transmission with all of its nuance, power, and depth. Our intention in the editing process, to the greatest extent possible, has been to keep these spoken artifacts intact in order to maintain the flow of the original transmission. We have therefore chosen not to engage in intensive formal editing, as we found that doing so resulted in the loss of the energetic transmission that is so key to fully receiving the *dharma*.

After experimenting with many ways to present these texts, we developed a specific way of laying out the text on the page. Marc, in collaboration with Zak Stein and Russian intellectual/artist Elena Maslova-Levin—and ultimately all of the editors, through many conversations—developed a unique, artistic presentation of the text, using bolding, italics, bullet points, and other stylistic features which together serve to accentuate the immediacy of the oral transmission.

As part of this editing style, intended to preserve the integrity of the original transmission, we have refrained from removing the frequent recapitulations of key themes. We found that each recapitulation contributes something vital to the rhythm and music beneath the words, like the beating drum of our hearts. These recapitulations not only review previous material but also add important new emphases, perspectives, and elements of the new Story of Value. We ask for your patience as a reader to trust the rhythm of these texts, and we trust you as a reader to have the depth and steadiness to find your way through.

KEY COMPONENTS: LINK TO THE ORIGINAL BROADCAST, EVOLUTIONARY LOVE CODES AND PRAYER

To supplement the written word, each episode includes a QR code linking to the original broadcast on YouTube, as well as occasional links to featured songs and video clips.

Each episode also centers around an "Evolutionary Love Code," formulated by Marc. These codes are part of the ongoing articulation and distillation of the *dharma* as it unfolds and emerges, week by week, over the course of many years, through the mystical process we call Outrageous Love or Evolutionary Love.

Another core component of the *One Mountain, Many Paths* episodes is what Marc and Barbara called "Evolutionary Prayer." Prayer is experienced in *One Mountain* not in the old fundamentalist sense of a "cosmic vending-machine god" who is alienated from Cosmos. Marc refers to this as the "god you do not and should not believe in"—and he often adds, "the god you don't believe in does not exist."

GOD IS THE INFINITE INTIMATE

In fact, in the *dharma* of CosmoErotic Humanism, a new name for God has emerged: the "Infinite Intimate," who appears in first-, second-, and third-person expressions. Marc first shared this name as he heard it whispered in 2023, although earlier intimations and formulations of the name appeared as early as 2010.

In first person, God is infinitely alive and as intimate as our own first-person experience.

In second person, God is the infinitely intimate Personhood of Cosmos that knows our name and holds us—the God about whom we say, *whenever we fall, we fall into Her hands*. This is the God who is our Beloved, Father, Mother, Lover, and Evolutionary Partner.

Finally, in third person, God inheres in all of the First Principles and First Values of Cosmos, and in the laws of science (both interior and exterior) that govern manifest Reality.

Therefore, we have a realization of God as not only the Infinity of Power but also the Infinity of Intimacy.

In *One Mountain, Many Paths*, we are reclaiming prayer at a higher level of consciousness. And we are reclaiming prayer as deep, alive, loving, and intimate conversations with God as the Infinite Intimate who knows our name.

EDITORIAL NOTE

THE INVITATION

We invite you to find your way into this revolution. Each one of our Unique Selves and unique gifts are desperately needed as we co-create this new Story of Value together, as part of the covenant between generations, for the sake of the whole.

Let's *play a larger game* and evolve the very source code of consciousness and culture together.

With mad love,

The Editors

LOVE OR DIE

LOCATING OURSELVES: ARTICULATING THE ESSENTIAL CONTEXT FOR THE ONE MOUNTAIN, MANY PATHS ORAL ESSAYS

SETTING OUR INTENTION

Intention setting is everything.

We're here—as da Vinci was with his cohort in the Renaissance—**to play a larger game, to participate in the evolution of love, which is to tell the new Story of Value rooted in First Principles and First Values.**

- Our intention is to recognize the critical historical juncture in which we find ourselves.
- Our intention is to take our seat at the table of history and to say, *we take responsibility for this.*
- Our intention is to participate as revolutionaries for the sake of the whole.

What we're here to do is revolution; revolution for the sake of the evolution of love.

It's a revolution for the sake of the trillions of unborn lives that will not manifest:

- The unborn loves
- The unborn creativity
- The unborn goodness
- The unborn truth
- The unborn beauty

All of it looks to us.

Not because we're engaged in grandiosity. Not at all!

- We're trembling before She.
- We're trembling with joy at the privilege.
- We're trembling with joy at the responsibility.
- We're trembling with joy at the Possibility of Possibility.
- We have to enact a new Story in this moment of time. Because it is only a new Story that can change the vector of history.

The most revolutionary act that we can do—the greatest moral imperative of this time—**is to articulate a new Story at this time between worlds and this time between stories.**

Story is not made up, as postmodernity suggests. **We all live in inescapable frameworks; our framework is the story we live in.** Right now, Reality lives according to win/lose metrics, a story that is generating existential risk. **We need to change that story.**

When we change that story, when we tell a new Story—not a made-up story, but a new Story of Value, rooted in First Principles and First Values—**then it all changes.**

We need to participate in the evolution of the source code of consciousness and culture, which is the evolution of love.

It's the most important, exciting, evolutionary, revolutionary act that we can do to alleviate suffering: to be lovers.

Like Rumi, the great poet of Sufism, we have to be "mad lovers," because it's the only sanity.

To be mad lovers is to see around the corner, to not be so obsessed with the details of the contractions of my life.

Let me see bigger.

Let me take complete care of myself in every possible way, let me completely attend to those in my circle of intimacy and influence, and then—*let me expand my circle.*

That's what we're here for.

- Our intention is to participate in the *LoveForce*, the *LoveIntelligence*, the *LoveBeauty*, the *LoveDesire* that literally animates Cosmos all the way up and all the way down.
- Our intention is to participate in the evolution of love.

[*In the next few pages we will cover some key concepts which are essential to locating ourselves and setting the context for all the One Mountain, Many Paths Oral Essays. —Eds.*]

OVERVIEW: EROS IS NO LONGER A LUXURY—IT'S LOVE OR DIE

Eros is life.

The failure of Eros destroys life.

Our lack of Eros is poised to destroy the world.

All civilizations have fallen because the stories that they lived in were, in some sense, stories based on rivalrous conflict governed by win/lose metrics. Every civilization was weakened by interior polarization caused by the lack of a shared Story of Value.

We now have a global civilization, but we haven't created a shared Story of Value.

We haven't solved the generator functions that caused all civilizations to fall. Our global civilization has exponential technologies and extraction models depleting the Earth of resources that took billions of years to create, which is going to lead to a civilizational collapse.

Existential risk is risk to our very existence.

The choice is clear: love or die.

It's that simple.

Eros is no longer a luxury. It is an absolute necessity for the survival of the individual and the planet.

In the last half a century, modern psychology has documented an age-old truth: a fully nourished baby who is not held in loving arms will die.

So too, our world, both personal and global—even with all the resources of intelligence and technology at our disposal—will die without being held in love, in the embrace of Eros.

We must embrace a personal path of love and a global politics of love.

Not ordinary love. Not love which is "mere human sentiment," but Eros, or what we sometimes call Outrageous Love, which is the heart of existence itself.

We live in a world of outrageous pain.

The only response is Outrageous Love.

EXISTENTIAL RISK AND THE EVOLUTION OF LOVE

WHAT IS EROS?

Eros is the experience of radical aliveness, moving towards, seeking, desiring *ever deeper* **contact and ever-greater wholeness.**[4] Eros is the core fabric of Reality's being and the motivational architecture of Reality's becoming.

Eros is what animates the evolutionary impulse itself, from the very inception of Cosmos all the way to our very selves, who awaken to the realization that the evolutionary impulse throbs uniquely in each of us.

The realization of human awakening and transformation that lies at the core of the interior sciences is the invitation—or even the urgent and desperate demand—of a madly loving Cosmos animated by infinities of power and infinities of intimacy.

The demand—the desperate invitation, the plea, the tender and fierce command of Cosmos that lives inside every human being—is to awaken: to awaken to our true nature as unique incarnations of Eros and Ethos that are needed and desperately desired by All-That-Is. Said slightly differently: Reality is Eros. Or: God is Eros.

The failure of Eros destroys life. The collapse of Eros is always the hidden (or not so hidden) root cause for the collapse of ethics.

This is true both personally and collectively. We live in a moment of a worldwide and personal collapse of Eros. Our lack of Eros is poised to destroy

---

[4] We define Eros through what we refer to as the Eros equation (one of a series of what we call interior science equations):

> Eros = Radical Aliveness x Desiring (Growing + Seeking) x Deeper Contact x Greater Wholeness x Self Actualization/Self Transcendence (Creation [Destruction])

There are good reasons for the formal language of the interior science equations in these writings, and the reader is invited to explore them on their own, in particular, in our work, David J. Temple, *First Principles and First Values: Forty-Two Propositions on CosmoErotic Humanism, the Meta-Crisis, and the World to Come* (World Philosophy and Religion, 2024).

the world. Humanity is currently experiencing what has come to be known as existential risk, a risk to our very existence, or what I will refer to as the Second Shock of Existence.

EXISTENTIAL RISK: THE SECOND SHOCK OF EXISTENCE

The first shock of existence is the death of the human being—the realization that we will die, which dawns in human consciousness at the beginning of history. We are not talking about the biological fact of death but the *existential* realization of death. Although the interior sciences disclose that death is a portal between two days (there is vast empirical,[5] philosophical,[6] and anthro-ontological evidence[7] for the continuity of consciousness[8]), death is also, in our own direct surface experience, a stark end. And that is obviously not a bug but a feature in the system.

---

5   We refer to evidence gathered by the most serious of researchers, beginning with Henry and Edith Sedgwick at Cambridge University and William James at Harvard University, and continuing in highly rigorous form for the last 150 years, as recapitulated by Whiteheadian scholar David Ray Griffin in multiple volumes. See also, for example, Dean Radin, *Real Magic: Unlocking Your Natural Psychic Abilities to Create Everyday Miracles* (Potter/TenSpeed/Harmony, 2018), *The Conscious Universe: The Scientific Truth of Psychic Phenomena* (HarperCollins, 2010), and other books. Or see the earlier classic by Frederic William Henry Myers, *Human Personality and Its Survival of Bodily Death* (Longmans, Green, 1907).

6   This requires a cogent analysis of materialism and dualism, and the introduction of the far more cogent third possibility which we have called "pan-interiority."

7   We discuss Anthro-Ontology in some depth in *First Principles and First Values*, and see also the fuller conversation in David J. Temple, *First Principles and First Values: Towards an Evolving Perennialism: Introducing the Anthro-Ontological Method*—both published by World Philosophy and Religion Press, in Conjunction with Integral Publishers. For now, we will simply define it as an "innate and clear interior gnosis directly available to the human being."

8   See Dr. Marc Gafni and Dr. Zachary Stein's essay in preparation, "Beyond Death: Anthro-Ontology, Philosophy, and Empiricism." This essay is slated to appear in the book *Towards a World Religion: Homo Amor Essays*. The essay is also the ground for a larger book by the same authors, *Twelve Portals to Life Beyond Death: Responding to the Second Shock of Existence*, in which we discuss three forms of material: the empirical, the philosophical, and the anthro-ontological, and show how each form discredits the notion of death as the end.

Our first-person experience is that death ends this life. It is not the *totality* of our experience if we go deeper inside, but it is obviously intended to be the central, potent, and painful dimension of every human life. Indeed, as Ernest Becker potently reminded us, the denial of death is at our peril.

All the stories and all the plotlines and all the threads of living end at that moment. Whatever happens beyond, we have an actual experience of ending. **Paradoxically, that ending, the experience of the finality of mortality, is what presses us into life.** From the implicit demand of the first shock of existence, human beings were activated and pressed into creative emergence, and what emerged was all of human culture, both interior and exterior.

The second shock of existence is the realization of the potential death of all humanity. After all the stages of human history—matter, life, and mind in all of their stages of evolutionary unfolding—we have come to this place in the evolution of humanity, in which the gap between our exponentially expanding exterior technologies and our stalled (or even regressing) interior technologies of value has created dire catastrophic and existential risks.

This gap generates extraction models and exponential growth curves, rivalrous conflicts based on win/lose metrics, tragedies of the commons, and multipolar traps, in which everyone has to keep producing to the nth degree, including weaponized exponential threats to our very existence because we are afraid that the other parties are going to do it and not be transparent—hide it from us and then dominate us.

GENERATOR FUNCTIONS FOR EXISTENTIAL RISK

Let's outline clearly the main *generator functions for existential risk*.

Rivalrous conflicts governed by zero-sum, win/lose metrics. Rivalrous conflicts generate extraction models at the core of the economic system and exponential growth curves. Both of these drive and are driven by a contrived system of artificially manufactured desires and needs, delivered into culture by ever more precise forms of micro-targeting to individuals and groups through the ever more immersive environment of the internet.

Next, rivalrous conflicts and exponential growth curves animated by win/lose metrics generate **complicated, fragile world systems** highly vulnerable to myriad forms of collapse. Fragile local systems are made exponentially more fragile on a global level by our inability to meet global challenges with social, legal, political, economic, and ethical infrastructures that remain largely local.

All of this is a direct result of the failure to develop more adequate interior technologies that would be sufficiently compelling to displace "rivalrous conflict governed by win/lose metrics" as the motivational architecture for the human life world.

This failure has led to the conditions that will cause the implosion of systems that are already and quite literally on the brink of collapsing themselves. That's what we mean by the *second shock of existence*.

To recapitulate: the second shock of existence is not the death of the human being, but the potential death of humanity.

It is the *Death Star* moment of our species.

THE DECONSTRUCTION OF INTRINSIC VALUE

We stand in this moment poised between utopia and dystopia, at a time between worlds and a time between stories. We need a new Story of Value, eternal yet evolving, rooted in First Principles and First Values, which would become a universal grammar of value and a context for our diversity.

This is exactly what the Renaissance was. It was a time between worlds and a time between stories. In the Renaissance, we had been recently challenged by the Black Death, a pandemic that swept across Europe. The Black Death destroyed between a third to half of Europe and a huge part of

Asia. People died horrifically, brutally, in the streets. They had no idea how to meet this challenge, and so, in response to the Black Death, da Vinci and Ficino and their cohorts understood that they had to tell a new Story of Value.

That story was the story of modernity. Did they get it right?

- They got part of it right, which birthed, to use Jürgen Habermas' phrase, "the dignities of modernity," such as new ways of gathering information and universal human rights.
- But they also deconstructed the source of Value. They lost the basis for the Good, the True, and the Beautiful.

The basis used to be divine revelation: *God told us*. But this claim was owned by religion, and every religion began to overreach and over-claim. The revelation was thus often mediated through cultural categories and wasn't fully accurate.

> *Modernity threw out revelation, but was unable to establish a new basis for value.*

Value was just assumed to be real. As it says in the founding document of the American Revolution: *We hold these truths to be self-evident*—that is, *we don't really have a basis for value; we just take it as a given*.

In other words, modernity took out a loan of social capital from the traditional world. The source of value was never worked out.

And then, gradually, value began to collapse.

- The Universe Story began to collapse.
- The belief that the Good, the True, and the Beautiful are real began to collapse.
- The belief that Love is real began to collapse.

As Bertrand Russell is reported to have said, "I cannot see how to refute the arguments for the subjectivity of ethical values, but I find myself incapable of believing that all that is wrong with wanton cruelty is that I do not like it."

What do you do if you grew up in a world in which value is not real? A world without a source of value, without a Universe Story, without a story of human identity, without a story of desire, without a narrative of power?

In the words of W.B. Yeats, *the center does not hold.*

- You have a collapse at the very center of society, because you no longer have Eros.
- You no longer have a Reality in which value is real, and so you have this lingering sense of emptiness.
- You have a complete collapse at the very center.
- We become *the hollow men and the stuffed men*, gesture without form.

And that's the source of our current existential risk.

THE DEEPER ROOT CAUSE OF THE META-CRISIS: A GLOBAL INTIMACY DISORDER

Above, I have outlined the major generator functions of existential risk. But there is a deeper cause for the existential risk that lurks underneath the rivalrous conflict governed by win/lose metrics and the fragile systems they engender.

And we cannot take the Death Star down without discerning and addressing this. We have already alluded to this root cause above, but at this point we need to make it more explicit so that, from this context, the adequate root response will become clear.

Modernity threw out the revelation, but was unable to establish a new basis for value.

This ostensibly surprising statement can be understood in a few simple steps:

1. All of the catastrophic and existential risk challenges we face are global: from climate change to artificial intelligence, pandemics, systems collapse, and exponential arms races.
2. Every global challenge self-evidently requires a global solution.
3. Global solutions can only be implemented with global co-ordination.
4. Global co-ordination is impossible without global coherence.
5. Global coherence is only possible if there is a global resonance between the parts.
6. Global resonance is only possible if we have global intimacy.

ONLY A SHARED STORY OF VALUE CAN GENERATE GLOBAL INTIMACY

Global intimacy—just like intimacy in a couple—is only possible when there is a shared story.

Not just a shared history, but a shared Story of Value.

- It is only a shared global story that can generate a new emergent quality of intimacy: global intimacy.
- A shared Story of Value must be rooted in shared ordinating values, or what we have called evolving First Values and First Principles.
- Intimacy requires a shared grammar of value as a matrix for a shared Story of Value.

The global intimacy disorder is the root cause for existential risk. The global intimacy disorder underlies the core generator functions for existential risk.

The global intimacy disorder is rooted in the failure to experience ourselves in a field of shared intrinsic value. This failure derives from the deconstruction of value.

Indeed, it is wholly accurate to say that **the root cause of the two generator functions of existential risk is the failed story of intrinsic value, or what we might also call the breakdown of Eros.**

1. The first generator function is **the success story**. Our modern success story is rivalrous conflict governed by win/lose metrics, which violates all the terms of the Intimacy Equation: there is no shared identity and no mutuality of recognition, feeling, value or purpose, and instead of *relative* otherness, there is *alienated* otherness. Such a story generates complicated fragile systems with no allurement or intimacy between the parts, systems which optimize for efficiency (as an expression of win/lose metrics) and not for resiliency and life.
2. The second generator function is **the deconstruction of intrinsic value** itself. The deconstruction of value is the sense that human value does not participate in the intrinsic value of the Real, for the Real is dogmatically declared to have no intrinsic value. Thus, there is no shared identity between the interior of the human being and Reality. There is no common participation in a field of shared intrinsic value. Instead of being intimate with value, we are alienated from value. And only intrinsic value can arouse will: political, moral, and social will.

To sum up, without a shared grammar of value there is no global intimacy, and therefore no global coherence, and no global coordination in response to catastrophic and existential risk, which means, put simply, there will be, quite literally, no future.

HEALING THE GLOBAL INTIMACY DISORDER REQUIRES THE EVOLUTION OF INTIMACY

But we are not hopeless. On the contrary, we are filled with great hope. Hope is a memory of the future. That memory of the future *is* the direct hit that takes down the Death Star, the culture of death. **The direct hit must be**—as it has always been in history—**the emergence of a new stage of evolution**.

Crisis is an evolutionary driver, and every crisis is, at its core, a crisis of intimacy: from the oxygen crisis of the single cells dying which generated multicellular life at the dawn of existence, to the existential risk in this very moment.[9]

> *The direct hit is therefore structurally self-evident: the evolution of intimacy itself.*

What is intimacy, as a structure of Cosmos all the way down and all the way up the evolutionary chain? We engage this inquiry in depth in other writings, but for now we will simply adduce what we have called the "Intimacy Equation":

> *Intimacy = shared identity in the context of [relative] otherness × mutuality of recognition × mutuality of pathos × mutuality of value × mutuality of purpose*

Intimacy is about the capacity of parts to generate a *shared identity* while retaining their otherness, or distinct identity. This requires multiple mutualities, including recognition, pathos (or feeling), value, and purpose. The parts must recognize and feel each other, even as they share value and purpose. But all of this must lead to intimate union—and not pathological

---

[9] We demonstrate this principle in some depth in the multi-volume series, The Universe: A Love Story (forthcoming) (https://worldphilosophyandreligion.org/early-ontologies), The Intimate Universe: Global Intimacy Disorder as Cause for Global Action Paralysis (forthcoming), and in other writings of CosmoErotic Humanism.

fusion, where the distinct identity of the parts disappears—like subatomic particles that successfully become an atom, or two people who successfully become a couple.

THE DECONSTRUCTION OF VALUE IS THE DECONSTRUCTION OF INTIMACY

We have identified the global intimacy disorder as the root cause of existential risk. But the underlying ultimate failure of intimacy is the deconstruction of value itself.

The deconstruction of value means that human value does not participate in any sense of intrinsic value of the Real. This is not about individual *values,* but about *the Field of Value* that underlies all of them. **When the human being**—moved, often sincerely or even nobly, by myriad cultural, historical, and psychological confusions—**claims to have stepped out of the Field of Value, then intimacy itself is deconstructed.**

The deconstruction of value is the deconstruction of intimacy.

In the absence of a shared Story of Value, a story that is an authentic expression of Reality's Eros, a story rooted in *pseudo-Eros* takes center stage and becomes the generator function for existential risk. Our modern pseudo-Eros story is *rivalrous conflict governed by win/lose metrics*. Such a story catalyzes in its wake the second generator function of existential risk: *complicated fragile systems with no allurement or intimacy between the parts*. It is in that sense that we have argued that the first generator function for existential risk is the success story.

- The failure of intimacy is precisely the impotent experience that there is no shared identity between the interior of the human being and Reality. **There is no shared identity in the sense of any kind of common participation in a field of shared intrinsic value.**
- **But only a shared Story of Value can arouse the global will**

required to engage catastrophic and existential risk. For it is only global political, moral, and social will—and we can even say *erotic* will—that can generate the most Good, True and Beautiful world that we have always known is possible.

THE EVOLUTION OF LOVE IS THE TELLING OF A NEW STORY

Coupled with the Intimacy Equation is the scientifically grounded realization, in both the exterior and interior sciences, that Reality is a progressive deepening of intimacies, or, said slightly differently:

Reality is Evolution. Evolution is the evolution of intimacy.

- The evolution of intimacy requires—both personally and collectively—a deeper, more accurate discernment of the nature of our universe, ourselves, and our beloveds.
- This new discernment generates a new global Story of Value.
- The new global Story of Value generates an emergent, heretofore unseen global intimacy and heals the global intimacy disorder.

The new Story of Value is the direct hit that takes down the Death Star and replaces it with the hope that invokes the memory of our best future.

Global intimacy facilitates global coherence, which facilitates global coordination, which activates the possibility of our creative and effectively coordinated global responses to the global meta-crisis in its entirety and its specific expressions.

To solve Bertrand Russell's challenge—the apparent argument for the subjectivity of ethical values—**we have to reground value theory in eternal yet evolving First Principles and First Values, and articulate a new Story of Value.**

This is what we call CosmoErotic Humanism.

CosmoErotic Humanism—together with other emergent strands—**needs to become the ground of a world religion as a context for our diversity**. We need religion, even as we need science, to articulate a shared global grammar of value.

As we said at the beginning, our choice is simple: love or die.

- To love means to participate in the evolution of love, which is the evolution of the human Story of Value.
- To love means to evolve and activate a new cultural enlightenment—rooted in a new narrative of identity, a new narrative of value, a new narrative of intimate communion, a new narrative of desire, a new narrative of power—all of which will birth new narratives of economics and politics.
- The evolution of love is the telling of a new Story.

The new Story that must be told is a love story, for in fact that is the deepest truth of Reality, rooted in the best exterior and interior sciences, that we have at this moment in time:

- Reality is not merely a fact. Reality is a story.
- Reality is not an ordinary story. Reality is a love story.
- Reality is not an ordinary love story. Reality is an Outrageous Love Story.

Story doesn't mean it's *made-up*.

It means doing the hard work of integrating the validated insights of the traditional world, the modern world, and the postmodern world.

This is the intention at the heart of telling the new Story of CosmoErotic Humanism.

ABOUT THIS VOLUME

Existential Risk and the Evolution of Love offers a bold philosophical framework aimed at addressing the meta-crisis that threatens both humanity's existence, and our very humanity. At the heart of this volume is the concept of "existential risk," a term that encapsulates the various crises—social, environmental, political, technological—that jeopardize humanity's very future. Through this series of what we have called "Oral Essays," based on edited talks given in the weekly One Mountain, Many Paths broadcast, we propose a powerful response to existential risk: the articulation of a new Story of Value leading to what we in CosmoErotic Humanism call a Planetary Awakening in Love through Unique Self Symphonies.

The realization of Unique Self is presented as a key to humanity's future. It refers to the deep recognition of each individual's inherent uniqueness as an expression of the deeper Field of Value. Through this realization, each of us is called to offer our unique gift to the collective, evolutionary project of humanity—to the evolution of love itself. As we do, we come together in Unique Self Symphonies, a manifestation of a more coherently intimate vision for existence, where our unique gifts coordinate to play an essential role in the unfolding of Reality as the evolution of love. This is the emergence of *Homo amor*, the new human and new humanity, the triumph of *Homo sapiens*.

This vision points toward a new Story of Value, named as CosmoErotic Humanism. This story emerges from the very fabric of Reality, the Field of ErosValue that underpins both individual and collective life. Through the lens of CosmoErotic Humanism, the text calls for an awakening to the deep, interconnected nature of Reality, emphasizing that the modern and postmodern deconstruction of intrinsic value is a main cause of humanity's current struggles. The collapse of the old value systems, which were once based on a shared sense of divine or intrinsic worth, has led to fragmentation, alienation, conflict, and to what we have called in CosmoErotic Humanism a "global intimacy disorder." To overcome this, humanity must develop a new Story of Value—a shared narrative that reconnects all people to their Unique Selves and to one another, thus fostering a global intimacy that can address the existential risks we face. This new story weaves together the leading-edge, validated insights of the premodern, modern, and postmodern wisdom streams.

The typical responses to existential risk we currently see are denial, domination, and doomerism. Denial attempts to wish our current situation away by not facing it. Domination is the response of the corporate tech plex, which is attempting to create a large surveillance state to address the dangers in our world. Doomerism seems wise and honest at first but is ultimately a capitulation and a resignation. Instead, according to CosmoErotic Humanism, the only true response is the Dawn of Desire, or the Dawn of Divinity. This is the telling of the new Story of Value that puts our sacred and clarified desire at the heart of Reality.

CosmoErotic Humanism has perhaps most importantly called for a new name for the Divine, the Infinite Intimate. To be human is to incarnate the Infinite Intimate. To incarnate the Infinite Intimate is to be intimate with Reality, understanding that your personal transformation is the transformation of the whole. This transformation begins through the transformation of intimacy and love itself—moving beyond the isolated narratives of our separate selves, to a deeper fabric in which intimacy means that I am omni-considerate and omni-responsible for the sake of the whole. In essence, existential risk is a radical demand to love or die. Either we evolve our consciousness, recognize love as not mere human sentiment but the heart of existence—what we have called Outrageous Love—and step into a future where humanity recognizes its unique and interconnected role in the Cosmos. Or we die. The choice is stark and simple, and it is ours to make.

This is a work written for this precise moment—what we are calling "a time between world and a time between stories." The message is clear, and we are its messengers: to navigate the existential risks of our time, we must evolve the core structure of our identity, as human beings always have done. We must realize that are not merely separate selves, skin-encapsulated egos with particular talents, but rather we are inseparable from the larger Field of ErosValue that lives uniquely in us, as us, and through us. We are Unique Selves called to play our parts in the Unique Self Symphony. The music we have to play together is rooted in a shared musical score, a new Story of Value, a new universal grammar of value, in which we are aligned with the evolutionary Eros that is itself the inherent nature of Cosmos—the animating energy of all of Reality, from mathematics to molecules to metabolics to Mozart to morals to mysticism.

Volume 23

These oral essays are lightly edited talks delivered by Marc Gafni between August 2020 and March 2024.

CHAPTER ONE

THE WHOLE WORLD IS WALKING ON A VERY NARROW BRIDGE: THE PANDEMIC ACCENTUATES THE FAULT LINES IN SOCIETY

Episode 201 — August 16, 2020

FIRST PRINCIPLES ARE NEEDED TO MOVE THROUGH THIS MOMENT

I want to introduce a new chant for this moment in time. The words are:

> *Kol ha'olam kulo gesher tzar me'od*—The whole world is walking on a very narrow bridge.
>
> *Veha'ikar lo lefached klal*—And the essence is not to be afraid, not to be afraid at all.

We're in this moment of pandemic.

- People are in life and death situations all over the world.
- People are also losing their basic economic security, which means fierce anxiety.
- The First Principles and First Values needed to move through this moment are not in place.

We are the First Principles. Before we articulate them, we have to *be* them, we have to live them. The core of the First Principles is envisioning a new human and a new humanity, a new possibility for the human being and a new possibility for humanity.

According to the latest surveys on depression in the United States, **1 out of 4 people aged eighteen to twenty-four have contemplated suicide.** Why? It's not the pandemic exactly. **The pandemic is accentuating the fault lines in society that are already there.**

I want to identify some of these fault lines and identify the First Principles and First Values that move us beyond them.

That's why we started One Mountain, Many Paths. **We are a revolution.** We're not a spiritual group. We're not a political group. We're not an economic group.

We're all of it.

> *We're a politics of evolutionary love. We're articulating love as religion, articulating First Principles and First Values that can take us through to the next level.*

If you don't want to take responsibility for evolving the source code and you're looking for a quick fix, you're in the wrong place. But if you're willing to play a larger game, this is ultimately going to be the most personally satisfying thing in the world.

There is no joy and no pleasure like the pleasure of evolving the source code. That's what we're here for. What's the distinction between self-help and transformation? Self-help is asking, *What can I get out of it?* Transformation is asking, *How can I step so deeply in that, oh my God, I just blow open?*

WE WALK THROUGH THE CONTRACTION, AND WE COLLECT THE JOY

What happens in a pandemic is that the fault lines that are already there get accentuated and deepened. *The very narrow bridge* means that in one conversation, you can fall off; in one missed moment you can raise the stakes too high. It's a big deal to make it through. It's a big deal. It's *gesher tzar me'od, a very narrow bridge.* You can fall in trying to get from one side to the other.

So how do you do it? How do you find your way through? **You find your way through by getting rid of all the fears.** The fear that:

- I'm not enough.
- I'm not loved.
- I'm not honored.
- My life doesn't matter.
- I'm an extra on the set.
- I'm insignificant.

I begin to know that *you love me.* **I turn to Reality and my Beloved, and I say,** *You love me.* Not *I love you.* I look at you, and *I'm not waiting for you to say, I love you.* In our deepest, closest relationships, we say, *you love me.* Let's get rid of our *I love you* tests. **You love me.**

We have to gather our moments. I got a beautiful email from a dear, dear friend of mine, a student and friend. We did a deep dive together in a course I gave some sixteen years ago. He was falsely accused of a serious crime, and he would have gone to prison for seven or eight years. He told me he was innocent. I know him. I trust him. We stood together in it. We literally stood together. It breaks my heart.

He wrote me an email this morning, remembering that day sixteen years ago when we held hands, and we were waiting for the verdict. I remember the joy. I don't think I've ever experienced joy exactly like that quality of joy. It was unbelievable. We were ecstatic. He was correctly exonerated. We literally danced. I remember dancing, just completely dancing. We've got to gather those moments.

We have to collect those moments. We have to collect the moments of joy. We have to collect the goodness and the delight—and *from that place, we have the energy to not fall off the bridge.*

We let go of the fear.

Let go of the fear that my life doesn't matter. Your life matters insanely and enormously. Your life matters beyond imagination.

All of Reality intended you. Feel into that.

No fear.

- You're in the right place.
- You're in the right time.

Every place you've been you needed to be.

We can walk through this pandemic with enormous power, and enormous joy, and enormous love.

Reality itself is literally on a narrow bridge like it's never been before. We face catastrophic risk.

We face existential risk. **And yet we have the capacity to scale the mountain and manifest a utopia that never has been seen on Earth.**

The essence is not to be afraid, not to be afraid at all.

We all contract. We all have moments of, *oh my God, it's so painful.* But we walk through them, and we collect the joy.

WAKING UP AND GROWING UP

We're about to pray. What does it mean to pray? **To pray is to know the nature of Cosmos.**

I sometimes tell a story about an exchange I had with John Welwood, a beautiful man who passed away. We just started talking in a friend's kitchen, and we loved each other; we just had a wonderful time. In a book called *Toward a Psychology of Awakening,* John initiated the phrase "wake up and grow up." As the West met Eastern Enlightenment, there was a sense that *you could wake up, you could have an experience of radical opening, of deep enlightened consciousness, and then you were home.*

People thought this was going to bypass psychology, that it would bypass working out the contractions. But people died because of it. People went off their medications. People didn't do the real work of working through their contractions.

You need both to "wake up" and to "grow up."

- To grow up is, in John's understanding, to work through your own psychological maturation.
- To wake up is to have an experience of *om mani padme hum,* an experience of fully waking up.

But it's even deeper than that.

Ken Wilber and I have talked about "wake up, grow up" in a different way for many years. Ken understands growing up as the movement through developmental levels of consciousness—to move from egocentric to ethnocentric to worldcentric to cosmocentric. John, Ken, and I revisioned this.

We now understand "wake up, grow up" as to wake up to your True Self. **But when you wake up deeply, you realize the unique dimension of your True Self, the utter uniqueness, which is Reality uniquely speaking through you.**

To **wake up** is to wake up to your Unique Self, the unique voice of your True Self. True Self is the Field of Consciousness. Your Unique Self is the unique expression of that field, so to wake up is to wake up to your Unique Self. You can't wake up to True Self. Classical enlightenment doesn't work, because every True Self is a Unique Self. So waking up is always waking up to Unique Self. You're blown open as the unique expression of consciousness.

In **growing up**, you don't just grow up to a generic level of consciousness; you grow up uniquely. Zak Stein and I are writing a book called *In a Unique Voice: On Unique Self and Developmental Theory*, where we show how, when you move through the developmental levels, it's your Unique Self that grows up to the highest levels of consciousness.

When you get to the highest levels of consciousness—what we call in developmental thought "second-tier consciousness"—**you begin to live from your Unique Self**. That is the demarcating characteristic.

The sign of developmental growth is when you step into your Unique Self and you live from that uniqueness, in communion with the larger Unique Self Symphony.

To grow up is to grow up as your Unique Self into the most fully present, developed, and evolved consciousness of cosmocentric intimacy.

Your Unique Self is giving its gifts to the entire Cosmos:

- You feel the pain of the Cosmos.
- You feel the responsibility of the Cosmos.
- You feel the call of the Cosmos.
- You can say, *I am evolution.*
- You can say, *I am a unique configuration of Evolutionary Love.*

That's what it means to grow up. To grow up means going through all the levels of consciousness. I get to cosmocentric intimacy and realize the answer to the question, *who am I?*

I am a unique configuration of Evolutionary Love. That's who I am.

PRAYER AND MEDITATION: DOGMA OR REALIZATION?

In my conversation with John we went deeper and started to talk about how we practice.

John said, "I understand that you talk about prayer, and I couldn't believe it. I heard you were intelligent. And now you're talking about this dogmatic, premodern idea? You're talking about prayer. Really? Why are you talking about prayer?"

In his book *Up from Eden,* my colleague Ken Wilber also essentially dismisses prayer. The whole notion of the personal God was dismissed by both John and Ken.

He said, "I do awareness. That's my practice. I meditate and access awareness."

I said, "John, why do you believe in awareness?"

He said, "Because it's a realization. I actually realize it in my body. It's not a dogma."

So I said, "John, *prayer* is also a realization."

John looked at me, and he just got it. He is the most humble, beautiful man. He said, "Oh, prayer is a realization."

But prayer is a realization of what, my friends? It's a realization that *She never drops you.* It's a realization that you can be walking on a narrow plank on the ground and you're not afraid at all, but when it's 20,000 feet in the air and you're walking across it you're in fear because you might fall off.

> *The prayer realization of God in the second-person is the realization She never drops you. You can never fall off. Everyplace you fall, you fall into Her hands.*

Let me tell you about Levi Yitzchok of Berditchev. He would make a blessing. **He would begin by saying, "*Blessed are you…*" and he couldn't even get to the rest of the blessing.** It's "*Blessed are you, God, King of the world…*" There's a whole formula. He would go, "*Blessed are you, you, you, YOU, YOU, YOU, YOU!*" **And he would faint in ecstasy from the realization of God in the second person, which is God as the Infinity of Intimacy that holds us in every second.**

So we're going to turn to God, and we're going to pray now.

- We're going to pray for the world.
- We're going to pray for ourselves.
- We're going to pray for our friends.

We're going to bring before She everything, our holy and our broken *Hallelujah*. So take us inside, Leonard Cohen's "Hallelujah."

And you know what, friends, let's shout an *Amen* if you're up for it. *Amen* is *Aleph, Mem, Nun* in Hebrew, and *Amen* means *I trust*.

- *Amen* also means the nursing mother, so it means *I trust that She's never going to drop me*.
- *Amen* means practice, *I'm going to practice all the time.*
- *Amen* also means *oman*; it means art, *the art of practicing so that I know that you love me, and She's never going to drop me, and the Infinity of Intimacy is holding me in every second.*

After every prayer, let's just shout out an *Amen*. [Prayer]

EVOLUTIONARY LOVE CODE: THE PLEASURE OF TRANSFORMATION

Reality is pleasure.

The pleasure of transformation is the highest pleasure.

Knowing that my transformation transforms the whole thing is the highest pleasure of transformation, and the pleasure of transformation is the pleasure of power.

Now, let's add one more thing to the code. This is the essence of the code. We think that in order to transform the whole thing we've got to be Barack Obama, Angela Merkel, or in some position of obvious power. But the power in positions of obvious power often has no power at all.

The true nature of a human being is to know the true nature of Reality. And the true nature of Reality is that the entire Universe lives in me.

I'm not just living in a Universe. *All of Reality is living me and lives in me.* Muons, hadrons, protons, electrons, cells, fungi, plant structures, fungi structures, animal structures, eukaryote structures, mammalian structures—they all live in me, all of it. The entire lithosphere, the entire biosphere, the atmosphere, the hydrosphere—it all lives in me. **All of the environment that I live in, the Universe I live in, actually lives in me and through me.**

As the physicist John Archibald Wheeler said, it's literally a *participatory universe*. A participatory universe demands a participatory politics and a participatory spirituality. I'm a participant in the universe. It's a participatory universe, which means that if I know myself, **I know that I have immense power, that my power impacts the whole thing.**

And it's not just *if I become prime minister.* **It happens within my own personal transformation.**

IN THE PANDEMIC WE'VE LOST NOT ONLY PSEUDO-EROS, WE'VE ALSO LOST OUR SOURCES OF EROS

Two things are happening in this pandemic:

1. **First, most forms of pseudo-eros are gone:**

   - The pseudo-eros of partying
   - The pseudo-eros of gossiping
   - The pseudo-eros of going out for dinner
   - The pseudo-eros of having a lot of extra money
   - The pseudo-eros of not feeling the pain of the other because I split it off from me

These are the arrangements I make with life to avoid the pain of emptiness because I feel alone, because I feel alone in my relationship, because I'm not sure that I'm loved, or I'm not sure I matter, or I can't actually find myself inside.

There's a low, dull, throbbing pain, and a billion little strategies that make up your pseudo-erotic arrangement to get you through. Most of it is now gone.

Addiction is one replacement. That's why addiction is going through the roof. There are ways that many of us are at the edge where we're barely holding on. Mental health is breaking down all over the place, and all of us are participating, even if not directly. Even if I'm not directly experiencing addiction, I feel this sense of contraction. It's hard.

2. **Second, not only is my pseudo-eros not there, much of my real Eros isn't there, many sources of my depth aren't there.** I can't embrace the people in person I wanted to embrace.

Lots of it wasn't pseudo-eros:

- The joy of being with another person;
- The joy of being touched and just hugging a person;

- The joy of being in a crowd of people and feeling the human energy.

Remember being at a basketball game a few months ago? Remember being together, all of us, at the festival last year in person? That's not there any longer.

Not only have we lost our pseudo-eros, but we've also lost a lot of the places that were the sources of our Eros.

So at this moment, sacred holy brothers and sisters, **we've got to reach deeper. This is our calling to reach deeper and find our Eros again in a way we never have before.**

- I've got to find my Unique Self.
- I've got to walk through that contraction.
- I've got to walk through the pain.

It accumulates.

- There's not enough time.
- There's not enough contact.
- There's not enough of a lot of things.

And so many things are cracking.

So we go inside and find the truth of our love. We go inside and find the truth. We collect the moments. **We collect the joy.**

We can see it in front of us. We live in it, we hold it, and we blow it open.

At that moment, it's not that we don't crack. **We crack, and then we find ourselves.** Of course we crack, of course we contract, but then **in that contraction, we stop everything and find each other in the contraction, and we walk through it holding hands.**

We're holding hands around the world, and we're holding hands not just for each other. We're holding hands for each other to walk through this together, and we're holding hands for everyone who doesn't have someone to hold their hand.

THE WORLD NEEDS FIRST PRINCIPLES AND FIRST VALUES

We're not just distributing fish. We want to share with the world how you learn to be a fisherman, meaning First Values and First Principles.

Among us all here, we can use the word *dharma*, but as we face the world and go to change the source code, let's find that term: First Principles and First Values.

- First Principles express the underlying, eternal yet evolving, universal principles of value that need to be the rudder of civilization's next stage.
- First Principles are urgently needed, personally and collectively, to respond to the catastrophic and even existential risk that challenges us, invites us, and demands our response at this moment in time.
- First Principles are ancient, time-honored, and venerable, even as they are evolutionary, emergent, and new.
- First Principles are a weaving together of the most crucial and validated truths from all the wisdom streams—premodern, modern, and postmodern—into a new whole greater than the sum of the parts.

We refer to First Principles as the new story, a new *dharma*, or a global ethos for a global civilization. First Principles are implicitly shared by all the many paths. They're the foundation of One Mountain. That's us. It's ours to do.

My personal transformation is a First Principle. When I contract—and we all contract—I find myself getting shrill, strident, too sharp, or angry. Something's accumulating in me and bursting through me. **Then I reach**

deep inside and I find myself, I expand into my true identity, and I realize, *Oh my God, you love me.*

Who am I? What's the answer to the question, "Who am I?" I realize that *I'm an irreducibly unique expression of the LoveIntelligence, and LoveDesire, and LoveBeauty that's the initiating and animating Eros of All-That-Is that lives in me, as me, and through me, that never was, is, or will be ever again. And as such there's something for me to do.*

THERE'S SOMETHING FOR ME TO DO, AND IT'S THE GREATEST THING IN THE WORLD

I want to tell you a short story about a holy teacher, one of the greatest masters of modern times. His name was Kalonymus Kalman, the Master of Piaseczno, which was near Warsaw. He perished in World War II, in the Warsaw Ghetto. He was called the "Master of Children." This master would say that children at five years old already need a master: they need someone to connect their souls to heaven.

So he gathered around him in Piaseczno literally a kingdom of children. He had a school with thousands of kids, and he was their father, their mother, and their best friend. Then he was moved by the Nazis to the Warsaw Ghetto in 1940. He wrote a most precious book called *The Holy Fire*, in which he wrote down on Saturday night the teachings that he gave during the day because he didn't write on the Sabbath. He was killed in the death camp of Treblinka.

I want to share with you the story of a man who met Kalonymus Kalman, someone who's so close to my heart. The person talking here is Shlomo Carlebach, a great master of song. I'm going to tell you the story in his first-person voice.

> When his book came out after the war was over, *The Holy Fire*, I couldn't believe its beauty. It so pierced my heart that I asked everyone, "Where are those kids of that holy master, the precious children who heard these teachings from him every week? I'd

love to speak to them." And I was told there was nobody left, nobody.

But one day, a few years ago, I was walking down HaYarkon… I saw there a hunchback on HaYarkon Street in Tel Aviv, a hunchback so broken. His body was so broken, and his face was beautiful, so handsome, but his whole body was misshapen. He was sweeping the streets. I had a feeling this person was special, and so I said, "Shalom aleichem. Peace unto you."

He replied to me in the heaviest Polish accent, "*Aleichem shalom.* Peace unto you."

I asked if he was from Poland, and he said, "Yes, I'm from Piaseczno."

I couldn't believe it. "Piaseczno? Have you ever heard of the Holy Master Kalonymus Kalman of Piaseczno?"

He said to me, "What do you mean have I heard of him? I've seen him. I was a student in his school. I was a child in his school from age 5 to 11."

I couldn't believe I had finally met one of the children of this great master.

Then this holy hunchback went on, and he said, "When I was 11 I went to Auschwitz, to the death camp of Auschwitz, and I was so strong they thought I was 17, and I was whipped and hit and kicked. They broke me. They broke my body, and I never healed. That's why I look the way I do now. I've got nobody in the world. I'm all alone."

And he kept on sweeping the ground.

I said to this man, this holy hunchback on HaYarkon Street in Tel Aviv, "My sweetest friend, do you know my whole life I have been waiting to see you in person, you who saw the Master of Piaseczno, a person who was one of his children? Please give me one of his teachings."

THE PANDEMIC ACCENTUATES THE FAULT LINES IN SOCIETY

The hunchback glared at me. He said, "Do you think you can be in Auschwitz in a death camp for five years and still remember teachings?"

I said, "Yes, I'm sure of it. I know. I know teachings that are real"—teachings that are First Principles. Teachings that come from the heart never leave the heart. The master's teachings, you can't have forgotten them."

So this holy hunchback said, "Okay, wait." He went to the water fountain to wash his hands, he found a tie and put on a jacket, and then he came back to me and said one more time, "Do you really want to hear the teaching?"

I said to him, "I swear to you I'll tell your teaching all over the world."

So he began. He said,

> "I want you to know there was never such a day as a Sabbath in Piaseczno when I was there. We danced, hundreds, maybe thousands of children, and the master would sing and greet the angels. At the meal, he would teach between every course, and after every teaching, this is what the master would say."
>
> "After every course he would say, '**Kinderlach**'—**which means children**—'**the greatest thing in the world is to do someone else a favor**.'"

The hunchback sighed, the holy hunchback, and he said:

> "You know, my parents are gone and my whole family, and there's no one anymore. I have no more family. Oh my God, when I was in Auschwitz and alone, I wanted to commit suicide. I wanted to break so many times."
>
> "**And at the last moment when I would go to the electrified fence, I would stop, and I would hear my master say, 'Kinderlach, children, the best thing, the holiest thing in the world is to do someone favor'.**"

"There I was in Auschwitz. Do you know how many favors you can do in a death camp at night? People are lying on the floor crying, and no one even has any strength to listen to their stories anymore. I would walk from one person to the other and ask, 'Why are you crying?' and they would tell me about their children, their wives, their people they'd never see in this lifetime again. And I would hold their hands, and I'd cry with them. Then I'd walk to the next person, and it would give me strength for another day. **When I was at the end, and I wanted to kill myself, I'd hear my Rebbe's voice.**"

"Then the war was over, and I came here to Israel to Tel Aviv, and I've got no one in the world. **Sometimes I take off my shoes, and I walk down to the beach late at night and go up to my nose in the ocean, ready to sink. And then again I can't help but hear my teacher's voice saying, 'The greatest thing in the world is to do somebody a favor.'**"

"'Remember, my precious children,' he would say, 'the greatest thing in the world.'"

And the holy hunchback stared at me for a long time, and he said, "Do you know how many favors you can do sweeping the streets of the world? Do you know how many favors you can do?"

THERE'S AN ACTION YOU CAN TAKE THAT'S YOURS AND NO ONE ELSE'S

Every time my heart closes, when I open my heart and look at the people in my circle who need me, I'm their angel—to be an angel means you're a messenger.

- There's an *I love you* you can say.
- There's a *You love me* you can do.
- There's an action you can do.

- There's a creation you can do that no one else in the world can create but you.

It's yours to do. For us together.

It's ours to hold hands; it's ours to love each other madly.

- We *are* the First Principles; we *are* the First Values.
- We *are* the *dharma*.
- We *are Homo sapiens* becoming *Homo amor*. It's not separate from us.

But we're not just committed to *did this fulfill me?* We're not just committed to *did this open my heart?*

We're committed to opening the heart of the world. We're committed to articulating First Principles and First Values that can take us from a suffering that you can't imagine into a utopia beyond all imagination. That's our commitment. That's where we stand.

It's not easy. **The whole world is walking on a very narrow bridge.**

Veha'ikar, **but the most important thing,** *lo lefached klal*—**is don't be afraid at all.** No fear at all because you can't fall off the bridge because *everyplace we fall, we fall into each other, and we fall into She.* Even at the moment of death there's a continuity of consciousness, and you know that *it goes on.* You know that *it's not over.*

CHAPTER TWO

THE CHALLENGE: THE META-CRISIS, THE RESPONSE: UNIQUE SELF

Episode 279 — February 13, 2022

WE NEED A NEW STORY—A NEW WORLDVIEW FROM WHICH EVERYTHING EMERGES

Welcome, everyone. We are first setting our intention. We're here in this place together, in this community of pioneering souls, at this moment poised between dystopia and utopia. There are two paths. Dystopia lurks through multiple forms of catastrophic and existential risk, of a kind that never existed in the history of planet Earth, which began in 1945, but has exponentialized since then.

We've spent a significant amount of time unpacking existential risk, and I want to call that, as we have many times before, the meta-crisis. **It's not one crisis; it's a series of crises in different domains**, which together create the meta-crisis. The responses to the meta-crisis, to date, have been rooted in infrastructure suggestions or new social structures: new sets of laws, new sets of government structures themselves. Infrastructure is more connected to the actual mechanisms of Reality: supply chains, the linear materials economy, etc. Those are all important.

But what we understand here—and what every great mind and heart has understood, what's actually lost in the dialogue today and essential—is that **the only thing that can**, from the perspective of the human being, **change the vector of history**, is not infrastructure, and it's not social structure. **It's what Marvin Harris called "superstructure," which means the story. It means the worldview that everything emerges from.**

So what we're unpacking here in One Mountain, Many Paths is that story is not made up, as postmodernity suggested, expressed by many in our culture. For example, like my colleague, Yuval Harari, who's a lovely human being, I'm sure, and a wonderful historical storyteller—but who's also an unconscious parrot of the weakest positions in postmodernity when he says that *all story is made up, all story is fiction, all story is a figment of our imagination, and all story is a social construction of Reality.* I'm quoting him directly. He says there's no ultimate difference between Libya's Gaddafi and universal human rights—they're both made-up stories.

But that's a tragic (and rampant) misunderstanding of the correct intuitions of postmodernity.

It's not by accident that a book like Yuval's becomes a favorite of Barack Obama, Jeff Bezos, and a host of other figures, who are in no sense shocked by these claims. That's what's new in the last twenty years. **They are in no sense shocked by a position that says the story is completely made-up, a total social construction, and that there are no actual intrinsic values in Cosmos.**

That's a disaster!

There are many reasons why that's happened, and one of them is that value has been hijacked by particular communities; value has come to represent regressive premodern values. The notion that there could be intrinsic value—what we call here in One Mountain, Many Paths, "First Values and First Principles in Cosmos"—is a notion that's been lost.

> *We're here to reclaim First Values and First Principles—not as fixed or preordained, but as the orienting simple rules that generate complexity.*

That's how complexity theory works. There's an orienting set of simple rules, which are the values in a mathematics equation (exterior sciences). **But there are also the values in the interior sciences.** So we're here to articulate *the Evolving First Principles and First Values of Cosmos*. They're Evolving First Principles and First Values—they evolve to infinity.

- Just like Gödel and Tarski, in their Incompleteness Theorem, essentially pointed out that there's not one mathematical set that completes everything.
- Just like in physics, there was a thought for a moment that "there's one set of physics equations, and now we've worked everything out." Then quantum physics exploded that.
- Similarly, in the values of interior sciences, there's evolution. We're evolving towards infinity.

But there's a vector of evolution. There are First Principles and First Values of love, Eros, intimacy, personhood, uniqueness, and choice. We need to unpack each of them, and we've got to enact a new shared grammar of value, a new Story of Value.

It's not enough to have First Principles and First Values; we need a plotline. We are storytelling creatures. **Story itself is a First Principle and First Value of Cosmos.**

WE ARE HERE TO TELL THE NEW STORY OF VALUE

What we're here to do is revolution: revolution for the sake of the evolution of love, revolution for the sake of the trillions of unborn lives that will not manifest, the unborn loves, the unborn creativity, the unborn goodness,

THE CHALLENGE: THE META-CRISIS, THE RESPONSE: UNIQUE SELF

the unborn truth, the unborn beauty. All of it looks to us—and not because we're engaged in grandiosity!

- We're trembling before She.
- We're trembling with joy at the privilege.
- We're trembling with joy at the responsibility.
- We're trembling with joy at the Possibility of Possibility.

We have to enact a new Story of Value in this moment of time *because only a new story can change the vector of history*.

Story is not made-up, as postmodernity suggests. **Value has been hijacked by particular communities**; value has come to represent regressive premodern values.

The notion that there could be intrinsic value—what we call First Values and First Principles in Cosmos—is a notion that's gotten lost.

- We all live in inescapable frameworks; our framework is the story we live in.
- Right now, Reality lives according to win/lose metrics, a story that is generating existential risk.
- We need to change that story.
- When we change that story and tell a new story—not a made-up story but a new Story of Value, rooted in First Principles and First Values—then it all changes.

It's the most important, exciting, evolutionary, and revolutionary act that we can do to alleviate suffering, to be lovers. Like Rumi, the great poet of Sufism, we have to be mad lovers because it's the only sanity. To be mad lovers is to see around the corner, not to be so obsessed in the details of the contractions of my life, my health, and my markers.

Let me see bigger. Let me take complete care of myself in every possible way. Let me completely attend to those in my circle of intimacy and influence, and then **let me expand my circle.**

That's what we're here for. We're here, as da Vinci was with his cohort in the Renaissance, to play a larger game, to participate in the evolution of love, which is to tell the new Story of Value rooted in First Principles and First Values. What an exciting beginning, and what a wondrous time to be together!

EVOLUTIONARY LOVE CODE: UNIQUE SELF SYMPHONY IN RESPONSE TO THE META-CRISIS

The question is the meta-crisis.

The answer is Unique Self and Unique Self Symphony.

The code is simple and straight. *The question is the meta-crisis. The answer is Unique Self and Unique Self Symphony.*

That's what we're going to talk about today. But first, let's practice. In practice, we open up a new eye. It's the Eye of Value, which was the essential eye for all the most subtle and speculative minds—premodern, modern, and postmodern.

SILENCE AND CHANT OPEN UP THE EYE OF VALUE

Let's first go for a second to India, to the tradition of Kashmir Shaivism, to the depths of Hinduism. We turn to She, to Devi, to the Eros that animates Cosmos, the Eros which is the Eros of value itself.

Let's just hold that. Let's hold it gently, and let it breathe you and you breathe it. Let's bring the East together with the interior sciences of the West.

We'll do just one more chant: *Mizmor Shir*. In *Mizmor Shir*, we sing not to the Goddess who is the force of Cosmos, but we sing to the face of She, the face of Eros, which is infinitely personal and intimate, that knows my name, that dances in the holy and broken *Hallelujah*s of my life.

So there's the She, the Goddess, that suffuses the East—the Shakti Eros that aggregates Reality, the evolutionary impulse. Then there's Her appearance in the West, in which She is Shakti but also infinitely and intimately personal.

> *Mizmor shir leyom Ha'Shabbat*
>
> It's good to be together in the depth of Sabbath.
>
> *Tov lehodot L'Adonai, u'lezamer leshimcha elyon*
>
> It's good to love each other, to speak of your love in the morning, and to trust you through the nights.

It's absolutely essential that we don't just access the Eye of the Mind: reason, conversation, etc. My colleague, Sam Harris, does a podcast which is pure mind and reason. But reason gets lost; reason confuses. **First you have to access the silence.** The silence that is not a materialist construct of Cosmos, that gives you a certain experience.

The silence speaks, the song speaks, and the chant speaks. It opens up the Eye of Value.

Value is intrinsic and innate. It's evolving; it's not preordained. But value is an innate structure of Cosmos; Cosmos generates value that's intrinsic.

THE INFINITY OF INTIMACY: THE PERSONHOOD OF COSMOS

One of the values of Cosmos is personhood. Cosmos is both third-person—the flow of the four fundamental forces, all animated by Eros—and first-person: I can feel a sense of my own consciousness in my first-person experience. Consciousness is the feeling of me, not reducible to any mechanical structure. **But Cosmos is also second-person, which is the Infinity of Personhood, the Infinity of Intimacy.**

It's my I-ness yearning to know your You-ness.

It's *I am Thou.*

It's the knowing that if my inner heart and all of its unique beauty doesn't speak to your inner heart and all of its unique beauty, life is drab, empty, and ultimately meaningless.

That knowing of personhood is itself a First Value and First Principle of Cosmos. That personhood lives not only between *I* and *thee*, *you* and *me*, between *he* and *she*, between the *I* and the *we*, or between different *we*'s. **Personhood is a quality of Cosmos itself.**

Cosmos is both impersonal, in the sense that it's beyond personalities—it's the supernovas in all of their immense and cascading gorgeousness—and Cosmos is also personal. But it's the personal beyond the impersonal. It's the personal that invests and animates the impersonal.

It's not just intimacy as a human construction. It's the intrinsic value of intimacy, located in the Intimate Universe, sourced in the Infinity of Intimacy.

That's the chant: *to speak of your love in the morning and to trust you through the night.* **We turn to the Infinity of Intimacy that knows our name, and we dance, and we hold hands. We impress our lips on Infinity, and we feel the press of Infinity's lips on our bodies, hearts, and minds.**

ENCAPSULATING UNIQUE SELF

We're going to be unpacking the Unique Self teaching that's central to the new story of CosmoErotic Humanism, to give the teaching its rightful place and to bring it into the world, to download it into the source code of culture.

THE CHALLENGE: THE META-CRISIS, THE RESPONSE: UNIQUE SELF

I want to clearly state the essence of Unique Self so we get a deep sense of what this notion of Unique Self is that lies at the very center of Cosmos itself. I don't generally believe in short encapsulations, but there's such a demand for it, so I want to really try and see if we can do it without losing integrity and depth.

The question is the meta-crisis. And the answer is Unique Self and Unique Self Symphony.

UNIQUE SELF IS A DIRECT HIT TO THE DEATH STAR OF EXISTENTIAL RISK

What's the meta-crisis? As a simple image, let's take the Death Star in that cinematic classic of the late twentieth and early twenty-first centuries: *Star Wars*. The Death Star is a battleship armed with existential risk, which has the ability to not just attack but destroy planets. That's existential risk. The forces of good don't have the capacity to engage the Death Star.

The Death Star is culture. It's a culture of death that leads to existential risk. **There's a realization in the cinematic version**—which is not about what the writers were thinking, but culture speaking through this epic story—**that the only way to take out the Death Star is with a direct hit.**

A direct hit that gets through all of the defenses and explodes culture into a new possibility. That's the direct hit.

When we're talking about the Death Star, we're talking about what we call the "second shock of existence."

The first shock of existence is the death of the human being, the realization that the human being will die, which dawns at the beginning of history. Although death is a portal between two days, death is also a stark end. Our experience is that death ends this life. All the stories, and all the plotlines, and all the threads of living end at that particular moment. What happens beyond is a different conversation, and there is a continuity of consciousness. But we have an actual experience of ending.

That ending—the experience of the finality of mortality—**is what presses us into life**. That's the first shock of existence: the realization of the death of the human being.

But there's a second shock of existence. Meaning, after we go through all the stages of human history (matter, life, and mind), we've come to this place in which the gap between our exterior technologies in their exponential forms and the paucity, dearth, and collapse of our interior technologies of value have created extraction models and exponential growth curves. It has created tragedies of the commons and multipolar traps, in which everyone has to keep producing to the nth degree—even weaponized, exponential threats to our very existence—because we're afraid that the other person is going to do it, not be transparent, and hide it from us. **All of these structures have created this essential collapse of systems that are literally on the brink of manifesting themselves. That's the second shock of existence.**

> *The second shock of existence is the potential death of humanity.*

What's the Death Star move? How do we respond to that imminent existential risk? The answer is: **we need a direct hit, and that direct hit is Unique Self.**

So what is Unique Self?

UNIQUE SELF RESPONDS TO THE QUESTION OF *WHO ARE YOU*?

Unique Self is not a declaration, and it's not a claim. It is the best realization about the nature of the human being. It's the answer to one of the greatest questions we can ever ask: *Who am I? Who are you?* Then there's the question, *Who are we?*

But those questions, those narratives of identity, are rooted in larger questions:

- Where are we?
- What's our Universe Story?
- What's there to do?
- What's there to do with our power?
- What's there to do with our desire?

All of those questions are answered by Unique Self.

Again, Unique Self is not just a fanciful conjecture. Unique Self is the result of decades of work that we've done, integrating in a form of "second simplicity." Second simplicity is the third stage: after simple, there's complex, and then comes the second simplicity—the best leading-edge insights and validated understandings of the exterior and interior sciences, in the entire premodern, modern, and postmodern period, woven together into a new Universe Story, into a new understanding of identity that we're calling Unique Self. The individual Unique Self combines with others to create the Unique Self Symphony.

That is what takes down the culture of death. It responds to the second shock of existence, existential risk, and even the first shock of existence, our individual death.

So what do we mean by Unique Self? Unique Self answers the questions of "who am I?" and "who are you?" Unique Self Symphony answers the question of "who are we?"

UNIQUE SELF ANSWERS THE QUESTION OF *WHO ARE YOU?*

Who are you? *You're an irreducibly unique expression of the larger Field of the LoveIntelligence, LoveBeauty, and LoveDesire that is the initiating and animating Eros of All-That-Is that lives uniquely in you, as you, and through you that never was, is, or will be in anyone past, present, and future.*

As a Unique Self:

- You have an irreducibly unique perspective.
- You incarnate an irreducibly unique quality of intimacy.
- You are a unique configuration of desire.
- You are a unique expression of power.

All of those come together to form your "unique gift."

YOUR UNIQUE GIFT

- Your unique gift is both your unique *quality of being* in the world—interacting, interfacing, inter-activating with Reality, your interbeing with Reality—and *the unique gift that you have to give to the world.*
- The unique gift is that which answers a unique need that can be addressed by you and you alone, in your unique circle of intimacy and influence.
- When you are addressing that unique need, in your unique circle of intimacy and influence, you are responding to Reality. That's your unique response-ability. That's your unique obligation. But obligation and love, in the original Semitic languages, are the same word. It's the unique expression of your *LoveIntelligence* that can be done by no one that ever was, is, or will be—other than you.
- When you're committing your unique Outrageous Act of Love, which is your deepest heart's desire, which emerges from your unique configuration of desire, you're giving of your unique gift.

UNIQUE SELF SYMPHONY

That's what it means to play your unique instrument in the Unique Self Symphony. The Unique Self Symphony is not a top-down command-and-control structure. Rather, the Unique Self Symphony is the emergent of evolutionary intimacy, which is the natural product of the self-organizing universe and the self-actualizing Cosmos. **The universe self-organizes to greater and greater levels of intimacy** because evolution is the progressive deepening of intimacy.

Whenever there's a crisis—and we're currently facing a meta-crisis—**the crisis is always a crisis of intimacy.**

The crisis of intimacy is responded to by a new configuration of intimacy, and the new configuration of intimacy, in this generation, at this moment of meta-crisis, is Unique Self Symphony.

Unique Self Symphony is not top-down, and it's not command-and-control. It is rather the human being self-organizing to their highest self, to their deepest self, to their most wondrous and beautiful self, which is their Unique Self.

In other words, **uniqueness is like the pheromones in an ant colony which self-organize the colony,** like the exchange of intelligence among bees. We know scientifically that beehives are wildly organized, allured, and uniquely emergent in wonderful expressions of intelligence.

So how does that work on the human level? Ants and bees are not human beings.

Human beings are, on the evolutionary chain, conscious expressions of evolution.

What drives us? What guides us? What's our North Star? What's our compass of joy?

Our compass of joy is our Unique Self.

- It's the unique set of allurements that call me forward to give my unique gift.
- It's the unique configuration of desire—not surface desire, not pseudo-desire, not lowest-common-denominator desire, manipulated by the internet, whose goals are bottom lines of profit and control—my deepest heart's desire, my clarified desire, which gives my unique gift.

My unique gift allows me to play my instrument in the Unique Self Symphony. Sometimes we play together. Sometimes ten or twenty or thirty of us, or a whole division, or a whole people, are playing different strands on the same Unique Self instrument. That Unique Self instrument gives a unique gift into society.

Who am I, as a human being? I'm a Unique Self, and I have an instrument to play in Unique Self Symphony, and I am needed by All-That-Is.

UNIQUE SELF: REALITY INTENDED ME

That's the realization of Unique Self. The realization of Unique Self is to "speak of your love in the morning" and to "trust you through the night." **Unique Self implies personhood**, and personhood means there's a personal relationship. Reality intended me—that's what uniqueness tells me.

Uniqueness tells me: *I'm unique; I'm not generic. I'm irreducibly unique. Reality intended me. Reality chose me. Reality recognizes me. Reality loves and adores me. Reality desires me. Reality needs me. Reality needs my own growth and my own transformation.*

THE CHALLENGE: THE META-CRISIS, THE RESPONSE: UNIQUE SELF

It's my transformation from a separate self (I'm separate from the field) to a True Self (I'm part of the field), to Unique Self (I'm a unique expression of the field), to an Evolutionary Unique Self (Unique Self in an evolutionary context), who feels the evolutionary impulse pulsing in him, pulsing in her, knowing that this evolutionary impulse has a personal face and that personal face is my Unique Self.

That's how I join in the Unique Self Symphony. **Unique Self Symphony is made up of Evolutionary Unique Selves, acting as unique expressions of *LoveIntelligence* all over the world.**

That's a new vision. That's what I was delighted to call with my dear friends, Barbara Marx Hubbard and Zachary Stein, a Planetary Awakening in Love through Unique Self Symphonies. Let's hold that for a second. That's Unique Self.

UNIQUE SELF AND UNIQUE SELF SYMPHONY IN RESPONSE TO THE META-CRISIS

The meta-crisis: The Death Star.

The response to the meta-crisis: Unique Self and Unique Self Symphony.

It responds to the second shock of existence by activating all of Reality as Unique Selves and Unique Self Symphonies. It's a bottom-up, self-organizing, self-actualizing expression of Cosmos, which is activating to a new structure of intimacy.

It's not a corporation or a government imposing. Of course, we need governments and corporations, as they have important roles. **But at the very core, we need a new cultural enlightenment; we need a new emergent order.**

Only in a closed society like communist China can you have a top-down imposition. An open society needs to have an emergent order, a cultural enlightenment, which self-organizes based on simple First Principles towards a complex and beautiful society, which is the most beautiful world we know possible, the highest, most stunning emergence of the Good, the True, the Beautiful—of intimacy, of love, of Eros.

Unique Self and Unique Self Symphony are the simple first rules. That is what we've learned from complexity and chaos theory: **simple first rules generate a complex and coherent system.**

UNIQUE SELF RESPONDS TO THE FIRST SHOCK OF EXISTENCE

Unique Self also responds to the first shock of existence because when you understand that you are a Unique Self and feel into your unique story, you can access the depth of yourself, the knowing that **as you approach your death,** *it's not over.* You know that you're in midlife. You know that there are all these threads that are still dangling.

You can feel it in the depths of yourself and the depth of your interior experience, what we call Anthro-Ontology (Anthro: human, Ontology: for real). That is, *the mysteries are within us*, and we can access in our own interior experience something real about the very nature of Reality.

I access and realize in my interior: *I'm in mid-play.*

I remember when I was in our dear friend Barbara Marx Hubbard's hospital room. I had just spoken to her that morning. Right before we were beginning a One Mountain podcast, she lost consciousness. I flew immediately to Colorado and was there at her hospital bed when she passed away. She never recovered consciousness. **But it was so clear anthro-ontologically that Barbara's Unique Self hadn't disappeared.**

- There's an enormous amount of very careful philosophy and empirical evidence today to support the continuity of consciousness.
- But even deeper, there's the anthro-ontological knowing, the realization that *I'm irreducibly unique,* and when I get to the

end of my life, I know that my story is not done.

It's Unique Self that tells me:

- We're ultimately going to transcend the first shock of existence.
- The story is not over—it's continuing in its next chapter, in its next unfolding.
- Everything we do in this world is part of the Field of Value, and everything we do writes the script of the next part of our personal passion drama, which participates in the great passion drama of Reality.

Because here's what we understand: **Unique Self is the principle of personhood**. It's the innate and irreducible value of the personal.

YOUR STORY IS CHAPTER AND VERSE IN THE UNIVERSE: A LOVE STORY

The personal is always a story, and our story participates in the larger story of Cosmos. What we understand about Reality, based on the interior and exterior sciences, is that:

- Reality is not merely a fact; Reality is a story.
- Reality is not an ordinary story; Reality is a love story.
- Reality is not an ordinary love story, and it's not a Pollyannish love story. It's an Outrageous Love Story; it's the Eros of Cosmos. It's the Eros that desires the progressive deepening of intimacy.

It's an Evolutionary Love Story.

- Your story is chapter and verse in the larger text of The Universe: A Love Story.
- Your evolution is chapter and verse in Evolution: The Love Story of the Universe.

- Your *Amor* is chapter and verse in *the Amorous Cosmos*.
- Your intimacy is chapter and verse in *the Intimate Universe*.

Your story matters.

It's not *a story you move beyond*. You move beyond your grasping, egoic, surface story and find the deeper outline and plotline of your sacred autobiography. **You find that the plotline of your personal story, your sacred autobiography, is precisely identical to the plotlines of Cosmos itself.**

THE PLOTLINES OF COSMOS ARE TOWARDS MORE UNIQUENESS

Stories have plotlines. The plotlines of Cosmos are simple:

1. The first plotline: the movement from simplicity to complexity.
2. The second plotline: the movement towards more and more interconnectivity.
3. The third plotline: the realization that the interior of interconnectivity is intimacy, and Reality is moving towards deeper and wider configurations of intimacy.
4. The fourth plotline: Reality is moving towards ever more creativity.
5. The fifth plotline: Reality itself is moving towards ever more Eros.
6. But finally, the sixth plotline, which is the mechanism, the engine, the animating *telerotic (telos+eros)* vector for everything:

Reality is moving towards more and more uniqueness.

More and more uniqueness means:

1. More and more complexity.
2. More and more interconnectivity: the node of interface is

always the unique node in a system.
3. More and more intimacy: we go from matter to life to mind, in which ultimately *my Unique Self meets your Unique Self, and we look in each other's eyes*—we see all of Reality, and we see irreducible uniqueness.
4. More and more creativity: creativity emerges from the matrix of my Unique Self.
5. More and more love: because love is Unique Self perception, *I look at you, and I'm blown away by your infinite beauty.*

So the movement towards Unique Self is the vector of Cosmos itself.

All of Cosmos moves towards the realization of Unique Self and Unique Self Symphony.

CHAPTER THREE

THIS POIGNANT MOMENT OF NEURO-CULTURAL PLASTICITY: A TIME BETWEEN WORLDS AND A TIME BETWEEN STORIES

Episode 315 — October 23, 2022

THE FIRST PRACTICE OF CHANT: WE ARE THE MUSIC

It is fabulous and beautiful to be with you. It is great to be with everyone. What we are going to be doing in the live, weekly Evolutionary Sensemaking broadcasts, is we're going to begin fifteen minutes before the hour, every week.

We're going to come together and just:

- Find each other in presence
- Find each other in chant
- Find each other in practice

Before we get to the *dharma*—to the new vision of First Principles and First Values embedded in a Story of Value, which is the single most important response to the meta-crisis—every week, we will begin with *yoga*.

And yoga means *practice*.

Just like there are First Principles and First Values, there are *First Practices*.

And one of the core First Practices—in all of the great traditions of value, in the great interior sciences, one of the most important practices is chant. And we are actually *scientifically* made of music. **We are music ourselves.** We are *constituted* by music. I gave a talk about it this summer, so I won't unpack the science of it now.

Science tells us that music emerges with space-time, and the intervals in space-time that create music quite literally live in us. **It's scientifically true to say that we, quite literally, are music—so when we chant, we find that dimension of ourselves that is music.**

We are going to do a little chant in the beginning, just to get started. We're going to pick up the pace of it a little bit, so we can *feel the feeling* of chant. I am going to do it once, a little bit off-tune like I always do, and we will pick it up and open it up.

We are spontaneous, we are here, we are just delighted.

It's "Let The Way Of The Heart"—and it's got some energy to it:

> *Let the way of the heart,*
> *let the way of the heart,*
> *let the way of the heart shine through.*
> *Love, upon love, upon love,*
> *all hearts are beating as one.*
> *Light, upon light, upon light,*
> *all appear as the one.*

Try it, wherever you are in the world. Together, all around the world!

This is the practice of chant—and the actual lived realization that *there's a way of the heart*.

THE WAY OF THE HEART INCLUDES THE MIND AND THE INTELLECT

The way of the heart *includes* the mind, the intellect, and rigorous thinking—and often lots of footnotes. The heart is both the organ of *feeling*—and, as we now know, with an enormous amount of research from the last twenty years—the heart is also part of our *cognitive function*, and you cannot split those two.

Our ability to think and our ability to feel are inseparable.

The Universe *feels*, and the Universe feels *love*.

I will tell you a little secret:

- I have, never in my entire life ever, like, ever, ever, ever, ever, ever had a good idea. I've never had a good idea, *not once*.
- I've had a *feeling*. I've only had a *feeling* that arrested me, that engaged me, that I *listened to*.

Often, we cut our feelings off, we split our feelings off—or we have a feeling, and then we don't *feel the feeling through to completion*.

And then the feeling gets *arrested*. It gets arrested in trauma, or it gets arrested in the golden shadow of our *unlived* self. It is an *unlived* feeling.

When you listen deeply, you realize that the world is not *only* a great thought, as the physicist James Jeans pointed out a bunch of years back: when you look at physics carefully, the world seems more like a great thought.

The world *is* a great thought, but it's not *just* a great thought.

If you look a little more carefully at physics, **the world is a great *feeling*.**

The Universe *feels*—that's scientifically accurate. **Reality is marked by *allurement*; cosmic allurement guides and *animates* Reality at every stage.**

So the world is not just a great thought, my friends; the world is a great *feeling*. The Universe feels, and the Universe feels love. And that love is One Heart, and it's One Love, and it's One Breath.

THE WAY OF THE HEART: REALITY IS EROS

Let the way of the heart means,

- Feeling *the interior quality* of Cosmos.
- Feeling the allurement that draws us *uniquely*, and that draws us *together* to create the most beautiful world that we know is possible.
- Knowing that *the heart is real.*

The heart is not a superficial function. The heart is not extraneous to the real stuff. **The heart is the most real dimension of Cosmos.**

Reality is, at its core, Eros. Reality is Eros. Reality is One Love and One Heart.

Our minds speak the languages of Eros. Our minds unpack the dazzling cacophonies and symphonies of elegant order, beauty, and truth, that are expressions of the feeling tone of Cosmos.

- **Cosmos is intimate.** It feels *intimacy*, and it *desires*.
- Alfred North Whitehead talks about the *appetite of Cosmos*. **Cosmos feels *hunger*.**
- **Cosmos is hungry for value**: for the Good, the True, the Beautiful, for love, for delight, for joy, for a heartbreak that becomes transformation.
- **Cosmos is evolution**, and evolution at its core is a series of transformations.

WE LIVE IN A TIME BETWEEN STORIES

Let us set intention on where we are:

- *Where* are we?
- *Who* are we?
- *What* are we doing here?

This is not a place for casual therapy. It's not a feel-good place, and it's not a doomer place where we say, *Oh my God, the world is about to explode!*

Although, of course there *are* reasons to feel good, and there *are* reasons for therapy, and the world *is* about to explode.

We are doing something very specific though. **We've got a very specific intention**—and I want to set that intention *very clearly* because it's easy to lose. I'm going to try and set it in a new way, with your permission.

Okay, are we in? Are we ready? Here we go.

We live in this time between worlds;
we live in this time between stories.

If you've been here before, that is the sentence you know well because we say some version of it every week. And we always point to the Renaissance, which was also, in its own way, a time between worlds and a time between stories. When the premodern story was breaking down, when pandemics were sweeping Europe and Asia, and people were dying on the street (almost half of Europe actually died), we understood then that **we couldn't use the old tools of premodernity, of the traditional world:**

- To heal the fracture
- To heal the break
- To heal the destruction
- To heal the breakdown

In order to move from breakdown to breakthrough, we needed to articulate a new vision, to tell a new story—because it's only a new story, and a new story of *value*, that changes the trajectory of history.

So da Vinci and Ficino, whom I mention all the time, and about a thousand other people gathered in Florence, under the patronage of the Medicis, opposed by almost all the other families in Florence, and **they began to *think* and to *feel*.** They felt in art; they felt in science.

They felt and asked the following questions:

- What is the feminine?
- What is Eros?
- What is sexuality?
- What is a relationship?
- How do we gather information?
- What's the nature of the human being?
- Who are you?
- Who are we?
- Where are we?
- What's there to do?
- Where are we going?
- What do we really want?

The new Story of Value that emerged, as we have shared many times together, was the story of modernity.

- To the precise extent that the plotlines were accurate, modernity birthed what Habermas, probably the greatest critical philosopher of the twentieth century, called *the dignities of modernity.*
- To the precise extent that they got the storyline *wrong*, which they did in the Renaissance, in major ways, it birthed the *disasters* of modernity. And those disasters have brought us to this moment in which we are quite literally not just poised

before *dystopia*—we are poised before a potential extinction, the death of humanity, or the dystopian death of *our* humanity.

But we are *also* poised before utopia. We have the potential to unfold a world of unimaginable beauty, unimaginable depth, unimaginable goodness, of *ever deeper* and ever wider truths, a world in which no one's left out of the circle, in which everyone can respond powerfully and accurately to the great questions: *who am I, who are we, where are we,* and *where are we going?*

But *not* in a way that occludes the uncertainty, *not* in a way which dissipates the Great Mystery. The Great Mystery is there, and we always live at the edge of mystery, reaching deeper and deeper into the mystery and unfolding it into the light. Even as we reach deeper, in the same moment, **the mystery itself deepens.**

We always hold uncertainty, and we always stand before the mystery.

WE HAVE THE CAPACITY TO CREATE A NEW SUPERSTRUCTURE WORLDVIEW TO CHANGE THE VECTOR OF HISTORY

And yet, we have the capacity to *integrate*, to *weave together* the validated insights from all the great stories of value, into a new source-code tapestry, into a new Story of Value, rooted in what postmodernity denied: First Principles and First Values.

We have come to the conclusion—after decades of study, practice, and research—that at this moment of meta-crisis, when everything is at stake, the *only* response that will change the vector of history is a **superstructure** change.

- An **infrastructure** response alone is insufficient. Infrastructure would mean: *let's create new sources of energy.* That's critically important; renewable energy is critically important but insufficient. *Let's find ways to check for waste in water to*

prevent a bioweapons attack—critically important but insufficient.
- A ***social structure*** change won't do it. Social structure means: *let's revision how democracy works, let's revision laws that demand that X amount of data scientists don't work for the tech world, but actually work for the government, in order to be able to appropriately bind or monitor what Big Tech is doing.* That would be a social structure change, a change in law. Those are also very important.
- **But the only response that will change the vector of history is a *superstructure* change.**

There's infrastructure, social structure, and superstructure—terms we are borrowing from the sociologist Marvin Harris—but the crucial insight is that **only a superstructure change can change the vector of history**, meaning only a change in the answers to the three great questions:

- ***Who*** are you? Who am I? Who are we?
- ***Where*** are we? Where am I? Where are we?
- ***What's there to do***, or where are we going, which is deeply related to *what do I really want to do*, and *what's my deepest desire*?

Those essential questions: *who, where, what*? Those are the questions, and our answers to them become the new story.

VALUE IS REAL, AND VALUE EVOLVES

We have to answer those questions based on First Principles and First Values that are *real*.

We have to move beyond the postmodern deconstruction of value. We have to realize that value *allures*, that *we are guided* by value, and that value *evolves*.

- Modernity and postmodernity were wrong when they said *value is not real*.
- Premodernity was wrong when it said *value doesn't evolve*.

Value is real, *and* **value evolves**—that's the *post*-postmodern understanding; that's the basis for the new Story of Value. Value is real. And so we're currently working together to articulate fifteen basic core First Values and First Principles, and to articulate the plotline of the story. And the story is a love story.

THE POTENTIAL FUTURE IS VAST—THERE'S SO MUCH MORE VALUE TO COME

Now, I want to try and say, *in a new way*, **why this insanely matters,** as part of setting our intention.

A thought experiment: **your actions taken now will affect all of your future lives.**

- Imagine for a second **that there are 100 billion people who have lived**—which is about accurate: there have been about 100 billion people in the world since the beginning of the species, around 300,000–400,000 years ago, when *Homo erectus* as it were, stood on the savanna of Africa and became some version of *Homo sapiens*. Now, from that moment till today, there's been about 100 billion humans.
- **Now imagine that in some sense, you are *every one* of those people.** Remember the chant we started with: *all hearts are beating as one*. And in some sense, you *are* every one of those people. We all share the same essential quality of consciousness, and we're all indivisibly part of each other in some fundamental way. But for now, let go of the ontology of it, let go of the reality of it. Just hold it as a thought experiment.
- **Let's say you live every single one of those lives**

THIS POIGNANT MOMENT OF NEURO-CULTURAL PLASTICITY

consecutively, one life after the other. And in some sense, you *are* all of those people (and Andy Weir, in a short story called *The Egg*, actually articulated some version of this thought experiment). Imagine 100 billion people, one after the other after the other after the other after the other—and you are *all* of those people—how long would it take for those people to go through their lives?

And so that means that…

> You're an early hunter-gatherer,
> and you're at the beginning of agriculture,
> and you're a man,
> and you're a woman,
> and you're a slave,
> and you're a boy,
> and you're a victim,
> and you're an apex predator,
> and you're a murderer,
> and you're the one who's murdered,
> and so on…

Do you get that?

> You're everyone.
> You're the rapist,
> and you're the one who is raped.
> You're the one who's filled with joy and goodness,
> and you're the one who's filled with black melancholy, who can barely move.

Imagine that you are *everyone*. You are literally all of those people, and all of those people live in you—that's going to take about 4 trillion years. About *four trillion* years.

- **Now imagine, for a second, the future.** If the average mammalian species lives about a million years, that means that at this point, four trillion years in, you still have 99.5% of your life left to live—meaning, if you unfold all of the future, you've only hit 0.5% of humanity. It means **you have an enormous amount of life left to live.**
- Now imagine, friends—**imagine that human beings actually learned how to take care of themselves to at least survive** in a way that earlier mammals are unable to do. And imagine we live *more* than a million years—we live two million, or three million, or four million, or we even live the fullness of the possibility of this earth and the star, until they burn themselves out—and we transmute into the next possibility. **Imagine you live *all of that*.**

Then, within the framework of that thought experiment, which is real and valid, we would be literally *taking our first breaths* outside of the womb; we'd have taken twenty or fifty breaths so far. **We're in the first seconds out of the womb right now.**

And to get a sense, my friends, the future is vast and large; **the potential future is vast and large.**

> Trillions and trillions of people.
> Trillions of boys and trillions of girls.
> Trillions of babies and trillions of loves.
> Trillions of pearls of laughter and trillions of holy tears.
> Trillions of transformations.
> Trillions of creative acts.
> Trillions of unique expressions of Reality, each one more dazzlingly beautiful than the last, each one with infinite value.

There are trillions of new emergents, of self-evidently precious value—each of which matters immensely and enormously—yet to come. There are trillions of irreducibly unique expressions of infinite value left to come, of infinite divinity left to come.

Or we could say:

There's more God to come. There's more value to come.

But *infinitely* more value to come, *infinitely* more God to come—not literally infinitely but virtually infinitely. Wow!

THE FUTURE DEPENDS ON WHAT WE DO NOW

Now, let's go to the next level of the thought experiment.

Now you realize that your actions taken now will affect all of your future lives.

Do you get that? What you do now will affect all of your future lives.

One possibility is that it will affect whether you even *have* a future life. In other words, you may behave in a foolhardy way now, which will ensure that you have no future life at all. Now, that's kind of a shocking notion.

Imagine you're a teenager, and there's lots of things you do as a teenager.

- You want to experiment, go deep inside, experience the pain and beauty of the world, and get new fields of knowledge.
- But you also have to be careful as a teenager **not to take risks that will prevent you from growing up.** And it's the job of society, your parents, and your own internal learned, trained discipline to prevent this. You don't want to take a risk whereby through some foolhardy act you actually die—you actually never grow up into the fullness of who you are. Wow!

And sometimes we don't even realize we're taking those risks.

I remember in Bexley, Ohio, where I grew up, we used to go jumping building from building, and it was intensely dangerous. And it didn't even occur to me it was dangerous; I was never hurt. But looking back on it, it's like, wow, *what was I thinking?* We could have fallen. Sometimes you do it unconsciously—and sometimes, we're actually aware that there's this immense risk in what we're doing, but we split off the risk.

Now, **we are not even close to the adolescence of our humanity.** And at this moment, what we do in the next ten, twenty, fifty, 100, 200 years from now, in this immediate period, will directly affect the future—according to carefully articulated and hard-crunched numbers, and an entire set of writings on existential risk, by people like Nick Bostrom, the student of Derek Parfit at Oxford who coined the term *existential risk*, along with quite a few other serious investigators. Some of Parfit's other students, Toby Ord and Will MacAskill, have also done very good work in this regard.

I think their work is deeply flawed in terms of *how to respond* to existential risk, but they did an excellent job in both coining the term, articulating the *possibility* of existential risk, and bringing it deep into consciousness.

So that's real. Existential risk is absolutely real. That's the death of humanity.

What we do in this period of time could actually prevent us from growing up. It could stop us from living all of those trillions of lives, in some fundamental sense. Or it could also cause the death of *our* humanity. **And the death of *our* humanity means, we don't actually go extinct, but we enter into a dystopian future.**

NEURO-CULTURAL PLASTICITY

I want to take a look at what that means—because it's a very big deal.

Right now, we are in a moment—if I could coin a term that emerged in conversations last week—of what I would call neuro-cultural plasticity.

THIS POIGNANT MOMENT OF NEURO-CULTURAL PLASTICITY

Plasticity is a term from biological systems research from the last fifty years. A brilliant brain researcher named Thomas Metzinger (who coined the term and whose material I've been reading for the last two to three years) talks about plasticity. Plasticity means that we used to think that the brain—very early on in infancy, or perhaps a little bit later—is essentially ossified, or frozen, and it doesn't ever change after that. The brain is a given, and this belief has had enormous implications. We now realize that that's not true, that **the brain is constantly rewiring itself.**

For example, after you have an accident, and you lose, for example, one part of the brain, the other hemisphere will often rewire some of the functions of the lost part. And that's true not only of the brain but of the entire body. The body is *plastic*. **The systems of the body, including the brain, are plastic, and they have the ability, at certain moments of crisis, to rewire themselves,** until they again get appropriately set in the mold or the pattern that they will be in.

That's called *plasticity*.

But **not only is there plasticity in the biological system. There's plasticity in the *cultural* system.**

MacAskill, in a book that's called What We Owe The Future, gives a very good example of this. In the sixth century, the Xiao dynasty ended in China, and then there was a period of 400 years of what was called "The Hundred Schools of Thought," in which you have major schools competing with each other: Confucianism, Taoism, and what was later called, retrospectively, Legalism, and also Mohism. You've got these major four schools of thought battling for dominance—until about 400 years later, when Confucianism wins the day, and for about a 1,000 years Confucianism dominates China.

He uses that as an example of these moments that are *in between*. That's what we mean when we say, *we are at a time between worlds*. When we say we live at a time between worlds and a time between stories, what we mean is that **there is neuro-cultural plasticity in this moment.**

EXISTENTIAL RISK AND THE EVOLUTION OF LOVE

We are at a time between worlds, we are at a time between stories. This neuro-cultural plasticity means that in this moment, it's not set; in this moment, it could go many different ways.

That's generally not the case. Generally, we are *in* a world, *in* a story, and you can't really even think outside of that story.

- You live inside of that story.
- That story lives in you.
- You can't even see the story.
- You can't make the subject into an object.
- You can't see the story. You're just in the story.

We are at this unique moment when, at least at the leading edge, there are many of us who have stepped *outside* of the old story:

- We realize that we are not just at a place where, after Covid we need to *get back to normal*.
- We realize, as I've been trying to say for a couple of decades, together with Barbara Marx Hubbard, our partner—with whom I founded One Mountain, Many Paths, and who was the co-chair of our Center for the last few years of her life—that in some deep sense this is a *phase-shift moment*.

We are at a phase shift in human history, unlike any that we've ever been in, in which *everything* is at stake, where all the old systems are breaking down, but the new system hasn't yet emerged.

This space *in between* is a completely creative space. And in the space in between, the relationships between parts *can be reconfigured*. **This space**

in between is a *neuro-cultural plastic* space, in which what we do affects everything.

That wasn't true 200 years ago, and it may well not be true 200 years from now. It may not be true 100 years from now; it wasn't quite true 100 years ago.

This time between worlds, this time between stories, is this space *in between*, where:

- We are either going to do **a reset by telling a new Story of Value** rooted in First Principles and First Values.
- Or there's going to be **a tragic, dystopian value lock-in.**

VALUES ARE NOT MERELY *PRAGMATIC*

Here's where MacAskill, Ord, and Bostrom go wrong. They are essentially beautiful people, highly moral, highly principled in their own lives. And yet, despite the fact that they come out of a what I would call Derek Parfit's "moral realism," **they can't quite articulate a genuine theory of value.** Value, for them, is, in one sense or another, *consequentialist*: value is merely based on its *utilitarian* effect in the world.

Once you try and do *consequentialist ethics*, they always break down, as the critics of consequentialism have pointed out, and they can't ultimately *motivate* you—because we are only truly motivated by an intrinsic sense of responding to value that's *real*.

You cannot deconstruct value and say that value is a mere fiction. This is the way the circle of postmodernity talks about value: *value is a mere fiction, value is a figment of our imagination, value is a story, and value is pragmatically consequentialist.* No.

Value is real; value is an intrinsic structure of Cosmos.

So we need to actually create *not* a world in which you just keep open, competing values—which is what MacAskill suggests. **No, we instead have** to download into Reality a vision of a set of First Principles and First Values that are *evolving*.

- One of the First Principles and First Values is that these values themselves are always evolving.
- These First Principles and First Values form a universal grammar of value.
- That universal grammar of value is **a context for our diversity**. It is a context for many plural, various, subtle, and nuanced understandings and applications of value.
- But at the center, there has to be **a shared sense of Evolving First Principles and First Values that are rooted in a Story of Value.**

We need to know that *uniqueness* is a value, that *truth* is a value, and that *peace* is a value. But these are all *real* values, not *pragmatic* values; we did not just make them up because it seems to be good for our ability to have a good meal today.

No, we actually feel and know that *value lives in us:*

- That justice is a real value.
- That kindness is a real value.
- That Eros is a real value.
- That sensuality is a real value. Sensuality means it's worth being sensual with someone, that it's valuable.
- That the exchange of pleasure is a value.

In other words:

- There is a set of First Principles and First Values that animate Cosmos, and that move all the way *up* the evolutionary chain and all the way *down* the evolutionary chain.
- In matter, life, and mind, there are evolving expressions of the same Field of Value.

- One of these values is *mystery*, meaning that it's not all worked out yet. One of the values that's part of mystery is *uncertainty*—but that these are *real*, and that what we do *matters* ultimately.
- Our lives are part of the Field of Value, and our lives are not over when they're over.
- We participate in the Field of Value, and value is *eternal*—not in the sense of unchanging, but in the sense of that which is *beneath* space and time. **We participate in the Field of Value which is beneath space and time.**
- **We need, in this moment of neuro-cultural plasticity, to *download* those values into Reality.**

Because the alternative is a value lock-in.

That's what MacAskill talks about accurately. A value lock-in means that at this time between worlds and time between stories, at this moment of what I'm calling *neuro-cultural plasticity*, **if we don't download First Principles and First Values**—which are valid and true, and which integrate the best of premodern, modern, and postmodern insights into a new "evolving perennialism"—**the alternative is a tragic dystopian value lock-in.**

IN RESPONSE TO NIHILISM, YOU GET CLOSED SOCIETIES

If we don't articulate a universal grammar of value, then the first country that achieves technological supremacy will dominate the world

This is a very big deal, so I want to try and articulate for you what that means. This is the key of everything we're talking about today.

Before people emerge in their fullest and most noble selves, they always go through certain stages. Often, people never get past going through what I'm about to describe before they die. Some people do transform. But it's not just people—**humanity as a whole goes through these same stages.**

These are stages in which there is **a seeking of dominance**: we want to dominate, and we want our vision of the world to dominate after we're gone:

- Alexander the Great wanted Hellenism to last forever.
- Hitler wanted there to be a thousand-year Reich.
- Chinese emperors, who reigned only fifteen years, spent that time planning for their dynasty to last forever, which of course it never did.

But there is a sense that we want our vision of the world to last forever. That's a big deal because we are in a world today in which **there is an enormous battle between open societies and closed societies.**

This is the way MacAskill tells this story. Although he clearly comes from the open society side of the world, **he refuses (in his chapter on value) to say that one set of values is actually better than any other set** because he has no *ultimate basis* to say that, other than consequentialism, which doesn't give you a ground in intrinsic value. Over the long term of history, he claims, we are actually not sure what works better. China is making a case that ultimately, over generations and generations, *their* system is going to work better.

So MacAskill cannot actually create a hierarchy of values. *Nothing can ever be ultimately better than anything else,* although there is lip service paid to that kind of claim—and beautiful lip service. For example, read Derek Parfit, his teacher, who is stunning. I have all of his books, and I've been reading through them the last seven or eight weeks. They are gorgeous.

But ultimately, we need to be grounded in the Tao, and the Tao is a Field of Value.

Once we step out of the Tao, we step into *the abolition of man,* as C.S. Lewis said it. The Tao is the Field of Value. Once we step out of the Field of Value—even if we have a couple of generations of benevolent articulators of culture, like Parfit, Bostrom, the young MacAskill and Ord, and blessings to you guys—ultimately, it's not going to hold.

Once you step out of the Tao, out of the Field of Value, you are ultimately in the realm of nihilism. When you are in the realm of *not* standing for actual value, then the nihilism emerges. **And in response to nihilism, you have various forms of closed society.**

That's what China is. That's what Russia is trying to be. It's what Hungary is becoming. That's what the Philippines is becoming. It's where Brazil is going. It's where Sweden—strangely—is going. It's where Italy is going. And France has very strong movements in that direction. And the United States has strong movements in that direction—movements towards some version of closed society.

Now let's look at a closed society, for example, from the perspective of China. This is a big deal. A closed society responds to this breakdown of value, responds to the sense that the West is not standing for value, and says: no, no—we are going to **superimpose values from above, and those values are going to be totalitarian.**

- Those values are going to create concentration camps around China.
- Those values are going to create a total surveillance system, without First Values and First Principles, in which there is no value to the individual:
    - There is no value to unique human personhood, and there is no sense of Unique Self.
    - There is no sense of the intrinsic value of goodness, truth, and beauty.
    - There is no sense of human personhood.
    - There is no ultimate sense of universal human rights, let alone governance through more advanced forms than top-down, totalitarian, brutal, and murderous dictatorship.

The Chinese Communist Party today is essentially a mafia, which engages in the most brutal tactics of murder and mayhem. Let me just say that clearly. Anyone who has studied and read seriously about the Chinese Communist Party knows that it's a degraded expression of what humanity can and needs to be.

THE CURRENT TRAJECTORY IS TOWARDS THE DEATH OF *OUR* HUMANITY

Let's say we *do not* manage to articulate a universal grammar of value. Let's say we just go about our lives, and we do our little projects and our little New Age engagements, and we do our transformations—but we actually ignore the fact that we are at this moment of *neuro-cultural plasticity*. We fail to download a compelling vision—a vision that's compelling to the people of China, a vision that's compelling to Russia—that begins to emerge as a *universal* grammar of value.

What's going to happen is that **the first country to achieve technological supremacy,** for example, to realize AGI (artificial general intelligence)—according to multiple estimates, there's a significant possibility in the next twenty to fifty years that this could happen—will have a huge advantage. If that country is China, **what China will seek to do is to *lock in its values*.**

Artificial general intelligence means not *local* artificial intelligence, in which you can do one particular action exponentially better than humans, but you can do *everything* better than humans. Right now you have an artificial intelligence that can do *one* thing. It's really good at playing chess and Go, but it's not good at ordering groceries. You have very, very localized, exponentially developed, local artificial intelligence—but it's not *general*.

If you get to an artificial *general* intelligence, and that general intelligence is owned by a closed society or a totalitarian state, within six months to a year, two years, the AGI will exponentially increase the rate of productivity and military power achievable by that country and **make

them the dominant force in the world, in a very, very narrow window of time.

In other words, the country that achieves that will dominate the globe. And when I say *dominate the globe*, it's not an old world. It means they dominate the entire planetary stack, all of the computational infrastructure. **The planetary stack of Reality will be completely dominated by that country.** Wow!

And that country will then download *their* value structure into the whole world.

In order to get food, to get a job, to participate in any way in society, you actually need to be part of what China today calls the *Social Credit System*.

- You have to be part of that world infrastructure. If you are not part of the world infrastructure, essentially, you die.
- And you only are allowed into the survival *infrastructure* if you assent to the imposed *superstructure* (worldview, value structure).

So within a generation or two, that downgraded, dystopian value structure becomes the value structure of humanity.

Wow! That's what I mean by the death of *our* humanity.

So there are two possibilities:

1. There's **the death of humanity**: extinction.
2. Then there's this other dystopian possibility, which is a second form of existential risk, which we've been talking about together in our Unique Self Symphony. It's not the death of humanity, it's **the death of *our* humanity**.

UP TILL NOW, WE HAVE NOT PRESENTED A COHERENT SYSTEM OF VALUE IN THE WORLD

What we've been saying week after week—and it's sometimes easy to lose the meaning—is that we are at a time between worlds, a time between stories. We are at this moment of **maximal neuro-cultural plasticity, when what we do *can* affect the future.**

That's a *very* rare place to be in history. There is no generation that's ever been, in all of history, at this place, where what we do can affect the future in this way.

Imagine we've lived for four trillion years, 100 billion lives. But we're just at the first 0.5 percent, as we said earlier. If humanity lives, like most mammalian species, a million years, we are at the beginning of all our future lives. **And what we do now could lead us to suicide; we could have *no* future lives**, meaning we will have essentially left, *in non-existence*, essentially *murdered* trillions and trillions and trillions of gorgeous, irreducibly unique expressions of *LoveIntelligence* and *LoveBeauty*. Boys and girls, and babies, and old men and old women, and wise ones. All of it!

Or we can engage in this great project, this overwhelming moral imperative of this time, articulate a new Story of Value based on evolving First Principles and First Values, and have the audacity to say that we want to download this and engage the world. And we want to talk to China, Russia, and every closed society, and *invite them* into this possibility, so they see that we actually *are* standing for value.

- **We are *not* trapped in nihilism.** We are not in what Putin thinks is a kind of weak and broken postmodern West.
- **We are actually standing strong for value and aligned with value in a deep way.** It is an evolving and coherent system of value. And it's a Story of Value that we are willing to place everything on the line for.

Up till now, the West has not presented a coherent system of value in the world. We haven't. Putin, Xi, and Orban have looked at the West in a kind of postmodern breakdown, no longer standing for value in any genuine sense.

There was a moment where the West came together around Ukraine, which was critically important, and we've talked about that here (and Elena has done a beautiful job of bringing those talks together, and we're going to share them shortly with the world)—but that's broken down in many ways.

We have to come together and stand for value. But we can't do that because:

- We actually don't have a *theory* of value.
- We don't have a vision of First Values and First Principles.
- We are stuck in all the postmodern critiques of value, which are valid, but we haven't moved beyond them.
- What we're here to do is to tell a new Story. **To tell a new Story of Value, rooted in First Principles and First Values, at this time of neuro-cultural plasticity, is the single most compelling moral act, with most consequences.**

What we do at this moment of plasticity, what we do at this time between worlds and time between stories, will affect *everything*.

What we need to do is give *new answers*. But not declarations, not *made-up* answers—the deepest, most beautiful, most gorgeous, most grounded, most validated answers we can—to the great questions of:

- Who am I? Who are we?
- Where are we? What kind of world do we live in?
- What's there to do? What's our deepest heart's desire?
- What does it mean to be a man and a woman?
- What does it mean to be in a relationship?
- What does it mean to create an economy?
- What does it mean to create politics?

All of that depends on these basic questions: *who*, *where*, and *what*.

That's what we are going to be doing. We are in this revolution, and our question is, are we ready to play a larger game?

Are we ready to participate, at this moment of maximum neuro-cultural plasticity, in the Evolution of Love and be brave and courageous enough to create a universal grammar of value, even a world religion—but a world religion as a context for our diversity? It's not *one* religion where we say, "we *own* truth, you don't," but a *universal* grammar of value as a context for our pluralism, as a context for our diversity.

Literally, the future of Reality depends on it. The suffering, catastrophic risk, existential risk, the death of humanity, or the death of our humanity—all depends on what we do at this moment in time.

PLACING OUR LIVES ON THE ALTAR OF HISTORY

The rare privilege of being those people, born at this time, to have that privilege—and of all the people on planet Earth, somehow, we, and colleagues of ours around the world, have been granted this privilege.

We have the capacity to be here together on Sunday, to be participating in evolutionary sensemaking projects, and in editing projects, and writing projects, and funding and resourcing, in order to make this true.

And we've got to take dramatic steps:

- What does that *mean* for each of us?
- What are we doing to show up, to wake up?

So that we can actually light this moment up with our mad commitment, our mad joy, because we can *see* it.

I want to tell you something. There are days when I wake up, and I'd rather *not* see it; I'd rather be blind. Because if you don't see it, you can just engage your life. But once She opens your eyes, once you can see it—if you could

THIS POIGNANT MOMENT OF NEURO-CULTURAL PLASTICITY

see it today—that means you are in. That means you have a place at the table of history.

This system that we are in is not an old-style system. It's not somebody downloading *dogma*. We are together as a Unique Self Symphony, creating this new Story of Value, resourcing and visioning it. **We are placing our lives on the altar of history and saying, we are here!**

We are here to do this. Wow, that's a big deal.

We are going to step into articulating this grammar of value. And we want to weave it together in a way so that:

- It's going to land in China.
- It's going to land in Moscow.
- It's going to land all over Africa.
- It's going to land all over Asia.
- It's going to land all over Europe.
- It's going to land all over the Americas.
- It's going to land in Greenland.
- It's going to land in Iceland.
- It's going to land in Australia.

And I missed a continent: Antarctica.

We want to articulate an evolving shared grammar of value that calls us to the best of who we are.

Not to our lowest common denominator, which is how the web is architectured (the web-plex appeals to the lowest common denominator of human being). Instead:

- We want to call forth **our nobility**.
- We want to call forth **our beauty**.

- We want to call forth the capacity for the fullness and gorgeousness of what a human being is, **a *Homo sapiens* who's becoming *Homo amor*.**

Homo amor, meaning the fulfillment of *Homo sapiens*.

Homo amor, who is omni-considerate for the sake of the whole.

Homo amor, who is an irreducibly unique expression of the *LoveIntelligence* and *LoveBeauty*, who is giving his or her unique gift, who participates in a planetary awakening in love through Unique Self Symphonies.

That's what we're here for.

TURNING TO THE DIVINE TO PARTNER WITH US

I cannot say *thank you* enough. We are going to finish today with a prayer, like we always do. And just thank you madly for being with us. We are going to finish with a prayer from Leonard Cohen.

Prayer is not an *old* idea. It's *not* a premodern idea. **Prayer itself is a First Principle and First Value of Cosmos, and it's the First Principle and First Value of *second person*:**

- There is not just *first person*, my experience with myself.
- There is not just *third person*, me *observing* Reality, looking at *it*.
- But there is *second person*: there's the space in between us. And that second person is relationship.

There are very serious writers in quantum physics who understand that **Reality itself, at its core, is *relationship*.** Reality is relationship; that's what it is. And it's relationships *between us*. There is a relationship between me and myself, but there is also a relationship between me and you. There are I-Thou relationships. But our relationships are *reflective*; they participate in the larger field of relationship.

Reality is not *just* third-person, objective fact. And it is not *just* my own internal experience. Reality is personal. There's an infinite Field of *Personhood*. Reality has a personal face.

- There is not just God as an Infinity of *Power*, all of the dazzling complexity and energies and forces of Cosmos.
- There is a second quality of Cosmos, which is a First Principle and First Value, which is *personhood*. There's a personal face to Cosmos that knows my name. We call that by many names—the Gods and the Goddesses of every tradition were an attempt, sometimes primitive—but it was a valid, correct intuition, that *there is a personhood to Cosmos that knows my name, that's holding me in every second.*

Leonard Cohen's song, "Hallelujah," has more covers than any other song because it speaks to that intuition. Leonard Cohen stands before the lord of song, the personal face of Cosmos, and says, *Hold me! Hold my holy and broken Hallelujah.* Because I know that, *There's a blaze of light in every word, it doesn't matter which you heard, the holy or the broken Hallelujah.*

So we turn to the Divine, and we say, *partner* with us.

- You live *in us*, as us, and *through us*.
- But you also *hold* us, and you are also *manifested in us*.

Those are somehow both true, paradoxically, so:

> Partner with us. Hold us in our *holy and broken Hallelujah*, and hear our prayer. Hear our prayer, even as we human beings hear *your* Divine prayer.

Because in the great lineages, **humans respond to the prayer of the Divine.** And God says:

> *I need your partnership.*
>
> *I need you to hold my hand.*

I need you to walk with me in history.

I need you to partner with me in creating the new world.

And we turn to the Divine, and we ask for everything.

- We ask for health, we ask for longevity, and we ask for energy.
- We ask for goodness; we ask for joy.
- We ask for ourselves, our neighbor, our family members, our children, our cousins, and then for people we've never met.
- We ask for the goodness of the whole thing; we are omni-considerate for the sake of the whole.
- We bring it all—nothing is left out. Every place we go, we fall into Her hands, into the hands of *She*, who hears every note of our holy and our broken *Hallelujah*.

We move into prayer, and as we hear Leonard Cohen, who's very loving. He comes to us, to One Mountain, every week, and we play this chant, this prayer.

It is a mad joy to be with you, with all of the urgency! The urgency is also lined with joy at the privilege. We feel infinite concern—and yet we *celebrate*, and yet we're alive. We are filled with joy in every second. And what a joy, what a delight, and for me at least, a great honor of my life to be with you.

CHAPTER FOUR

THE ULTIMATE META-CRISIS IS GOD'S CRISIS OF INTIMACY

Episode 334 — March 5, 2023

LISTENING TO THE GODDESS

It is a wildly important day. I got up early to try and work on the *Intimate Universe* book, but Goddess had other plans. And *She* whispered a bunch of things in my ear.

Now, you might say, what does he mean: *Goddess whispered a bunch of things in his ear?*

When we say, *Goddess whispered in my ear*, what we mean is, **there are moments in which we feel this experience of being *taken over*.** It's an experience that we have in creativity, but creativity is just one expression of it. We can feel it in many different places like sexuality and ethics, this feeling of being taken over by an ethos.

We feel it—and I want to be very precise—**we feel it the more we practice.**

Occasionally, we'll have an inspiration—but inspiration generally comes because we *prepare* for inspiration. The notion that you're simply living your life, and then along

comes inspiration—it's not really how it works. A reliable inspiration generally comes from two places:

- One, **from grace**. It's a gift. It's an utter, complete, total gift.
- Two: **you are listening for it**. You may listen for it in different ways, but practicing means: you *listen* for it. **You dedicate your life to listening for that moment in which Reality is speaking uniquely through you.**

Reality speaks through each of us in particular ways, and we each have different roles and scripts. But we are part of a shared symphony.

I first started the process of thinking and teaching about these things forty-five years ago, and I've been, give or take, pretty much in this process, practicing in one way or the other, since then. And so you think, *wow, we got this.*

That's not how it works.

It keeps deepening, it keeps evolving, it keeps crystallizing—and then there are these moments when *She* takes us over. Everything that we already knew—through decades of realization, practice, transmission, receiving, reading, studying, and then practicing again—all of that crystallizes again, and **we can tell the story again in a clearer way.**

What we're here to do is tell a story—but not a casual story: we are here to tell the new Story of Value in response to the meta-crisis. It is our understanding here that the new Story of Value is the most important single response we have to the meta-crisis, and the meta-crisis is the most important single source of massive suffering or extinction we've ever experienced. Telling the new Story of Value is huge, and being able to crystallize the new Story together, to deepen the new Story, and to evolve the new Story—that's the seat of the revolution. That's what we do here at One Mountain.

We are exactly where we are supposed to be this week: we are going to talk about Outrageous Acts of Love. I want to try and capture what we mean by Outrageous Acts of Love, and in doing so, unpack this Story of Value at a new level.

You have to listen to the Goddess—and by *the Goddess*, I mean the voice of *She*, **the voice of creativity that is not reducible to anything that came before.**

Alfred North Whitehead writes that there is an *occasion*, and the occasion *prehends* (or receives) all of the previous moment. That's where karma comes from. **The new moment receives all of the previous moment, and yet it is inherently creative, so the occasion allows for something new.** These moments when we are seized by the Goddess are not some strange New Age apparition. They are the quality of Reality that moves evolution forward, where we see with new clarity. We are on the Inside of the Inside, and in the new moment, something new emerges, some new configuration of intimacy.

That's what a new Story of Value is: a new configuration of intimacy. And the story evolves when we put together the parts we already know. We put it all together in a new way, and then it *sharpens*. **This is the story that can actually *re-vivify* humanity.** We can actually move to the next level. *Homo sapiens* can actually become *Homo amor*.

In response to the meta-crisis, we can generate a new Story of Value that changes who we are as human beings: a new human and a new humanity. And that new human and new humanity, that *Homo sapiens* who becomes *Homo amor*, is able to become the response to the meta-crisis.

I am wildly, madly excited to share with you this new crystallization.

EVOLUTIONARY LOVE CODE: OUTRAGEOUS LOVE

> *Homo amor* is vocationally aroused to commit Outrageous Acts of Love. S/he commits the Outrageous Acts of Love that are a function of his/her Unique Self. Outrageous Acts of Love are almost always that which we can "get away with not doing."

An Outrageous Act of Love might be smiling when we want to withhold or opening our heart when it is more comfortable to keep it closed.

An Outrageous Act of Love might be changing your tone of voice. It might be sending a text with an overflowing heart.

It might be taking a stand when we can get away with not taking a stand.

Outrageous Acts of Love are when we give ourselves outrageously—beyond our traumas, our rackets, our issues, and our patterns.

With true Outrageous Acts of Love, we can always rationalize to ourselves why we don't have to do them. Genuine Outrageous Acts of Love are the fabric of the Intimate Universe realizing its Omega Point as you. What moves us to commit Outrageous Acts of Love is evolution herself. Goddess Herself. She.

We are poised between utopia and dystopia. We are confronted by a meta-crisis. Our understanding is that neither an *infrastructure* response nor a *social structure* response will be sufficient. Those are both very important, but we need new *superstructure*, a new Story of Value rooted in evolving First Principles and First Values.

That's what truly changes the story.

That's what evolves the story.

We are in a particular part of the story:

1. We live in a world of outrageous pain, the only response is Outrageous Love.
2. Who am I? **I am an Outrageous Lover**.
3. What does an Outrageous Lover do? **An Outrageous Lover commits Outrageous Acts of Love**.
4. Which Outrageous Acts of Love does an Outrageous Lover commit? **Those that are a function of his/her Unique Self**.

That's enough for now; that's the general context. There's a lot to say about each of those points, and we've previously said a lot about each one. But that's just a simple recapitulation.

We also distinguish between Outrageous Love and ordinary love:

- Ordinary love is beautiful. It lives only at the human level. It's a strategy of the ego for comfort and security, which are legitimate but insufficient. It's a very particular form of love. Ordinary love is a very short love list, with maybe one or two people on it.
- **Outrageous Love is not mere human sentiment. Outrageous Love is the heart of existence itself.** When I awaken as an Outrageous Lover as a human being, I realize that I am participating in the Field of Outrageous Love, and I'm participating in the Field of Outrageous Love uniquely. Outrageous Love doesn't move through me *generically*; it moves through me *uniquely*. That's what Outrageous Love is.

What does the Outrageous Lover do? The Outrageous Lover commits Outrageous Acts of Love.

Last week, we focused on the word *outrageous*. There is this dimension of outrage that's necessary to arouse the experience of Outrageous Love: the outrage of the prophet who rejects the status quo. Now we want to focus more directly on Outrageous Love.

What are Outrageous Acts of Love?

At the end of last week, I shared a story of someone who had jumped onto a subway track to save someone else, with no rational benefit to themselves, in an instantaneous decision. We talked about that story in depth.

The main point is that **there's a moment in which you just realize the true nature of Reality.**

- You realize you are not disconnected from the whole.

EXISTENTIAL RISK AND THE EVOLUTION OF LOVE

- You realize that in that particular moment, there is a unique act of Outrageous Love that can be done by you and you alone.

That gentleman, a fifty-year-old construction worker, sees a young art school student fall onto the tracks, and he is the only one there.

He is the only one who can do it.

He is the only one who has that capacity.

He is the only one who can step in.

He realizes it's only him, and then everything disappears, and he realizes that **everything depends on him**.

He is, in that moment, an atheist. But by *atheist*, I mean **there is no God who is going to step in and pluck the person from before the train**. He *is* the God of that moment—and he steps in and transforms the moment, at great risk.

That's an Outrageous Act of Love moment.

That's where we left off last week. The sense that there is this moment in which you are Cosmos, and you realize directly in your own embodied being:

- I'm not a separate self.
- I am the wholeness of all of Reality.
- I am the only expression of Reality in this moment, in this place, in this time, in this unique intersection of the space-time continuum.
- It's all on me. Everything that happens is determined completely by my willingness to be an Outrageous Act of Love.
- I become the God of that moment.

Today, I want to deepen what we mean by an Outrageous Act of Love.

I BECOME MORE *ME* IN OUR *WE*—ALL THE WAY UP AND DOWN THE EVOLUTIONARY CHAIN

Here we go. Step one.

- **The ultimate Outrageous Act of Love is when I *bracket myself* for the sake of intimate relationship.**

That's step one. *To bracket* means that I step aside, I give up something of myself for the sake of an intimate relationship.

Step two is—and here's where it gets wild:

- **It's only when I bracket myself for the sake of intimate relationship, that I *become myself*.**

It's only when I bracket myself for the sake of *We*, for the sake of a new shared identity, an intimate relationship, that I become myself.

This is because **intimacy equals shared identity in the context of otherness**—this is the first part of our intimacy equation in the interior sciences of CosmoErotic Humanism, this new Story of Value that we're telling.

- **When I bracket my *Me* for the sake of *We*, that's an Outrageous Act of Love. It's an Outrageous Act of Love for you, but also for me because I become *Me* in our *We*.**

Let's see if we can get this clear.

You become you through intimate relationship.

When I sacrifice or give up a dimension of *I* in order to become a *We*, and I enter into intimacy, then *through* that intimacy, through that relationship, through the creation of the depth of relationship, I become myself.

It's very beautiful.

WE LIVE IN A PARTICIPATORY UNIVERSE

Let me just give you an example of that.

There is a core principle in hermeticism and in early Hebrew wisdom (and it exists in different ways across the interior sciences): *As above, so below.* A better way to say this is: **we live in a participatory universe.** That which happens above happens below.

When you say *as above, so below*, it's too strict. It looks like: there's Heaven, there's an Earth, and things that are happening in Heaven are also happening on Earth. That's an old view of the world. It's rather not about *above* and *below*, about a structural analogy between Heaven and Earth. It's not the old chain of being that Arthur Lovejoy wrote about, where matter (below) is on the bottom and Spirit (Heaven) is on top. Rather:

- **We live in a participatory universe, and whatever happens in the depth of the interior face of the Cosmos, in the world of what we might call Spirit (interiors), also happens in exteriors.**

There is no split between Spirit and science. The interior sciences and the exterior sciences are one. That's step three.

Here's step four. This is very beautiful and very interesting. In the first nanoseconds of the Big Bang, neutrons disappear if they don't form a stable relationship with protons. That's just true. It's a structure of Reality. If the neutron doesn't create a stable relationship with the proton, the neutron disappears and becomes a proton. In other words, it loses its identity and becomes something else. Does everyone get that? That's the structure of Reality. In other words, I become Me through the depth of our We. That's the principle at play here.

We're just getting started, this is wild.

That's not only true about neutrons. As above, so below. But not *as above, so below* in a superficial structural way. (And I'm going to ask you not to search for analogies with familiar ideas for now. All the analogies are right, but we are going to try and *emerge* something. And the second I put it into another idea, I cannot hear anymore. So, I am going to suggest to everyone, just be in this flow, and *then* we can do the cross-comparison.)

This notion that I become Me only when I enter into the miracle of We—and *We* means we create shared identity in the context of otherness, with mutuality of recognition, pathos, value, and purpose—**that idea is true all the way up and all the way down, every level of Reality** (as above so below—we live in a participatory universe). Again, I'm using "up" and "down" here more as *interior* and *exterior*. All the way up and all the way down the evolutionary chain. This means **it's true even for the Infinite Divine**, so I want to introduce this wild idea:

- **The Infinite Divine—who both participates in Reality and who holds Reality, in whom we participate—only becomes fully divine, fully God, if She/He/It creates intimate relationship with *us*.**

That's shocking! Now I'm going to say it in brute simple terms, then we are going to bring in more complexity:

God becomes God in the fullest sense, or God becomes more God, when God creates intimate relationship with us.

But not just with *us*, but with *every single one of us*. In other words, because we are all irreducibly unique, **in every intimate relationship between God and an irreducibly unique conscious being, God becomes more God.**

From the divine perspective, you could say: God becomes more *We* through God's *We* with *Thee*—with you, with me. God becomes more God. Or if we're talking as God, in the first person: I become more *Me* through my relationship with *Thee*.

Does everyone get that? God becomes more Me through His relationship, through Her relationship, with Thee, with you.

Through every unique relationship, God actually becomes more God.

You can't even conceptualize it; you have to *feel* it. This is a direct realization.

This is what I've called, in the *Unique Self* book, the evolution of God. We've been talking about this for several years, but I want to deepen it in an entirely new way here.

DIVINE KENOSIS

At the very ground of Reality, there is an Outrageous Act of Love.

What's the Outrageous Act of Love at the very ground of Reality? It's that the Infinite manifests Reality.

> *The Infinity of Power, in an outrageous explosion of Eros, manifests Reality—that itself is an Outrageous Act of Love.*

But that Outrageous Act of Love is not creation in the classical sense. It's something else.

It's not that God/Goddess *thrusts forward*.

It's that God/Goddess *steps back and empties*: divine kenosis.

God/Goddess empties Herself *out* of the space, to make room for Thee, for Me, for We. And in that stepping back, the human being steps into the space.

In order for God to become fully God, the human being has to become fully human. In that space in which God has emptied out and the human

THE ULTIMATE META-CRISIS IS GOD'S CRISIS OF INTIMACY

being steps in, in that space, the human being assumes power—and God becomes, as it were, *dependent* on the human being to be more fully God.

That's what it means to be madly in love.

That's what Outrageous Acts of Love mean.

Let's just start at the beginning.

What Outrageous Love means, or what love means at its very core is:

- I love you so crazy much that I can't be Me without Thee, that without us loving each other that much, I actually cannot be who I am.
- It's the willingness to *recognize* that. It's the willingness to say: *I love you, I need you, and I can't be me without you.* **Without our intimate relationship, I am actually not Me.**

A neutron can't be a neutron unless it creates a relationship with a proton. As above, so below. We live in the participatory universe, all the way up and all the way down.

God can't be God unless God creates an intimate relationship with a human being—but not just with humanity as a whole, but with every irreducibly uniquely individuated human being. That's what intimacy means. Intimacy is shared identity in the context of otherness.

So Divinity says:

- I'm going to love you so much that we are going to share identity. But you're still going to be You, and I'm going to be Me—but then we're going to create a larger We, and in that larger We, I'm going to be Me in a way that I could have never been before.

Let me see if I can get this to you in a couple of stages:

- **First, you have to be you.** I've got to be me, and you've got to be you. We can't be codependent in a negative sense. It's not about codependency. Our response to codependency is, I've got to be *me*, and you've got to be *you*. **We all have to be individuated. We can't be codependent.** That's only step one, though.

- But here's step two: opposites are joined at the hip. This is the paradox. Step two is, I am me because you are you in relationship to me, and you are you because I am me in relationship to you.

It's more than *interdependency*. Interdependency is a structural term from systems theory, and I'm specifically *not* using those words. I am trying to create, if you will, a new language. All systems theory literature is filled with the term *interdependency*, which is a good term, but I'm trying to create a new language. I don't want to reduce it to the old terms. Something's happening here. It's *more* than interdependency.

I'm only *Me* because we are *We*.

GOD NEEDS THE HUMAN BEING

What does that mean? It means that it gets completely crazy.

Let me say it in a new way.

There is a crisis. But the crisis is a crisis in God.

The ultimate meta-crisis is a crisis in God.

We talk about the meta-crisis as the meta-crisis in the human realm, and the animal realm, in the realm of matter, life, and mind, in the manifest world realm—but the deeper meta-crisis is a crisis in God.

What's the crisis in God?

- God says, *There is a way in which I'm broken. And I can't be whole without you.*
- God is actually saying, *I need you.*

That's why we understand that God is not just the Infinity of Power. **God is the Infinity of Intimacy.** That's what we mean by that. That's why we say the new name of God is the Infinite Intimate.

God is the Infinite Intimate, and God's desire for intimacy leads Divinity to manifest Reality.

Why does Divinity manifest Reality? This is Fichte and Schelling's great question in German evolutionary spirituality, but it's been asked by everyone for thousands of years: *why is there something rather than nothing?* It's because the Divine is actually the Infinite Intimate, and there is no infinity in the Divine independent of the Infinite Intimate.

The Infinite Intimate, God who is the Infinity of Intimacy, desires *relationship*.

The paradox of relationship is that I'm madly committed to Thee, but it's only through my Outrageous Love for Thee and my Outrageous Acts of Love for Thee that I become Me. I become Me only in my Outrageous Love—and in my manifest Outrageous Act of Love, I create, I manifest Reality for Thee.

All of manifestation is an Outrageous Act of Love sourced in the Infinite.

This is step one. But then step two of the Outrageous Act of Love is:

I am so insanely in love with you that I am willing to not be Me unless there is a We.

That's amazing. It means you can't walk out easily. You can't walk out easily, because there is no Me without our We. I lose something unimaginable when I break the depth of our intimacy.

The name of God, in the interior sciences, is the structure of Reality. All of Reality is names of God. The DNA of Reality, if you will, is the name of God—and the name of God is the Infinite Intimate.

> ## *The Infinite Intimate means: I cannot be Me unless there is a We.*

Now, stay with us, this gets wild. This is so gorgeous!

I opened up Schleiermacher again this morning, an English version with translations. He talks about the right relationship of the human being to God is *Abhängigkeitsgefühl*, which means the sense of absolute dependency. That's what Schleiermacher talks about. He has this sense of *Frömmigkeit*, which means a kind of piety, which comes from *Abhängigkeitsgefühl*, this feeling of ultimate and radical dependency. That's how Schleiermacher understands the relationship of the human being to God.

But here's the thing.

He only got half of it, friends. He understands *Abhängigkeitsgefühl*, this radical dependency, as the relationship of the human being to God. But here's the thing: **it's also the relationship of God to the human being.** Wow! In other words, God says, *I love you so much that I, God, Infinity, am absolutely dependent on you.* That's an Outrageous Act of Love.

In other words, the source of Reality is this Outrageous Act of Love in which Infinity turns to finitude and says, *Abhängigkeitsgefühl*: "I am completely dependent on you." Not because I *have* to be—because God/Goddess is the Infinity of Power. It's not because I'm codependent in the jargonized sense of the Human Potential Movement.

No, **my ultimate power is my willingness to make myself utterly dependent on you.**

My *frumkeit* (which is the way they say it in Yiddish), my piety, is the experience that I'm actually dependent on the Divine—that's Schleiermacher's read. This utter sense of radical need, which is true. But the opposite is true as well.

That's why there is this new model of relationship, which is **the lovers model**.

- It's not the king-servant model.
- It's not the father-son model.
- It's not the mother-child model of the Great Mother traditions.

No, it's the new model. It's CosmoErotic Humanism's evolution of relationship, in which **there is *Abhängigkeitsgefühl*, radical dependency, on both sides. God needs the human being.**

God is desperately in search of man and woman, the human being, and the human being is desperately in search of God.

It's what Plotinus intuits when he talks about *the flight of the lonely one is the lonely one*. In other words, there's this desperate need of gorgeousness. **There's nothing more gorgeous than desperation when it's the desperation of love, and we meet each other in the desperation of love.**

The Infinite and the finite meet each other in the utter desperation of love.

OUR HEARTS DON'T JUST BREAK, THEY BREAK US OPEN INTO DIVINITY

The original crisis is the crisis in God.

That's called in the interior sciences *shevirat ha-kelim*, "the shattering of the vessels."

But I want to be clear: I am not just repeating the interior sciences here. We are evolving the source code. We are taking pieces from different places and weaving them together in a new configuration of intimacy. We are weaving them together into this new Story of Value.

The allusion to this idea in the interior sciences is *shevirat ha-kelim* "the shattering of the vessels." There is a three-step process:

- The first step of the process is *tzimtzum*: divine contraction/withdrawal, in order to make room for Reality. Or divine kenosis: **God empties Herself out to make room for Reality**.
- Two, is that emptying out real, or *as if*? The fancy way to say that is, is that emptying out *ontological* or *epistemological*? But people say fancy things for dumb reasons. It means, is it real? Does Goddess *really* empty Herself out? Or is it *as if*, it only appears that way? That's a deep conversation, but ultimately, it's *as if* because Divinity is always there. **Step two is: Divinity empties Herself *into* the world because the withdrawal is only *as if*.** Divinity is actually there—but the manifest world, finitude, cannot handle the intensity of the light, so finitude breaks. That's the image, the "breaking of the vessels." A world in which infinity and finitude meet is unimaginable. The contradiction shatters the paradigm; paradox is unable to be held. The vessels shatter. **Then the shards of broken vessels spread through Reality.**
- Then we get to the third stage, and **the third stage is the *tzadik*, "the avatar."** But the avatar is no longer, in our teaching of CosmoErotic Humanism, just the elite. **Every human being has the potential to be an avatar, and every human being is a unique avatar.** Then the avatar, the *tzadik*, the righteous one, the *axis mundi*, what the Sufis called *the pole*, the human being, liberates the spark of light from the broken vessel—**that liberation of the spark of light from the broken vessel is step three.**

THE ULTIMATE META-CRISIS IS GOD'S CRISIS OF INTIMACY

Step three is *tikkun*, and *tikkun* means not *fixing* in the way that we make it unbroken like it was before.

It's not *restorative* fixing. It's *evolutionary* fixing.

It's not restorative rectification. It's evolutionary rectification.

- We don't fix it by going back to Eden and rewinding history back up, to get back to the place before The Fall.
- No, we actually *experience* all the breaking of the vessels. We experience all the breaking of the vessels, and then we bring it home, and we fix the whole thing.

The original breaking of the vessels happens before there are any human beings.

In the realization of the interior sciences, the breaking of the vessels is built into the structure of Reality—the crisis in God. **The crisis in God is a crisis of intimacy.**

The Infinite desires the intimate—there is a crisis of intimacy.

The crisis can only be met by generating a new intimacy.

The new intimacy that's generated—that's finitude, that's us, that's Reality, that's the manifest world.

Once there is a manifest world, then we *participate*. It's a participatory universe: as above, so below. **We participate in that experience of the breaking of vessels. That's what it means to live a life of a broken heart.** Our hearts break. Our hearts break for a thousand reasons, again and again and again.

When we experience our heartbreak, and instead of:

- Breaking and destroying ourselves
- Becoming narcissistic
- Becoming win/lose metrics and rivalrous conflict
- Becoming lost in the illusion of separate self

- Becoming lost in the illusion of a world without value (that's an illusion, you can actually never step out of the Field of Value, because we're always in it)

Instead of getting lost in the illusion of having *stepped out of the Tao*, we actually step *in*, and we let our hearts not just break, but break open. They break open to this unimaginable breakthrough, which is the new human.

In other words:

- When I actually realize: no, my heartbreak breaks me *open*
- When I realize that there's nothing more whole than a broken heart
- When I step in and become whole
- When I transform myself

In that transformation of myself, Goddess becomes whole, God becomes whole.

The *tikkun*, the third step, the fixing is the evolutionary rectification of the Divine.

That's the evolution of God.

The evolution of God happens through me experiencing my broken heart, and instead of that broken heart making me small and degrading me, it breaks me open into my divinity.

My shattered heart is healed—not by going to the place *before* the shattering but by *embracing* the shattering. Embracing, if you will, my holy and my broken *Hallelujah*. That's my holy and my broken *Hallelujah*.

THE ULTIMATE META-CRISIS IS GOD'S CRISIS OF INTIMACY

GOD NEEDS YOU TO LIVE YOUR STORY

The ultimate intimacy on the human level is: I become intimate with the broken parts of myself and my heartbreaks.

I've got broken *Hallelujahs*; I've got all these split-off parts of myself. I'm split, I'm broken. **When I become intimate with myself, and I weave those broken-off parts back into the wholeness of the fabric of my story, I become intimate with myself.**

And how does that happen?

It happens when *subject* becomes *object*.

When I am subject, I'm in myself, and I cannot see the broken-off parts of myself.

- I cannot see the broken *Hallelujahs*.
- I cannot see my pathologies.
- I cannot see my contractions because they're all in my subject.

But then subject becomes object. Now I can see that which was inside of me. And **by seeing it, I can transform it. I can weave those split-off parts into a new whole, into a new configuration of intimacy.**

When I do that to myself:

- When I heal myself by turning all the broken *Hallelujahs* into holy *Hallelujahs*
- When I realize *it doesn't matter what you heard, there's a blaze of light in every word.* (And that blaze of light is the spark of the broken vessel. The spark that's in the broken vessel, the holy and the broken *Hallelujah*, are part of the same wholeness.)
- When I actually become whole, when I transform myself—not just by *accepting* my shadow. It's not that. No, I actually integrate my split-off parts, and I become more whole. I

become more kind, more generous, and I live the full agony and ecstasy of my story):

Then **my story becomes part of the Sacred Autobiography of God.**

My story, which is a story of transformation, my story when I experience "the crossing," I cross over from *Homo sapiens* to *Homo amor*—which happens in each of our lives uniquely.

My story is not your story. Your crossing is different from my crossing.

We're all unique, and we're all the same.

We're all the same in that we all have to experience a crossing, but we all experience the crossing uniquely.

God needs your transformation, my transformation.

God needs your story.

But *your story* means that you've included in your story *all* of its beauty: **all of its contradictions turned into paradoxes, and** *all* **of the broken parts become the design of the new humanity.**

You've got the main vessel, and there's a scratch in the main vessel, and you don't know how to fix the scratch, so you turn the scratch into part of the design. In other words, my unique shadow becomes part of my Unique Self. **My unique brokenness, my broken *Hallelujah* becomes the ground for my holy *Hallelujah*.**

When that happens, then you become the fullness of your story. You are in your Unique Self story. You are not in a victim story anymore; you are a player on the scene.

You are a Unique Self. And then your story becomes part of the divine sacred autobiography—so much so that God can't be fully God without your story. In other words—and stay close if you want to feel the inherent intention of Cosmos, the reason you exist, the reason I exist, the reason we exist—**this brokenness is not just a bug but a feature of the system.**

THE ULTIMATE META-CRISIS IS GOD'S CRISIS OF INTIMACY

The reason we exist uniquely, irreducible uniquely, is because:

- Reality needs your service and my service.
- Reality needs my *Me* and your *Me*.

Reality, or the Real, or God (it's all the same) manifest you uniquely as a unique story. And by transforming your story—not by *pathologizing* your story, not by denying or medicating it, but by *mythologizing* your story—**you participate in the myth of the Divine.**

By *myth*, I don't mean that which is not real, I mean *the ultimately real*. Your story is a great myth. It's the ultimate myth. The ultimately real is in crisis, and that crisis can only be healed uniquely and particularly through *you*—healing, transforming, embracing, and integrating your holy and broken *Hallelujah*.

God needs your service. But your service doesn't mean the particular ritual attention to a particular ritual act in a particular way, which is how *The Zohar*, the Book of Radiance from the thirteenth century, would understand it. No, what *God needs your service* means is: **God needs you to live your story.**

God needs you to live your story because your story is chapter and verse in the Divine story.

I AM NOT WILLING TO BE WRITTEN IN THE BOOK OF LIFE WITHOUT YOU

To do that, you've got to take a unique risk—all of us, every one of us.

And the unique risk is not just, *fulfill my own narrow needs and be in my own path.*

This is really important.

EXISTENTIAL RISK AND THE EVOLUTION OF LOVE

In order to know how to live your story, to become your Unique Self, you've got to be willing to take your unique risk.

And here's the nature of unique risk:

- You can totally get away without doing it, no one's going to call you on it.
- You can explain to yourself in beautiful pietistic, spiritual, New Age or classically religious terms, why you're *not* doing it.

But your unique risk isn't just about your self-fulfillment. It's not just about your path. It's not just about your edification.

Your unique risk is your Outrageous Act of Love. Your Outrageous Act of Love is your unique risk.

Your Outrageous Act of Love is where *you step out of yourself*. It's not just a clever disguise for your own self-fulfillment. It's actually an act of sacrifice.

- You step *beyond* yourself.
- You pour yourself into something larger than yourself.
- You empty yourself out in order to become full.

And there's something painful in it. You bracket yourself.

Why am I involved in creating a Center?

Why don't I just write and be a meta-theorist?

Because there's something that happens here—when we come together as a Unique Self Symphony, and I bracket myself, and we actually do this together. Instead of the old way—*let's just be a great thinker*. No:

- We are going to do this together.

THE ULTIMATE META-CRISIS IS GOD'S CRISIS OF INTIMACY

- We are going to love each other in it.
- We are going to give things up in it.
- We are going to work with our early traumas in it.
- We are going to work with a place where we're hurt, or disappointed, or don't feel seen.

When we commit our Outrageous Acts of Love, we say:

- I am willing to take my unique risk, and my unique risk means there's a unique way that I'm going to bracket myself for the sake of We.

But not in a pre-personal way. I don't give up my Unique Self. It's not some messed up cult thing. No, it's not pre-personal. It's *trans*-personal. You get the difference?

I move *beyond* personality, and I find my full Unique Self in intimate relationship with the We, in which I become Me, in our shared service to She, to God/Goddess. What that means is that **I am a unique Outrageous Love Story, and the plotline of my unique Outrageous Love Story is the Outrageous Acts of Love that are mine and mine alone to commit.**

Do you understand what's actually happened here? It's unimaginable. We've now realized the ultimate human nobility:

- We participate in healing the meta-crisis.
- The meta-crisis at its core is a crisis in God.
- Every crisis—this is one of the core principles of CosmoErotic Humanism—is a crisis of intimacy.

The original crisis of intimacy is a crisis of intimacy in the Divine, and every crisis of intimacy that we experience in our lives participates in that original crisis of intimacy.

Here's the thing: we cannot just heal it in romantic relationships. Our love lists are too short. Our intimacies are too narrow. We have to love each other outrageously.

Ordinary love is beautiful and gorgeous, but it doesn't even *begin* to exhaust Outrageous Love.

Outrageous Love means we love each other for real. We are part of this Unique Self Symphony, in which we realize that we need each other. We participate in each other; I become *Me* through our *We*. That's what we say to each other. That's what we mean when we say in CosmoErotic Humanism:

> *I am not willing to be written in the Book of Life without you.*

But who said that originally? God, Goddess, the Infinite said it to finitude. The Infinite said to finitude: *I, Infinity, am not willing to be written in the Book of Life without you.*

OUR HANDS ARE GOD'S HANDS

Here's the paradox: **We cannot solve the meta-crisis in the manifest world unless we solve the meta-crisis in God.**

The motivational architecture of the human being, which is the motivational architecture of Reality, **the only motivational architecture that works is one that honors our nobility.** It's when I realize I'm ultimately needed, and my entire story is needed, by All-That-Is, uniquely.

My story is uniquely needed by All-That-Is, and it's only my becoming whole that makes the Divine whole. **My transformation, quite literally, transforms the entire thing.** This is what we might call *personal myth*.

When I was in my thirties, which is longer ago than I'd like to admit, I started something called The School of Personal Myth. The School of Personal Myth means: **I am a unique myth, and that myth participates in the myth of the Divine.** *Myth* doesn't mean "not real," but "ultimately real."

THE ULTIMATE META-CRISIS IS GOD'S CRISIS OF INTIMACY

- My personal myth is the way I cry, so I wrote a book on tears.
- I wrote an unpublished book on laughter.
- I wrote an unpublished book on silence.
- I wrote another unpublished book on pleasure.

Those are all The School of Personal Myth. It's only by living my pleasure, and living my creativity, and living my silence, and living my tears, and living my laughter that I can live my personal myth.

But it's more than that:

- It's the evolution of my tears.
- It's the evolution of my pleasure.
- It's the evolution of my laughter.
- It's the ever-deepening evolution of my silence.
- It's the evolution of my creativity, dance, art, kindness.
- It's responding to the unique needs in my unique circle of intimacy and influence, meaning activism.

When I live those uniquely, then my hands become God's hands. That's the secret.

My master died, I don't know, almost 200 years ago. He has a famous teaching where he says, *all is in the hands of Heaven*. What does this mean, *all is in the hands of Heaven?* The way scholars read it, it means, the human being is completely dependent on God.

I love my master so much, I spent two years in the library, nineteen hours a day, trying to understand what his teaching was. And I realized—based on thousands of Aramaic texts that I wove together in a kind of *Da Vinci Code* insanity over two years in the Oxford library—I realized that what he meant, if you read him carefully, is that **the hands of Heaven are the hands of the human being.**

He was hiding his true position, so it seemed like a pietistic position, *frumkeit*: humans are utterly dependent on God. But when you read all the texts together, what he really meant was that actually the hands of Heaven are *our* hands (and this is an entire chapter in a book I wrote called *Radical Kabbalah*).

- Our hands are God's hands.
- We are God's verbs.
- We are God's dangling modifiers.
- We are God's adjectives.
- We're *not* nouns. We have to de-nominalize ourselves. We are verbs. We are the verbs of the Divine.
- We are love in action uniquely as us, through which God becomes more God.
- We are the more God to come.

That's the beauty. That's the insanity which is the only sanity.

That's the realization of my life: I get that my life *matters*.

Why does my life matter? My life matters *not* because it's a subjective, interesting, humanist, poetic moment, which then disappears when I die, and is ultimately dust and ashes.

No, it's because my dust and ashes, my poignant, fragile, fleeting humanity, participates in the story of God, and my wholeness becomes divine wholeness. And when I become whole, God becomes more God.

Through my relationship to you, you become more You, and I become more Me.

A neutron can only fully become a neutron if it creates a relationship with the proton.

I can only be Me through the depth of our We.

That's Outrageous Love, and the commitment to that is the committing of Outrageous Acts of Love. I commit Outrageous Acts of Love because the entire structure of Reality is an Outrageous Act of Love.

- **Infinity manifests finitude**, Outrageous Act of Love.
- Infinity says: I won't be Infinity without us being madly in love with each other. **Unless you are You, I won't be Me.**
- It's not just that we have to be madly in love with each other, but you've got to become more whole. **Unless you transform—unless you become more potent and more beautiful and more good and more true and more powerful—I can't be Me.**
- I am willing to love you so much, so outrageously, that **I make myself dependent on you.**

That's an Outrageous Act of Love: I step out of my separation, out of my splendid isolation, out of my splendid power, out of my own autonomy, even as God, and enter in intimate communion with you. And in intimate communion with you, in which I recognize my full dependency on you, I become me.

Wow!

This is a space where we try and deepen the Story of Value, in this kind of conversation. You can feel the contours crystallizing, outlining, deepening.

We retell the same story, but in a whole different way. Something happens. And that's why that key line in the *dharma* is *Your need is my allurement*. That's the ultimate dignity of need.

The ultimate dignity of need: **God's need is our need.**

They interpenetrate each other.

CHAPTER FIVE

THE META-CRISIS OF GOD, PART TWO: SHE DESPERATELY NEEDS US TO TAKE OUR UNIQUE RISK (WITH Q&A)

Episode 335 — March 12, 2023

EVOLUTIONARY LOVE CODE: OUTRAGEOUS LOVE

Homo amor is vocationally aroused to commit Outrageous Acts of Love. S/he commits the Outrageous Acts of Love that are a function of his/her Unique Self. Outrageous Acts of Love are almost always that which we can get away with *not* doing.

An Outrageous Act of Love might be smiling when we want to withhold or opening our heart when it is more comfortable to keep it closed.

An Outrageous Act of Love might be changing your tone of voice.

It might be sending a text with an overflowing heart.

It might be taking a stand when we can get away with not taking a stand.

Outrageous Acts of Love are when we give ourselves outrageously—beyond our traumas, and our rackets, and our issues, and our patterns.

With true Outrageous Acts of Love, we can always rationalize to ourselves why we don't have to do them. Genuine Outrageous Acts of Love are the fabric of the Intimate Universe realizing its Omega Point *as you*.

What moves us to commit Outrageous Acts of Love is Evolution herself. Goddess Herself. *She.*

WHEN *SHE* SPEAKS IT FOR US

The meta-crisis is the crisis of God, which is a crisis of intimacy.

This is a change-everything moment.

It's so deep, it's so beautiful, it's so real, it's so good, it's so true.

It's so filled with mystery.

It's so unfolding.

It's so evolving.

This is a pivotal moment.

I am not claiming that everything we say here is in any sense infallible. That would be absurd (we gave up infallibility with the Pope, and the Pope got it wrong himself).

But I *am* saying that we are thinking very carefully. These are not blind declarations; these are not just claims. I wouldn't dare speak a sentence if I hadn't meditated on it for decades and spent tens and tens of thousands of hours poring through the interior sciences, parts of the exterior sciences, and different strands in world philosophy. I've spent five decades on this and been in deep conversation with some key interlocutors across the world, who are at the leading edge of their fields.

All of that weaves together, and then *She*—Reality, the Goddess, Eros Herself—speaks it for us.

I am not saying we get everything perfectly right, but we are making mistakes in the right direction, and we are not being casual. None of this is a casual declaration, so you can take it with a certain amount of gravitas, and then take it in. And anyone who wants to become a master of the *dharma*—to step in, to read the books that have been written, to step into the process of preparing the next ones—and enters in all the way, and fully takes it in, and becomes somewhat of a master in any part of it, then start to contribute. **Everyone is welcome.**

At the center of this revolution:

- This One Mountain, Many Paths
- This new Renaissance
- This responding to the meta-crisis through a new Story of Value rooted in First Principles and First Values

There are no gurus. There is a Unique Self Symphony—and in the Unique Self Symphony, everyone has a role, everyone has a place, and everyone has an instrument. Everyone has to play their instrument in the Unique Self Symphony, and I can't play mine if you don't play yours.

We need each other.

We love each other (and to say *I love you* is to say *I need you*).

And at the very center is value Herself.

At the very center is Goddess Herself, is *She*.

We're in devotion to *She*.

She is the *dharma*.

She is the First Principles and First Values.

SHE DESPERATELY NEEDS US TO TAKE OUR UNIQUE RISK

She is the mystery unfolding in response to suffering, participating in the evolution of love—which is the evolution of consciousness—in this particular moment in history, when we are faced with a meta-crisis and a potential dystopia: the potential extinction of humankind, the death of humanity, or perhaps even worse, the death of *our* humanity.

Our understanding is that the response has to be a new Story of Value. Only a new Story of Value raises all boats, and only a new Story of Value transforms the very source code itself, which then trickles down and transfigures all of our economics and politics.

That's what we are going to be doing together.

THE UNIQUE SELF IS A UNIQUE CONFIGURATION OF OUTRAGEOUS LOVE

Let us briefly recapitulate, add a couple of pieces, and then open it up for questions.

We are talking about Outrageous Love.

One: this distinction between *ordinary* love and *Outrageous* Love:

- **Ordinary love:** Love which is a particular social human construction, at a particular cultural moment in time, which is often a strategy for security or comfort. Legitimate as those are, it's *not* Outrageous Love.
- **Outrageous Love**: Another word for it is *Evolutionary Love*, and another word for it is *Eros*. It's the very heart of existence itself. It's that which *incepts* (or births) Reality, and it's that which *suffuses* Reality.

In one text from Solomon, in an incredible chronicle called *the Song of Songs*, he writes *tocho ratzuf ahava*, "Its insides are lined with love." Outrageous Love suffuses Reality.

Another text from the sacred interior sciences reads *olam chesed yibaneh*, "The world is constituted, constructed through Eros."

Let's *feel that* together:

- The world is incepted by Eros, by Outrageous Love.
- The world is constituted, constructed through Eros, Outrageous Love, Evolutionary Love.

Charles Sanders Peirce, one of the most important polymath theorists of the last 150 years, who was influenced by James Mark Baldwin, and who was probably Piaget's greatest inheritor, was a critical forerunner to the Story of Value that we're telling in CosmoErotic Humanism, an incredibly important thinker. He was an incredibly important influence on Alfred North Whitehead, who wrote *Principia Mathematica* with George Bertrand Russell in Cambridge. Peirce's name for what we're calling Eros or Outrageous Love was Evolutionary Love. I came up with that name independently of Peirce, back in 2010. And then Zak Stein, who's my colleague, interlocutor, student, and friend, pointed towards Peirce who had used the term before. Beautiful!

Two: once I realize that Reality is suffused by Outrageous Love, I then realize that I am an *expression* of that Reality.

I am evolution. I am Evolutionary Love.

I am Eros.

I am Outrageous Love.

Three: I'm a *unique configuration* of Eros. I am an irreducibly unique configuration of Eros. I'm an irreducibly unique configuration of Outrageous Love. **I am an irreducibly unique configuration of Evolutionary Love.**

I am not just a *separate self*. I am *True Self*.

True Self means: I'm *not* just in this narrow, limited, trauma-informed story as separate self. Although that's extremely important to work with and deal with, it doesn't exhaust who I am. I am also True Self, and **True Self is an affront to narcissism.**

In other words, I get narcissistically involved in my separate-self story. I should work with it and do my trauma work, of course. But when I get into a recursive loop and keep repeating that same story, and I don't have consistent and direct experiences of True Self, then I get lost in a narcissistic recursive loop. And so, True Self is an affront to narcissism.

But then, I transcend and I move beyond even just True Self. I realize I am not *just* a True Self. I am not just inseparable from the Field of Outrageous Love. I am not just part of the Field—I am an irreducibly unique expression of the Field.

That notion—that I'm an irreducibly unique expression of the Field that's needed by the Field—that's *Unique Self*. And if True Self is an affront to narcissism, then **Unique Self is an affront to shame:**

- The shame which feels like I am unnecessary
- The shame which feels like I'm not worthy, like I'm an extra on the set
- Even worse, the shame that feels like I'm broken and can't be fixed—they stopped making the part that you would need to fix me at the factory; I'm not fixable.

True Self is an affront to narcissism. Unique Self is an affront to shame.

THE OUTRAGEOUS ACT OF LOVE OF THE INFINITE INTIMATE

Unique Self is a unique configuration of Outrageous Love.

What does the Unique Self do?

The Unique Self commits Outrageous Acts of Love—and that's the subject of our code this week.

Now, let's add to that. What we talked about last week was the realization that, actually, *as above, so below*. But when I say *as above, so below*, I don't mean it as a kind of classical hermetic principle. That principle is easily understood as a *structural* principle. We now understand that that's not accurate. It's not that there is an above and below that are *parallel* universes—but **we live in a *participatory* universe**.

We *participate* in the Field of True Self.

We participate in the God Field, and God participates in the human field.

In this participatory universe, Outrageous Acts of Love are that which are the very expression, fabric, and purpose of Cosmos.

I am a unique expression of Reality. I don't live *in* Reality—Reality lives *in me*.

I don't live in evolution, and I don't live in a world driven by evolution—the world driven by evolution, quite literally, lives in me.

I *am* evolution. The evolutionary impulse itself, quite literally, beats in my heart. Can you feel that?

I am evolution. I am the evolutionary impulse. I commit Outrageous Acts of Love:

- I am Outrageous Love.
- I am part of the Field of Outrageous Love. I'm not just Outrageous Love that lives in my separate self. I am the Field of Eros itself. I'm the Field not just of Consciousness or Awareness—but also the Field of Desire, Eros, Outrageous Love, Evolutionary Love.
- It all lives *uniquely* in me, so I am a unique expression of that Field. **As a unique expression of that Field, I commit**

Outrageous Acts of Love that can be committed by no one else that ever was, is, or will be.

But remember our structural principle: *as above, so below.* **If I am committing Outrageous Acts of Love, then *She*—Goddess, Source— must be committing Outrageous Acts of Love.** Does everyone get that structural principle?

What is the Outrageous Act of Love that's committed by God—or by Source, or by the Infinite Intimate?

The Infinite Intimate is the name of God that we are using in this generation, in our new Story of Value, which we call *CosmoErotic Humanism*. We have introduced a new name of God—and the name of God always means, in the interior sciences, the constitutive structure of all of Reality. All of Reality is names of God, so if I want to understand the constitutive structure of Reality, the way you ask this in the interior sciences is, *what is God's name?*

Not the God *out there*—the God that holds it all and inheres in it all. The God that animates me and holds me at the same time.

The new name of God is the Infinite Intimate. God is not just the Infinity of Power, God is the Infinity of Intimacy.

What is the profound desire of the Infinity of Intimacy?

What is the great Outrageous Act of Love of the Infinite Intimate? *She*, God, Source, the Infinity of Intimacy, the Infinity of Power says:

- I can't be *Me* without us being *We*.
- I'm willing to love you so madly, so desperately, so insanely, that I am going to step back and make room for you.
- Even though I am the Infinity of Power, I am going to empty myself out and make room for you.
- Even more, I am going to make myself dependent on you.
- I cannot be complete without you. I am going to make the entire mood of the Universe, the mood of Divinity, dependent on you.

THE INFINITE INTIMATE NEEDS YOU DESPERATELY

Just to make this clear, let me give you a human expression of this, so you can get a sense of how this works. Let's say you are very close with someone. It could be a beloved, a brother, a sister, a friend, but you are really close. Let's say they are in a terrible mood, and you're in the same place as them. Does that affect your mood? Completely! You're gone. It changes everything.

Let's say they are in a terrible mood because they are needing you, and you are not needing them? Does that affect your mood? It affects, quite literally, *everything*. Their mood completely redefines your mood.

It is their willingness to be madly in love with you, which is their act of self-emptying. What they are saying is: *Oh my God, I love you so much that if you are in a bad mood, my day is ruined.*

The Outrageous Love of Infinity is to be the Infinite Intimate.

Reality intends uniqueness. Reality moves towards ever more crystalline forms of irreducible uniqueness—and so, **if Reality didn't have *you*, then something would be essentially missing from Reality**. A love note from Reality to itself that wouldn't happen—because that love note, that shocking self-recognition, not just self-recognition, but self-completion, self-perfection, self-evolution, self-transformation of the Divine can only happen through *your* love notes. It's the only way it can happen.

In other words, what the Infinite Intimate is saying is: *I'm going to manifest conscious Unique Selves all over the world, who become conscious of their uniqueness.*

- It's only when that Unique Self becomes conscious of her expression of me and begins to be my hands, and to be my legs, and to be my phallus and to be my yoni, and to be my

belly, and to be my arms, and to be my ankles, and to be my knees, and to be my fingers.
- It's only when that Unique Self realizes: my hands are the hands of the Divine.
- It's only when this consciously unique being realizes: *I am the evolutionary impulse Herself, I am Evolutionary Love uniquely expressed and committing Outrageous Acts of Love.*

Only *then* I become fully God.

She, Source, the Infinite Intimate needs us—not us just as a homogeneous collective, but **each of us individually as Unique Selves**. Not *just* each of us individually, in a kind of monadic world—but each of us individually playing our instruments together in a Unique Self Symphony.

- When I pick up my instrument, I *attune*—**I play the tuning fork of my life**. That's why I should do trauma work, and that's why I should do therapy if I need it, and that's why I should do my work at the separate-self level—because that is my tuning fork.
- I clarify my tuning fork, and then I realize my True Self; **I affront my narcissism**.
- Then I tune, tune, tune, until I begin to feel the unique set of allurements that move through me, and **I go to commit my Outrageous Acts of Love.**
- Then **God becomes God**, because it's actually God/Goddess who's committing those Outrageous Acts of Love—because *She* is both *holding* me and *being* me, and *She* both protects me and needs me desperately. She needs each of us desperately.

This means, of course, that *we* need each other desperately—and **there's nothing more dignified than to need your beloved desperately.**

We are so afraid to be desperate; we have exiled desperation to some pathological expression. But, friends, we *should* be desperate for each other.

EXISTENTIAL RISK AND THE EVOLUTION OF LOVE

If you want to know the true state of Reality, imagine if you've ever had a sexual experience (and if you haven't, maybe you've read about sexual experiences), a sexual experience where:

- You've crossed that line.
- You are beyond choice, in a state of choicelessness.
- You're all the way on the inside.
- You're ten seconds before entering heaven in ecstatic explosion.

You desperately need your beloved, and **at a certain point, the split between you and your beloved disappears, and you begin to pulsate and throb in union in this larger We**, in which there's also *Thee* and *Thee* as irreducible Unique Selves—ultimate Unique Self sexing as one and yet individuated beautifully.

> *This sense of desperate need for the other is actually the true nature of our experience.*

It's the true realization of Reality in every moment.

That's what we mean when we say, *the sexual models Eros*. That moment when we cry out: *Oh, God, yes*, and the name of the beloved—that's when we are on the Inside of the Inside.

That is why, in Solomon's temple, there are these two cherubs making love above the Sanctum Sanctorum of the Ark of the Covenant in the inner Temple. What the interior sciences are saying is that it's in this place that we know the true nature of Reality.

That's why temples in India are filled with *Yab-Yum*, with images of God/Goddess making love—because when the true nature of Reality discloses itself, we realize we are desperate for each other—and not to be desperate for each other is to be dead.

To be alive is to be desperate—holy desperation, ecstatic desperation, delighted desperation.

YOU HAVE TO TAKE THE LEAP

Let me just add one piece, and we're going to open up for questions.

To play your instrument in the Unique Self Symphony is to commit your Outrageous Acts of Love.

Your instrument in the Unique Self Symphony is committing your Outrageous Acts of Love, which are a function of your Unique Self—but **in order to commit your Outrageous Acts of Love, you need to be willing to take your unique risk.**

Now, here's the key: you can explain away to everyone why you *shouldn't* take your unique risk. If you think that the culture around you is going to easily support your unique risk, then it's *not* your unique risk. **The nature of your unique risk is such that it's a risk.**

Of course, the true risk is *not* taking it—because **if you don't take it, then the very purpose of your life disappears.** You are unable to commit your Outrageous Acts of Love, your irreducibly unique Outrageous Acts of Love, which is *She* being *Thee*.

God comes alive through your Outrageous Acts of Love in that unique way, and you're born for this. You become divine.

When you become divine, then you have continuity of consciousness. As long as I'm a limited human being, then when I die, I die—but if I step into being Divinity, if I step into my Outrageous Acts of Love, which are the unique expressions of Divinity awake and alive in me, I've stepped into immortality. I have stepped into that which has ultimate continuity of consciousness because I'm not locked in my separate self anymore. In order to step into immortality, in order to transcend death, in order to actually cheat the angel of death, as it were—but in the most sacred sense—I have to be committing my Outrageous Acts of Love.

- I can only commit my Outrageous Acts of Love if I am committing the acts of love that are a function of my Unique Self.
- But I can only know which Outrageous Acts of Love are a function of my Unique Self if I am willing to access my unique risk.

There's always a unique risk; there's always *a leap*. The net *will* appear—leap and the net will appear—but **you've got to take the leap**, and the leap is not going to be easily and obviously supported by everyone around you. That's just true.

If you'd like an award at a dinner for committing your Outrageous Act of Love, well, then you're *not* committing an Outrageous Act of Love. When you get an award at a dinner for committing it, you can be pretty sure it's *not* an Outrageous Act of Love.

The nature of an Outrageous Act of Love is:

1. **No one can demand that you do it.** No one can tell you: this is what you need to do. It has to be self-authoring.
2. **It's not going to be easily culturally translatable.**
3. **You'll be able to explain to yourself and to anyone else exactly why you're *not* doing it.** You can critique whoever you need to critique, you can figure out why the system's not working that you should be contributing to, you can figure out who did what wrong that lets you off the hook. You are always going to have a very plausible narrative for explaining to yourself why you're *not* committing your Outrageous Acts of Love. It's very easy to justify.
4. **When you commit your Outrageous Act of Love, when you take your unique risk, you become completely and totally**

alive. That's when you become divine.

In other words, when you take that leap, it's not a leap into the absurd.

It's not anti-reason. It's not anti-rational. None of that.

It's trans-rational—it's beyond rational.

It speaks the language of the rational—and then, when the rational can no longer speak and the rational becomes silent, then a new eloquence emerges from the silence—*that* is your unique risk.

- Those are the Outrageous Acts of Love that are yours to commit, and that's where you become alive.
- That's where you step into second innocence.
- That's where you take your seat at the table.

It's an Outrageous Act of Love, and you can't actually succeed in *anything* else unless you do that.

It's the structure of Reality.

IT IS THIS SET OF REALIZATIONS THAT BIRTHS *HOMO AMOR*

There is a meta-crisis in God.

She needs us. And it's only when we realize that we are needed by All-That-Is, that our Outrageous Acts of Love and our instrument in the Unique Self Symphony is the very nature and joy of our existence, that we can solve the meta-crisis in this Reality.

It is this set of realizations that births *Homo amor*.

This is how we move to the fulfillment of *Homo sapiens* which is *Homo amor*.

This realization is the place where we do the crossing. This *is* the crossing.

When I take my unique risk, and I begin committing my Outrageous Acts of Love, and I play my instrument in the Unique Self Symphony, I am omni-considerate for the sake of the whole, even as I'm completely in my stunning uniqueness.

When the split between autonomy and communion disappears in the ecstasy of Outrageous Acts of Love, *Homo amor* **is born.**

When *Homo amor* is born, and when the world self-organizes as *Homo amor*, then the meta-crisis is solved. Then we have a bottom-up, self-organizing, self-actualizing Cosmos, which commits Outrageous Acts of Love through local Unique Self Symphonies all over the world, and Reality transfigures, quite literally.

That's the political-economic structure of the New World.

Anything less than a source code change will not take us home.

QUESTIONS AND ANSWERS

IS HOMO AMOR AN ATHEIST?

This is a question from a dear friend of mine. She wrote (and I don't have permission to use her name): *In the moment of an Outrageous Act of Love, I'm an atheist.*

She is referring back to our earlier conversation about how you have to be an atheist, meaning you've got to almost *bracket* God. God is not going to do it, it's up to me to do. I am evolution. So she writes: *In the moment of an Outrageous Act of Love, I'm an atheist. Homo amor is someone who lives as Outrageous Love, that is, in a continual act of Outrageous Love. So doesn't it*

SHE DESPERATELY NEEDS US TO TAKE OUR UNIQUE RISK

follow, like day from night, that Homo amor is an atheist? In other words, to become Homo amor, you have to become an atheist.

In other words, if you think God is going to take care of it, then you don't step in. If I think it's going to happen anyways, I don't step in—but **when I know it's really me, it's *only* me, it all in some fundamental sense depends on me, then I step in, in a very big way.**

There is this notion from Nachman of Breslov, one of the great masters of interior sciences, who says that when you see a poor person, and you have to decide, *do I help that poor person?* In that moment, I become an atheist, for that instant. There's no one else but me.

At that moment, there is no difference between what I would call *ultimate pantheism* and *atheism*. **It's an atheism which means there is no God out there, and it's just me—but that *just me* is the Divine.**

I am God. In other words, there is no other God who is going to do it. I am the face of God, who can respond in this unique moment.

In this unique moment I'm not thinking about being one with God. It's just me. God is awake and alive in me, but I'm not *religious-ing* it. I'm just *being* it. There is no split between me and God.

There is no God out there that's going to do it.

The question was: does *Homo amor* need to be an atheist?

The answer is: *Homo amor* needs to be a complete atheist and completely God at the same time.

That's the exact point. There is a holy atheism, or what we call *heresy which is faith*.

Heresy which is faith means that I reject any small notion of God, any caricatured Divine. I am a heretic, I reject all small gods who were going to take care of this. But I'm a heretic who has faith.

I embrace my direct realization of:

- A meaning-infused Cosmos
- A value-infused Cosmos
- A Cosmos which is the Infinite Intimate
- The Cosmos which is all a love story, in which even the question makes no sense without the love story

Then, in this moment, I have this irreducible knowing, even when I can't work it out, that value *matters*, value lives *through me*, and I have to respond *now*.

In that moment, I merge with the Divine. There is no separation between me and the Divine.

I am beyond thought.

What we're doing is **we are liberating the spark of holy atheism**.

John Grey, a professor at the London School of Economics, wrote a book called *Seven Types of Atheism*. Half of the book is wrong, but in the other half, he gets a sense of this. Late last night, I was skipping through the book, and I was like: *Oh nice, John*. My grandmother would say, *halevai, would were it that* all atheists were like John Grey. In other words, at least parts of this book are faith which is heresy—a refusal to let myself be bought out by the small god, to let myself off the hook. **It's only when my conception of the Divine expands that I both participate in the Divine *and* am held by the Divine.** I am an atheist, and I am the most passionate, ecstatic, devotional servant of the Divine in the exact same moment.

But I can't *remove* that. **There cannot be *Homo amor* without that dimension of taking the void seriously**. So the answer is, yes, there's a moment like that.

It's a dialectical moment.

It's a paradoxical moment.

But what a strange and beautiful paradoxical moment. So gorgeous.

HOW IS THIS DIFFERENT FROM CODEPENDENCY?

Codependency, for Melody Beattie who wrote a popular book about this, means two separate selves that can't take responsibility as separate selves. They don't assume their separate-self dignity, and they say, *No, I am actually completely dependent on you, and if you disappear, I'm dead. Without you, I cannot function.*

That's the litmus test.

When you are, instead, in a sacred, mutual, desperate dependency—if you disappear, if my partner disappears, I'll be broken-hearted, I'll be shattered, I'll cry forever, but I'm going to go on, and I'm going to fight, and I'm going to cry, and I'm going to laugh, and I'm going to create.

Your beloved—whether it's your one beloved, your two beloveds, or your ten beloveds (if you are Outrageous Lover, that circle expands)—your beloved is not the sun. **Your beloved is a rock, on which the sun shines and makes luminous.** If the rock disappears, the sun is still there. It's the simplest way to say it. The sun is Eros itself.

That's why you can't rely on the guru. The guru may incarnate, for a moment, Outrageous Love, which is beautiful—but so do you at your best moments.

At the center is Eros itself. That's what we mean when we say that God is at the center.

I can love my partner, my outrageous beloveds, madly and insanely, and know that we are madly, completely dependent on each other, but we are not codependent. If—tragically—my beloved disappears, I would go on loving.

One of the most beautiful examples of this is that dear man, Elie Wiesel. Wiesel won the Nobel Prize in literature, and in a book he wrote called *Night*, in the 1960s, he talks about being in a death camp in 1944 and seeing a boy hanging on the gallows. He writes, *I looked, and there was God, dead, hanging on the gallows.* Wiesel comes out of World War Two, comes out of the kingdom of the night, and he slowly begins to rebuild his language. He meets Marion, an Austrian woman, whom he falls in love with, and he begins to build his life. He slowly starts writing another book called *Dawn*, and then eventually a book called *Souls on Fire*, and another called *Messengers of God*. After the tragedy, **he writes an entire new literature in which Eros comes alive again.** The boy remains on the gallows, and yet the boy is also the *dharma* that we pick up and dance with at the same time.

Eros is at the center, and when you feel Eros alive moving through you, you don't use it to offer a religious explanation of why God killed that boy. No, you hold the mystery. But you know that you can scream *God is dead* on the gallows in protest, only if that's a violation of the great fairness and justice that the world needs to be if the world is a world of Outrageous Love in which fairness and justice inheres in Reality. It makes sense to write the book *Night* only if your soul is on fire—so you hold that paradox in the very depth of your being.

Tragically, nothing that we are saying is held in the world today.

We live in a world of polarization—fundamentalism on the one hand, and the rejection of the Field of Value and Field of Spirit on the other.

We are trying to create a new Story of Value, in which everyone has a place at the table. Remember, **no great system is smart enough to be entirely wrong**. Every great system has a place at the table, and we weave it together into a new whole.

Okay, so we're not codependent, but we're *interdependent* in a real and a gorgeous way.

HOW NOT TO GET STUCK IN THE TRAUMA SPACE, AND HOW TO MOVE FORWARD?

I am never saying skip your individual trauma. No, we must *work* on our individual traumas.

There is a reason that we were born into our stories, and our stories matter, and we need to work those stories. And that's the script of desire, which is the script of my life.

But don't get caught in the narcissism of the recursive loop of that story.

Understand that your life didn't start when you were born. That's the best way to get it. Your life, my life, our lives didn't start when we were born. That's such a great realization. In other words, I'm born into this journey that's ongoing. I'm born in a particular place at a particular time, and if you ever notice, you didn't choose *where* to be born, and *to whom* to be born, and *when* to be born, and with what qualities and skills to be born. You had nothing to do with that.

This story wasn't incepted by you.

You are being lived, I am being lived, we are all being lived.

When you realize that, you realize it doesn't all come from the first three years of my trauma. **The hidden premise of the perpetual tyranny of my early trauma is reductive materialism.** Does everyone get that?

There's a hidden premise in the therapeutic obsession with the first three years of my life, and that hidden premise is reductive materialism. Meaning, there is nothing *before*, and since there was nothing before, everything has to have been formed in those three years. Because there's nothing else, so where else could it have been formed? Then if you think you can move beyond it, you're an idiot because that's the only formative part of your life. That's reductive materialism.

If you live in the Field of Value, and you're pulled by your future self, and not only pulled down by your past self, then you are called forward by the action of evolution, which needs you and demands your presence. That's critical to understand.

That's why we need new modalities of working with trauma that are not rooted in reductive materialism. And one of the key works that we're working on with Lori Galperin at the Center, which is just about complete, is something we call *Unique Self Recovery*, which is a whole new trauma modality. If you visit our website, you'll see a couple of dialogues with Dick Schwartz, who developed this modality called Internal Family Systems. He was on our board for a bunch of years.

It's a really important conversation. Essentially, you cannot do real trauma work without Unique Self and True Self. It can't be done effectively—it just doesn't work. **Trauma work at the separate-self level always breaks down, it can't *not*.** That's really important to understand.

LOVE EVERYBODY MADLY

What a delight to be here! What a pleasure!

Let's just take our last minute and go back to the code. Let's read the code, and let's pray it, and conclude.

Homo amor is vocationally aroused to commit Outrageous Acts of Love.

She commits the Outrageous Acts of Love that are a function of his or her Unique Self. Wow!

It might be taking a stand when we can get away with *not* taking a stand.

> *Outrageous Acts of Love are when we give ourselves outrageously, beyond our traumas, our rackets, our issues, and our patterns.*

With true Outrageous Acts of Love, we can always rationalize to ourselves why we don't have to do them—but our unique risk, genuine Outrageous Acts of Love, are the fabric of the Intimate Universe realizing its Omega Point is you.

SHE DESPERATELY NEEDS US TO TAKE OUR UNIQUE RISK

What moves us to commit Outrageous Acts of Love is evolution Herself, Goddess Herself, *She*.

Oh my God. Maybe we can pray that together, our *holy and broken Hallelujah*, and we'll offer our prayers. And ask for everything, love everybody madly.

Thank you, everyone. Oh my God. Oh my God!

CHAPTER SIX

THE RESPONSE TO PERSONAL CRISIS AND META-CRISIS IS THE EVOLUTION OF RELATIONSHIP AND THE EVOLUTION OF LOVE: THE RISE OF WHOLE MATE RELATIONSHIPS

Episode 340 — April 16, 2023

GOD LOVES STORIES

We have this realization of what we call *the second shock of existence.*

The *first* shock of existence is the realization of death at the dawn of civilization—and death presses us into life. And then we go through all of the stages of human history, and we've now arrived at the *second* shock of existence, which is the realization that—after all the dignities and disasters of modernity—something new is on the table. After all the beauty and all the breakthrough but also all the breakdown and all the ugliness, something new is on the table.

We are, quite literally, confronting the second shock of existence, which is not the death of the individual human being, but the potential death of humanity.

We're going to talk about it today in a whole new way—relationships, Barbara Marx Hubbard, whole mates, and the future of relationships.

But I want to place this in this wildly important context.

What we are understanding is that **the only way to change the vector of history is to tell a new story**. To tell a new Story of Value—but not just to make up the story, not a conjecture, not a contrived story, but to gather the best strands of information, and to be covered with paint, as we paint this new story into history. This new story is drawn from all of the deepest colors:

- The validated insights of all the great strands of traditional ancient wisdom.
- All of the most profound insights of modernity, with its sciences, psychologies, and new ways of information-gathering and re-understanding human identity and the Divine.
- The best of the postmodern insights.

All of these are integrated together in a seamless weave, which is a new Story of Value that we can share deep into China, and deep into Russia, deep into Asia, deep into New Zealand, deep into the Americas, North and South, deep into Europe, and deep into the Middle East.

Story is not contrivance. It's not something human beings made up.

Story is real. It is the ontology of reality, the structure of the real, and it exists and lives all the way down and all the way up the evolutionary chain.

Story means that there is a sequence of events that are intrinsically related to each other:

1. They are *not random*. That's the first element of story.
2. A story follows *a plotline*. There's a plotline in the story.

3. That plotline follows *intrinsic desires*, desires that are inherent in that plotline.
4. Those desires are desires *for value*.
5. There is some dimension of *freedom* in pursuing those values. It might be elemental *proto*-freedom at the level of matter, but there is some expression of aliveness and freedom that lives all the way down, even at the subatomic level.

As Richard Feynman, the physicist, pointed out, there is a kind of *proto-freewill*, as it were, a proto-freedom, even at the level of matter (and Stuart Kauffman has done some very good mathematics on this). Because a story means it's not a tech manual.

Story is a structure of reality.

There's a story that lives in the world of matter, and then story evolves in the world of life, and then also at the different levels of the biosphere, and then into the human realm. And then, at every level of the human realm, story evolves, evolves, evolves until:

- We realize that we are actually actors in the story.
- We can see the whole story: the First Big Bang: the world of matter, the Second Big Bang: the world of life, the Third Big Bang: the birth of culture. We *see* the story.

We realize that the whole story lives in us.

We realize that the story is evolving.

We realize that we are *actors* in the story.

We realize that we are *storytellers* in the story, and we realize that we are *the authors* of the next chapters in the story.

That's called *conscious evolution*.

That's when we realize that our story is chapter and verse in The Universe: A Love Story.

The masters summarized this in three words when they said, *God loves stories*. It was an elliptical way of saying everything that we just said.

CHOOSING TO TELL THE MOST ACCURATE STORY

There's always more than one story that you can tell.

My bedtime reading these days is *Evolution: A View from the Twenty-first Century*, by James A. Shapiro. I recommend it to everyone. He's a great geneticist at the University of Chicago. He points out, in the section called *DNA as poetry*, that you can have multiple messages in a single sequence of DNA. What *multiple messages in a single sequence of DNA* means is that you don't only have one story. DNA is telling a story—but within one sequence of DNA, there are multiple messages, and those messages can be activated by the receiver. It's the receiver who decides, as it were, which message to activate.

There is not *only one* story of Reality you can tell. You can cogently build a number of stories of Reality—but **there is one story that organizes the information in the most adequate and elegant way.**

There is a *pluralism* of stories, meaning there is more than one possible story. Stories are not all equal. Some stories are better than others because they account for much more empirical information—so if you dismiss entire realms of interior information in telling your story, then it's not going to work.

Just to give you one example, I talk every other week to a great man whose name I won't mention now. He's one of my favorite people in the entire world, an incredibly brilliant scientist, mathematician, and really important thinker. We are working on some key projects together, and at some point, we always come to the issue of the continuity of consciousness, meaning death, and what happens after death.

Of course, we don't know exactly what happens after death—but what we do know is that the most plausible understanding and explanation of all the empirical information we have is that death is not the end of the story, that there *is* a continuity of consciousness. Now, every time we get to this set of information and I ask him to look at a book, an article, or a set of evidence, he always ignores me and says: *I can't do that, I can't go there*. What he is basically doing is taking off the table an enormous set of empirical data and, therefore, constructing his story *without that data*. But if you construct your story without that data, it doesn't work.

The best story covers the most data from the most realms and the most wisdom streams: from the most forms of exterior science and the most forms of interior science—so there is the best story we can tell. Having said that, it's not that you can only construct one story. You can construct multiple plausible stories. Some of the plausible stories don't take as much information as they should into account, but there still is more than one plausible story that you can construct.

There *is* an ontological pluralism of stories, but that means that **the most powerful thing you can do is choose to tell the most accurate story**. Since story is the source code of Cosmos:

- Choosing to *construct* a story
- Choosing to tell *the most accurate* story
- Choosing to bring the most human beings possible into a shared global story, a shared global Story of Value

That is the single most potent, cogent, and powerful act we can do today.

That new story has to answer three questions:

- What does it mean to be a human being? The question of **who we are**: our identity.
- **Where are we**, what kind of world do we live in? Is it a cold, materialist, indifferent Cosmos, or is it the Cosmos in which there's a welcome sign?
- **What's there to do**, what's our response to the world? Do we have a response-ability?

It's only those questions handled in a Story of Value that can generate a bottom-up, self-organizing universe, a self-actualizing Cosmos—the interior rules of Cosmos iterated exponentially, simple first rules. Simple answers to these questions: who, where, what? Only that can change the fabric of Reality and birth a new human and a new humanity.

A NEW CHAPTER IN THE NEW STORY: WHOLE MATE RELATIONSHIPS

That's what we are doing here: we are telling this new story. That's what we are committed to.

We don't go straight to "let's say something inspiring." No, the inspiration is when we are breathed anew.

Hallelujah. Leonard Cohen writes "Hallelujah," and he borrows this word from the Book of Psalms:

Hallelu: the pristine praise, and the drunken intoxication of life, is *Yah*: the breath of the Divine. *Yah* means "inspired, I am *breathed*."

- What breathes me anew, what gives me a new breath?
- What allows me to catch my breath?
- What makes me breathless with ecstasy?

A genuine new Story of Value, in which I can locate myself, and which organizes elegantly, beautifully, and artistically:

- The most information we have about interiors and exteriors
- The most feeling we have
- The most pathos we have
- The most longing we have

- The most yearning we have

In other words, information is not just quantitative and commodifiable. **Information is the information about my longings, my yearnings, my deepest knowings, that which is non-commodifiable, and that which is immeasurable.** *All of that* needs to be taken into account and articulated in a new Story of Value.

We've got to be able to tell this Story of Value to seven-year-olds and ninety-year-olds, to every color, every country, every region, and every form of belief or disbelief. It's got to be a shared Story of Value.

That is actually doable. That is what will change the course of history, without question.

History is about story. History is *his*-story or *her*-story. It's about the realization that there is a plotline. We get to participate in changing the vector of history by recognizing the contours of the story, by getting beneath the headlines and asking, *what's happening here, what's driving this?*

And the realization that emerges from all of this is:

- It's a love story.
- Reality is animated by Eros.
- Eros is the movement of Reality, in its radical aliveness, towards *ever deeper* contact and ever greater wholeness.
- It's the movement of separate parts to form larger wholes.
- It's the movement of new forms of relationship.

That's what all of Reality is.

This is why Barbara Marx Hubbard, my dear beloved friend, who was a partner in founding One Mountain Many Paths, completely committed her life to telling the new story.

What we want to do today is tell a new chapter in the new story.

THE EVOLUTION OF RELATIONSHIP

I am going to tell it in a new way because I spent the last three or four days deep in a particular plotline of the story, and I want to share with you some of what's emerged.

And I want to tell it to honor Barbara.

I just have to say—it brings tears to my eyes—that I miss Barbara immensely.

She was an evolutionary whole mate and beloved.

She was filled with a kind of radical positivity, radical wonder, and radical delight.

She fully understood the political, economic, social, existential, moral, spiritual impact of telling this new Story of Value, and we spent all of our time together crafting the plotlines of the story.

There was one particular part of the story that I was privileged to share with Barbara, that she got very excited about, and talked about a lot. We are dedicating this week to Barbara. Barbara passed away four years ago, on April 10th. I was there at her bedside.

And I miss you enormously, Barbara. You knew of the continuity of consciousness. I'm a bit mad at you that you haven't come to visit me.

I'd like you to come visit, talk, and be with us.

But I know that you're here, and I know that we're holding hands in this, in the deepest way, and holding hearts, and we're doing this together.

Today, we want to dedicate this to Barbara Marx Hubbard, and we want to do that by telling a new chapter in a new way.

The whole story re-contexualized itself for me this week, and it's about the future of relationships.

It's the most personal intimate story—and it's also the broadest cosmic strain.

It's a key dimension of our response to the meta-crisis, our response to the second shock of existence.

EVOLUTIONARY LOVE CODE: WE ARE CONFRONTED BY CRISIS

Cellular crisis, personal crisis, and meta-crisis. Every crisis is a crisis of intimacy. The meta-crisis, for example, is a global intimacy disorder.

A crisis of intimacy can only be solved by the emergence of a new level of intimacy.

The root of the meta-crisis is in the alienated relationship of the part from the whole. The part is non-intimate with the whole.

A crisis of intimacy is a crisis of relationship. The crisis is resolved by a new level of relationship.

We call *Homo amor* relationships whole mate relationships or evolutionary relationships.

Whole mate relationships are an essential dimension of the new Story of Value in response to the meta-crisis.

Whole mate relationships are also—not coincidentally—a crucial dimension in response to the personal crisis of love experienced by every human being, whether they are in a role mate or soul mate relationship, or they refuse to enter such a relationship because it does not address their deepest longing.

EVERY CRISIS IS SOLVED BY A NEW STRUCTURE OF INTIMACY

There is a meta-crisis, and at its core are two generator functions and an underlying root cause.

- The first generator function: **we are telling a bad story**. We are telling a story that is a success story, in which every individual is an atomized separate self, engaged—at one level or another, in their company, in their family, in their life, in their nation, between nations, between divisions of companies—in rivalrous conflict governed by win/lose metrics, different versions of zero-sum, win/lose metrics.

- That generates **a fragile world**. A world optimized for efficiency and not resiliency, with vulnerable supply chains, vulnerable resources, vulnerable health care for human beings, vulnerable social structures with a massive gap between haves and have-nots—a world in which the very foundational ecosystems are at risk in the next relatively short period of time. **All because everyone is involved not in a relationship to the whole but in an atomized relationship to the particular rivalrous conflict governed by win/lose metrics**—that generates a fragile system, subject to breakdown at the most fundamental of levels.

Underlying those two generator functions, there is something deeper, which we call *a global intimacy disorder*, a failure of relationship to the whole.

This is the inability to feel the whole, to be omni-considerate for the sake of the whole, to be madly in love with the whole. To participate not just locally but globally, and ultimately, galactically, and to realize that everything affects everything else, that I have no identity without the whole, without the plankton under the ocean, without the topsoil, without all the different dimensions of the biosphere, without the bugs or caterpillars or fish. That **I don't exist—there is no *Me* outside of the broadest frame of *We*.**

What do we need to do?

We need to tell a new Story of Value, which re-weaves our identity and locates us in the whole, and locates our nature as *Homo amor*—as human beings who are not merely separate self but also:

- True Self (we are the whole)
- Unique Self (unique expressions of the whole)
- Evolutionary Unique Self (we evolve the whole)

That's a new form of relationship.

- It's a new form of relationship to self.
- It's a new form of relationship to Reality.
- From that place of *Homo amor*, it's a new form of relationship to each other.

That's the background, that's the context. Now, let's see if we can sharpen it. Let's go much deeper—in these eight simple steps:

1. The core of Reality is evolution. That's what Reality is. **Reality is evolution.** Evolution is a series of transformations.
2. Reality is relationships. All of Reality is relationships, all the way down the evolutionary chain and all the way up.
3. Reality is the evolution of relationships.
4. What *drives* evolution? How do relationships evolve? They evolve in two ways. Relationships evolve because there's an inherent drive in Cosmos to seek ever more Eros, which means *ever deeper* forms of relationship. But the second driver of the evolution of relationships is crisis. **Crisis is an evolutionary driver.**
5. Every crisis is a crisis of relationship, which is another way of saying that every crisis is a crisis of intimacy. Intimacy is when a relationship is formed in which we realize we have a *shared identity*, where we can *feel* each other and *recognize* each other, and we have *a shared Field of Value*, and we have a *shared purpose*. Intimacy is a form of relationship, and **every crisis is a crisis of intimacy.**
6. You can't solve a problem at the level of consciousness which created the problem. This was Albert Einstein's famous and correct observation (made by many people before but a

correct observation).

7. Every crisis in relationship, every crisis in intimacy, is solved by a new level of relationship, by a new structure of intimacy. That's structural to Cosmos.
8. That's true about *every* form of crisis. Every form of crisis, without exception, is solved by a new level of relationship and a new level of intimacy because every crisis is a crisis of intimacy and a crisis of relationship.

Every form of crisis, without exception, is solved by a new level of relationship and a new level of intimacy.

FROM ROLE MATE TO SOUL MATE

Let's look at three forms of crisis.

The **biological crisis**, what's often called the *oxygen crisis*—the oxygen crisis at the dawn of Reality, when single-celled organisms were being destroyed by oxygen because of their cellular makeup. We were literally killing the cellular life on the planet. **This crisis of intimacy, this crisis of relationship generated a new form of life: multicellular life, prokaryotes to eukaryotes.** Multicellular life leads directly into animals, mammals, and human beings. A crisis of intimacy between oxygen, the elements, the biosphere, and the single-celled organisms generates a new structure of intimacy—multicellular organisms, which are able to be nourished by oxygen.

Personal crisis. Personal crisis is always a crisis of relationship, and it can only be solved by a new level of relationship—either a new level of relationship to self or to others. If I've split myself off from my second innocence, if I've split myself off from my capacity to take a seat at the table, I can only solve that by re-embracing and re-integrating the parts of myself that I've split off. In other words, **whether it's a relationship to self or a**

relationship to another, it's only a new level of relationship that allows us to solve personal crises.

There's a huge crisis today in love. **Relationship is not working.** I want to say that clearly: *relationship is not working.*

Marriage, in most of the world, is not ultimately working. Either people are not getting married because they can't find a partner who meets their deepest longing, or people are getting married and feel deadened and trapped in the relationship. **The marriage structure in the world isn't quite working.**

Our structure of relationship doesn't work.

Let's just notice what happened in relationships in the last, let's say, several hundred years. Fifty, sixty, seventy, eighty years ago, the basic structure of relationship, at its core, its center of gravity was *role mate*: we share roles. Our context for relating was shared roles.

- Homemaker, mother, nurturer, bearer of children—that was the role of the woman, the feminine.
- The masculine: protector, provider, breadwinner.

That was the basic structure, and everyone was in their particular role. That was the context for relating. There was a profound need that lived between people, and there was a mutual, radical dependency. We were utterly dependent on each other for survival and for thriving. **The context for relating was surviving and thriving, and each person played their own role.** End of story.

Occasionally, there were deeper trends in relationship. There were deeper forms of relationship. There were ideals of courtly love in the Cathar world, and in the medieval world, there were ideals of love in different sections of biblical literature. But **the center of gravity of relationship was always the role mate, in one form or another, for the preponderance of history the world over.**

THE EVOLUTION OF RELATIONSHIP

But in the last forty to fifty years that became insufficient, and there was this enormous desire for:

- Depth
- Sharing our vulnerability
- Genuine communication
- Sharing our mutual senses of trauma and wounding
- An ability to have empathy of a whole different kind, to feel each other in a whole different way

This was the introduction of the notion of *soul mate*, and **soul mate became the preeminent desire for relationship in most of the world.**

The problem is—and it's a profound problem—that **soul mates didn't quite know what to do with each other.**

They loved the personal fulfillment of looking deeply in each other's eyes, and looking deeply in each other's eyes is the great soul mate activity—and sharing wounding, brokenness, and personal history. And, of course, there were three famous soul mate books:

- One by Harville Hendricks, my dear friend, called *Getting the Love You Want*, a guide for communication for couples.
- One by John Gray, another dear friend, who wrote *Men Are from Mars, Women Are from Venus*, another manual for communication.
- And one by Gary Chapman, whom I don't know, who wrote *The Five Love Languages*, also a manual for communication.

These are all the new soul mate books, and they all were very important. It was a great momentous leap forward, a great evolutionary leap forward. There was an evolution of relationship. There was a crisis in relationship at the level of role mate, and then this crisis was met by this new form of relationship called soul mate.

SOUL-MATE CONTRACT WITHOUT A ROLE-MATE DIMENSION DOESN'T WORK

But the *soul mate* structure is not holding because, at a certain point, **there is something fragile and devastating in a soul-mate relationship: there is no genuine sense of shared urgent purpose.** We are looking deeply in each other's eyes, and in some sense, the personal fulfillment of looking deeply in each other's eyes is no longer personally fulfilling. It feels too alienated from the larger context.

- We don't have a sense of a shared world.
- We don't have a sense of a shared Field of Value.
- We don't have a sense of genuine mutuality of recognition.

We've let go of the role mate: we don't need each other in the old role-mate way to survive; we could each, theoretically, survive independently. We are coming together because we *choose* to come together.

- At the level of role mate, we say to each other: *I need you, and I need you desperately to survive.*
- At the level of soul mate, many women are working, and lots of men are not working. The balance has changed. Lots of men are not providers and protectors, some are. Lots of women are providers and protectors.

The old deal in relationship is no longer in play, so when I say *I need a woman* or *I need a man*, it means something very different at the level of soul mate than it does at the level of role mate.

It doesn't mean *I need you for survival.*

It means *I choose you.* I don't need you in the old survival way, at least an enormous amount of the world doesn't. An enormous amount of the world still does—but there is a huge leading-edge swath, all over the world, where we are not getting together because we're at a role mate level of *I need you.* No, it's actually *I choose you.*

THE EVOLUTION OF RELATIONSHIP

- I choose you because I don't want to be alone.
- I choose you because I want us to mutually resonate and feel each other.
- I want us to share stories and history, and share brokenness, and share the stories of our trauma, and hold our wounds together, and love each other, and look deeply in each other's eyes.

And then, at some point, that doesn't quite cut it.

At some point, that's not quite enough.

It's a momentous leap forward—but it's not enough. There is insufficient ground.

This is what I meant when I said that it's not working; the soul mate contract is not working. And this is heresy, you're not allowed to say this. This is heresy, but it's true. The soul mate contract isn't working. It doesn't actually hold.

Soul mate without a role mate dimension doesn't hold.

But we don't want to go back to the role-mate model. We don't want to go back to the old world.

We don't want to go back, we want to evolve.

Now watch as it gets really wild and beautiful.

We are at a crisis in relationship, in which, although no one will say it out loud, the emperor has no clothes. Soul mate relationship is not working. It is an insufficient ground to hold relationship—so you've got this new crisis in relationship.

This crisis of relationship is happening at the exact same time as the meta-crisis. Does everyone catch that?

- **There is a global meta-crisis**, what we called at the beginning the second shock of existence, the realization that we face the potential death of humanity or the death of our humanity: two different forms of the meta-crisis.
- **A second crisis is this personal crisis in our relationships**.

We are not satisfied by the soul-mate relationship. There's something tragic about that relationship. It doesn't feel like it has ground. And as many love songs and harlequin romances as we write, it just doesn't quite hold. **There's something fundamentally missing in the very foundation of relationship.**

Now, whenever there's a crisis, it's always a crisis of intimacy. Whenever there's a crisis, it's always a crisis of relationship—so the crisis in love is a crisis in intimacy, a crisis in relationships.

We don't want to regress to the old breadwinner/homemaker, forced role-mate relationship, where you don't have any other options. That's the forced role, that's the enforced role, that's the coerced role. You're stuck in that role; that's just the way it is. We don't have clarity that that's the way it should be. It's *not* the way it should be.

There are lots of other options. Men want a wider vision of being a man, women want a wider vision of being a woman, and these prescribed roles simply don't hold anymore as a necessary form of relationship.

We think soul mate is the answer, but it doesn't quite hold us. It's not quite enough.

We don't want to just sit and look in one person's eyes and exile everyone else—and so there's a need for a new form of relationship, for a new form of intimacy.

THE EVOLUTION OF RELATIONSHIP

FROM SOUL MATE TO WHOLE MATE

We call that new form of intimacy whole mate relationships, evolutionary relationships, or *Homo amor* relationships.

The essence of a whole-mate relationship is that there is a new context for relating, a new set of values at play.

> *In the whole mate relationship, the two parties to the relationship are not just looking in each other's eyes, they're looking at a wider horizon together.*

It is unimaginably lonely not to be able to look at a wider horizon, at a shared horizon, with your partner. It's not enough to look in your partner's eyes, and at a certain point, that doesn't hold. You have to be looking together at a shared Field of Value, at a shared horizon. When you look together at a shared horizon, then you can turn and look back to each other, then love explodes again, in an entirely different and deeper form: this new form of relationship, whole mate, meaning both partners in the relationship are in service to the larger whole. Wow!

I'm going to talk about it much more next week, but **both parties come to the relationship with their own prior wholeness.**

- In a role-mate relationship, neither side is whole; they don't even exist, they can't survive without each other. Neither side has wholeness by themselves, neither of the beloveds, the masculine or the feminine, or however that expresses itself.
- In a soul-mate relationship, the same is true: I feel completely incomplete without you. Without you witnessing me, I don't exist. I'm masculine, but I need your feminine in order to be whole. And I'm feminine, I need your masculine in order

to be whole. We both come broken, incomplete, and you're going to complete me. I don't have wholeness without you.
- In a whole-mate relationship, we come with a certain sense of wholeness already in place.

This means three different things. First, it means that I come *whole* to the relationship, and then, in the relationship, I *evolve and deepen my wholeness* with you.

But it's more paradoxical. I don't come because I don't exist without you. I exist without you, and I'm powerful without you. I've established some interior sense of wholeness myself, and then I bring that wholeness to the relationship. So, I am a whole mate in two ways:

1. I have a sense of integrity, autonomy, and wholeness within myself that I bring to the relationship. It's not a survive-thrive codependency. I have a kind of emotional wholeness that I can hold within myself, which I bring to the relationship.
2. We are both in service to the larger whole.

This is an evolution of relationships we've just described: from role mate, to soul mate, to whole mate.

Now watch carefully. It's very beautiful.

This evolution of relationships is not this new, strange social construct that happens to emerge at this moment in history.

Reality is relationship, Reality is evolution, and Reality is the evolution of relationship. Relationship evolves because of the inherent drive for new forms of relationship, and relationship evolves through crisis. **Crisis births a new form of relationship.** That's true all the way down and all the way up the evolutionary chain.

At this moment in history, when we are facing a crisis of love, a crisis of relationship, **a new form of relationship has to emerge, we have to go from soul mate to whole mate.**

Whole mate includes soul mate, but it *transcends* soul mate. It has all the best dimensions of soul mate, but then it transcends: we are sharing a vision together, we can see together, we are looking at a shared horizon.

THE META-CRISIS BEGINS TO BE RESOLVED BY A NEW FORM OF RELATIONSHIP

The entire point of everything we did today was to get to this last piece, which is, **the meta-crisis is also an intimacy disorder.**

Just like the personal crisis in a relationship is a crisis of intimacy, the meta-crisis is also an intimacy disorder. It's an intimacy disorder in which our story is a success story based on win/lose metrics. We produce a fragile system in which parts don't actually recognize or know each other. We create financial instruments in China that wreck American markets, but people don't even know each other. We are not thinking; we are not omni-considerate for the larger whole.

At this moment, when relationships—the basic structure of Reality—are all based on win/lose metrics, this iterates exponentially into a fragile system that breaks down and generates an extraction model:

- That extracts resources
- That depletes reality
- That creates violent caste systems
- That generates all the structures that will undermine our very existence on the planet

So what do we need?

We need our basic structure of Reality— which is relationship—to evolve.

How do we evolve it?

We evolve the basic structure of relationship from win/lose metrics (even a couple together, a couple between themselves are caught in win/lose metrics, and then as a couple, they're in win-lose metrics against everyone else).

We want to evolve the basic structure of relationship from soul mate to whole mate, and whole mate means:

- We are whole as a couple, but we are also whole individually.
- We are also in relationship, in service to the larger whole.
- We have a shared horizon, and part of our shared horizon is the meta-crisis, and part of our shared horizon is a shared vision of value.

And imagine: **what if all couples in the world become whole mates?**

Instead of them being a nuclear family, involved in success stories and win/lose metrics with everyone else—every couple, every relationship, whether it's a romantic couple or a friendship couple, whatever kind of couple, it's a whole mate couple, in which it's not just us looking in each other's eyes, but:

- We are looking at a shared horizon.
- We are acting together.
- We are not just joining genes, we are joining genius, to co-create a new Reality.

And as the basic structure of Reality—relationship—evolves, so **the meta-crisis, which is an alienation from the larger whole, begins to be resolved by the introduction of a new form of relationship, whole mate, which is relationship to the larger whole.** If the meta-crisis is a failed story, a story of alienation from the larger whole, then it's a new story, a story of being omni-considerate to the larger whole, that resolves the meta-crisis.

And an essential part of that new story is a new story of relationship.

THE EVOLUTION OF RELATIONSHIP

What's that new story of relationship?

The movement from role mate to soul mate to whole mate, to evolutionary relationships, to *Homo amor* relationships.

You begin to see how beautiful it is?

Both the personal crisis, as a crisis of intimacy, is resolved by a new structure of intimacy, and the meta-crisis—a global intimacy disorder—is *also* resolved by a new global intimacy, a new story of shared value, and a new structure of relationship, which is the core structure that creates intimacy.

- The new structure of relationship is no longer soul mates, separate-self soul mates sharing each other's wounding as the basic structure of their relationship.
- No, it's whole mates, who love each other passionately, who do share wounding and personal stories, but they are also connected to the larger story, to the larger whole. They're in service to a larger whole. Wow!

That's one of the things that Barbara was wildly excited about. This is just literally in the last years, as Barbara and I were whole-mating together.

And of course, friends, you can have more than one whole mate. **A whole mate is a kind of sacred polyamorous relationship.** You can be a whole mate with a number of people. Because you're loving each other madly; you're in service to the larger whole.

Imagine if the fabric of Reality is evolutionary whole mates, what a different world we would live in!

CHAPTER SEVEN

THE URGENT NEED FOR WHOLE MATE RELATIONSHIPS, PART 2

Episode 341 — April 23, 2023

OUTSIDE THE FIELD OF VALUE, NO ONE IS HUMAN ANYMORE

What are we doing here, friends, together? Who are we? What are we here to do and to be?

We are establishing—articulating—a universal grammar of value, as a ground, a context for our diversity. That's a big deal because the root cause of *every* form of existential risk is, in the end, the collapse of a universal grammar of value.

Now, I want to say something a little bit painful but really important to understand.

When you look at the last decades—in particular, I am going to talk about the United States, but this is something that all of Europe has witnessed, and the whole world has witnessed—you have this horrific phenomenon called *public shootings*. Shootings in a school, in a bank, in a

church, in a restaurant—when someone feels hurt, and their response is shooting people.

Now, let's be very clear. There have always been lots of guns in America, and America has a very major issue with guns. And it's part of the American ethos that armed force is not only owned by the government. Government doesn't have a monopoly on force, and the government not having a monopoly on force actually ensures democracy. That's part of the Constitution. I'm not here to debate that question right now.

But what does it *mean* that someone gets hurt, someone gets devastated—and they go and shoot up a school? It's impossible to even imagine. How does someone get to that, and how does that become a phenomenon, where every fifteen days, there is a public shooting?

I am going to say something that's controversial but accurate (my friend, Warren Farrell, pointed it out and did a lot of the research on it): there is an incredibly high correlation between children cut off from the father—no father in the picture or an absentee father in an extreme way—and acts of violence, in particular, school shootings.

Why?

It's part of something that's even deeper, which we may call *the death of the Father*, which we talked about three or four weeks ago. There is the personal father, and there is *The Father*, our Father in Heaven. By *our Father in Heaven*, I don't mean the mythic, ethnocentric, homophobic God of the old religions—I mean **Father as the source of value.**

- **The blessing of the Mother is the experience that I am always welcome** in the Universe because I can always go back to the Mother—and in the arms of the Mother, I am always welcome no matter what, which is the beauty of the Mother. I can always fall into Mother's arms. I am always welcome. That experience of being radically and always welcome is the experience of the blessing of the Mother, and it's absolutely necessary, and you can't be a healthy human being without it (an enormous amount of attachment theory is about the ways in which the blessing of the Mother wasn't received).

- But there is also, friends, **the blessing of the Father—the call of value, the *demand* of value.**

There is a very subtle dynamic that's happening all over culture, all over the globe.

In the premodern world, in which value was central, people were always massacring other people, but the people who were massacred were always the enemy; they were thought to be, in some sense, less human. That is one of the tragedies of the ethnocentric, premodern view—that the enemy is somehow less human than I am. As Margaret Mead points out, everyone agrees that you can't murder, but murdering only means killing human beings—and those outside of your tribe are somehow less than human, so different laws apply to them.

I am in no way suggesting a naive, strange, historically inaccurate thought, in which violence starts with American school shootings. Obviously, that's not true.

But what *is* true? What is true is that for the people who are doing these school shootings, **the sense of responsibility, of ultimately being held to account for those killings, is lost.** It's something like a premodern ethnocentric tribe killing the next tribe. That next tribe is somehow not human; they are less than human—and because I am doing God's will, I am not held accountable for it.

There is this sense that we have killed the Father, which means we have killed the Field of Value.

This means that, ultimately, Raskolnikov is not held accountable for killing the old woman—or at least he thinks it should be so, in Dostoevsky's famous story.

There is this new sense—and it is a creeping, pervasive sickness at the very heart of society—in which people begin to experience themselves as living outside the Field of Value. **And if I experience myself as living outside the Field of Value, it's not only that the human beings who are not in my tribe are not human,** *no one* **is actually human anymore.**

Does everyone catch that sentence?

No one is human anymore.

Everyone is outside the Field of Value.

When we attempt to build our world on that false premise, it begins to fall apart.

THERE IS A STRAIGHT LINE FROM POSTMODERNISM TO SCHOOL SHOOTINGS

I am going to say something very painful now, but I think it is accurate.

A dear friend of mine has been sending me some quotes from Irvin Yalom's book, *Existential Psychotherapy*, which I perused fairly extensively many years ago. He is a mainstream figure, at the very center of American society—tenure chairs, major universities, the iconic book read by generations. And what Yalom basically says is:

- The human being does not live in a Field of Value.
- There is no actual Field of Value.

He is a Sartrean, and bases his philosophy on Sartre's *Being and Nothingness*. He says, we need to *create* value, but it doesn't really *exist*. Therefore, every human being is ultimately alone—**love cannot bridge the chasm of aloneness**. Yalom is also strongly influenced by Heidegger. It's one of

Heidegger's primary positions that you cannot ever move beyond your aloneness.

Every human being is ultimately alone.

There is no Field of Value. There is no intrinsic value in Cosmos—and to be free is to know that only you are creating it, but there is no intrinsic value at all.

Yalom is echoing and parroting that postmodern position which says there is no Field of Value—a flawed, horrific, and dogmatic position. There is a straight line from Yalom to my colleague, Yuval Harari, who says that all value is a figment of our imagination, a fiction, a mere social construct. **And then there is a direct line to the lonely individual, displaced from the Field of the Father, which is the Field of Value, who is hurt and devastated, and who picks up a gun and shoots up a school.**

It is not just that too many guns are available.

One of the tragedies of the liberal worldview is that all evil, all breakdown is caused by someone or something *outside* of me. It might be guns, it might be racism—but there is always something out there, whatever it might be. It might be any manner of things that cause me to be broken and therefore act out—whether it's handguns, fundamentalists, or bad religion, whether I've been victimized by some version of bad psychology, or whether it's abuse.

All of those things are real—but what the liberal world fails to do is ask, *how do I participate?*

The liberal world always says, *transform society*. We *do* need to transform society, but **transforming society can't come at the expense of transforming myself**. I've got to transform myself. If I'm always locating the locus of the problem outside of myself. I spend all of my time transforming society, and I never turn to transform myself.

The conservative world errs on the other side. The conservative world says, well, *transform yourself*, and if you haven't transformed yourself, you're accountable because you haven't pulled yourself up by the bootstraps. The conservative world often ignores the need to transform society, and holds the person accountable in a way they shouldn't be—but actually, it's a dual moment and movement of transformation: I need to transform myself *and* transform society.

WE DESPERATELY NEED TO RECONSTRUCT THE FIELD OF VALUE

For our purposes, what we need to do is reconstruct the Field of Value.

We need to step back into the Field of Value.

And here's the key, friends: it's not about *values*. There is always a fight about values.

- *Values* is not the issue.
- *Value* is the issue.

Do you get that distinction, my friends?

"Values" means: let's fight for my values. That's not the issue.

The issue is: we are both in the Field of Value, and if we're both in the Field of Value, then **whatever values we hold are emerging from that field.** Those values need to be in relationship to each other, they need to synergize with each other, and they need to impact each other—and we go from polarization to paradox.

But if I am *not* in the Field of Value, then whatever my values are, they don't matter. My values become just another form of identity. They are socially constructed, so they're not intrinsically meaningful. And then, I create a world in which not only is *the next tribe* considered not human (as in the ethnocentric moment)—but *no one* is human.

No one is human because *human* means that I have an irreducible and intrinsic dignity, and I have infinite value. **My irreducible uniqueness confers intrinsic and infinite value on my life, and therefore, *Thou shall not murder*.**

Even if I am furious with you, I can't kill you, I can't murder you. I've got to somehow work out that fury, rage, and pain.

We just have to get what it means. It's so easy to look away! What does it mean that every fifteen days there is a school shooting in the last several years?

We desperately need to reconstruct the Field of Value. It is the single most sacred and ecstatically urgent moral imperative of this moment in history.

That's why we have spent so much time constructing and enacting One Mountain Many Paths as the place in which we are going to try and articulate a new set of First Values and First Principles embedded in a Story of Value. **You need both—you need First Principles and First Values and you need the narrative arc of the Story of Value—in order to literally *re-soul* Reality, to re-inform Reality with value.**

It has never happened before, friends.

What *has* happened before is that we placed particular groups of people outside the Field of Value. We argued that only our group is truly in the field, therefore, only we are fully human—but we've never actually gotten to a point where *no one* is in the Field of Value because it doesn't exist.

That's what we mean here when we talk about two kinds of existential risks: the death of humanity and the death of *our* humanity.

- The death of humanity is extinction.
- The death of our humanity is the extinction of our humanness: we are no longer human in the way we understand *human* to mean.

That's a big deal. That's the position that informs the leading edges of culture today—that there is no Field of Value. It informs the MIT Media Lab and Alex Pentland's work. It informs Irvin Yalom's work. It informs popular historians like Yuval Harari's work. It informs Sam Harris's work. It's a given in most of the major intellectual trends in Europe. It's a big deal.

We cannot go to the old premodern value—we need to reconstruct and re-energize the Field of Value.

- We *are* unique value in the Field of Value, and we are here to participate in the evolution of value.
- Value evolves through us, even as it is eternal. We participate in value.
- Value is real. The Father is real.
- The irreducible dignity of every human life is real—every human being is an irreducible depth of value.

That's the beginning of the new Story of Value. No one is outside the circle.

EVOLUTIONARY LOVE CODE: FROM ROLE MATE TO SOUL MATE TO WHOLE MATE

We are confronted by crises: cellular crisis, personal crisis, and the meta-crisis.

Every crisis is a crisis of intimacy. The meta-crisis, for example, is a global intimacy disorder.

A crisis of intimacy can only be solved by an emergence of a new level of intimacy. The root of the meta-crisis is the alienated relationship of the part from the whole; the part is non-intimate with the whole. A crisis of intimacy is a crisis of relationship, and this crisis is resolved by a new level of relationship.

We call *Homo amor* relationships whole mate relationships, or evolutionary relationships.

Whole mate relationships are an essential dimension of the new

Story of Value in response to the meta-crisis.

Whole mate relationships are also, not coincidentally, a crucial dimension in response to the personal crisis of love experienced by every human being, whether they are in a role mate or a soul mate relationship, or they refuse to enter into such a relationship because it doesn't address their deepest longing.

By the *role mate* model, we mean a relationship based on shared roles, in which the masculine is the breadwinner, and the woman's the homemaker. Well-defined roles.

In the *soul mate* model, we step beyond those roles. We look to each other not for roles—we don't need these roles for survival—but for communication, vulnerability, depth. We can share our trauma stories. We can hold each other. We look deeply in each other's eyes.

In the whole mate model, we are not just looking deeply in each other's eyes, but we have a shared horizon.

There is a crisis of relationship, and I want to name it clearly:

The soul mate model doesn't quite work.

That's generally heresy to say, but it's true. Soul mate doesn't quite work. We thought we would go from role mate to soul mate, and we would be in Shangri La. We'd be in blissful heaven forever, looking deeply in each other's eyes—but the soul mate model, in some fundamental way, is not working.

Now, that doesn't mean we want to go back to the role mate model. We don't. We don't want to go back to prescribed roles and the rigidity of what a human being was allowed to be as woman or as man. We don't want to go there.

We also don't want to go back to a place in which men can't engage their feminine and women can't engage their masculine, for sure.

We don't want to go back to a place in which men were forced to perform at very, very dangerous jobs, in order to be recognized in any way.

We don't want to go back to a place where women didn't have their full dignity and place in the job market.

We don't want to go back to any of those things—we don't want to go back to role mates.

And yet, soul mate hasn't taken us home. That's a very, very big realization.

THE TRAGEDY OF SOUL MATES

Let's go deeper.

I want to put two structures next to each other:

- Pre-tragic, tragic, and post-tragic.
- Role mate, soul mate, and whole mate.

Pre-tragic is clarity: role mate, everything is clear. Soul mate is tragic, and whole mate is post-tragic.

But why is soul mate possibly tragic? Soul mate is supposed to be the apex of our experience!

The soul mate relationship is tragic because it has no ground. It is not rooted in the Real.

Let me try and explain what we mean by that.

Number one, role mate and soul mate, in the vast majority of the population, is an expression of separate self and ordinary love:

- Separate self: I am a skin-encapsulated ego separate self.
- Ordinary love: love as the social construct of these last few centuries.

That's utterly insufficient to be the ground of relationship.

If, in the role mate relationship, we say *I need you, I need you to survive*, then in the soul mate relationship, we say *I choose you*.

But if it is *I choose you* in the soul mate model, **what's that choice based on?** Ultimately, today, that choice isn't based on *anything*. It's not grounded in the Field of Value—and **if my choice is not grounded in the Field of Value, then there is no choice that will ever be ultimately compelling**.

If there is no Field of Value, choice itself is not a value. Choice itself is attacked and thought to be illusory.

- There is no real choice.
- There is no value of choice.
- There is no value of freedom.

Basing my relationship on *I choose you* makes the relationship tragic because there is no ground for that choice—which is why, in the majority of couples in the United States, for example, and in many parts of Europe, we *un-chose*. More than fifty percent of couples divorce because the choice is not compelling.

In many ways, divorce was a great step forward because, as role mates, we were forced, and choice was taken away from us—so we reclaimed choice in the act of divorce. That was beautiful.

But then we thought: once we are soul mates and we are actually choosing our partners, we won't need divorce anymore—but of course, divorce still skyrocketed.

Part of the reason is that we make bad choices because we think we're choosing, but actually, there are hidden scripts that are choosing for us. We need to clarify those hidden scripts in order to be able to really choose. That's true, and that's beautiful.

But there is a deeper ground for the collapse of marriage.

The collapse of marriage is both the collapse of people *staying in* marriage and the collapse of joy *within* marriage, where joy is no longer available, sexuality is no longer available, and real intimacy is no longer available. It becomes tragic on both sides:

- One: the choice isn't followed through because we lose access to the memory of what brought us together, and we wind up splitting, usually in a horrifically traumatic and acrimonious way.
- Two is when we stay in, and we lose access to the Field of Joy. We lose access to our aliveness. We enter in a routinized *un-We* and deadness that no one is allowed to name.

There is an enormous tragedy to soul mate relationships.

That's an incredible realization!

To summarize, role mate is pre-tragic because it has clarity, and soul mate is tragic because:

- It's not clear *who* to choose.
- It's not clear *when to abide by the choice* and when to reverse the choice.
- There is no Field of Value in which choice is affirmed as a value.

Therefore, we assume, as most popular therapy books tell us, that who we choose is actually not emergent from our choice but from our unfinished business with our parents or attachment styles that we need to heal.

That's why *I choose you* is tragic.

I LOVE YOU MEANS I CHOOSE TO NEED YOU

In the whole mate relationship, we don't exclude—but include and transcend—the best of both role mate and soul mate:

1. We include the role mate model in the sense that we are both looking beyond ourselves. As role mates, we're looking

beyond ourselves at our immediate circle—our family, our children. As whole mates, we are looking at a much larger whole.
2. In the whole mate model, we are an expression—a unique expression—not of ordinary love but of Outrageous Love.
3. In the whole mate relationship, we are coming from our own original wholeness.

The core structure of self that animates whole mate is:

- *True Self* = the Field of Wholeness.
- *Unique Self* = I'm a unique whole expression of the Field of Wholeness.
- *Evolutionary Unique Self* = my unique wholeness can evolve the whole itself. And I can then play my instrument which is whole in itself and yet participates in the larger Unique Self Symphony.

All of this is whole mate.

- It is not *I need you* in the old sense, "I won't survive without you."
- It is not *I choose you* without a ground of choice.
- It's *I choose to need you.*

I want to just stay in this for just a couple of minutes because it's so beautiful, and it's so deep. The experience of *I choose to need you* is:

Yeah, I can make it myself. Yeah, I could find a way.

Yeah, I could re-narrate my life story.

Yeah, you're wrong about a lot of things.

Yeah, there's a lot I can blame you for—but *I choose* to stay. Not only do I choose to stay, **I choose to allow myself to love you so much that I need you.**

THE URGENT NEED FOR WHOLE MATE RELATIONSHIPS

I choose to need you.

Even though I am whole unto myself, I choose to need you, and only through you can I become more whole.

Even though I am powerful, I choose—in some way—to be powerless, so that when you get upset with me, even if you are completely wrong and inappropriate and blowing something way out of the water that doesn't need to be blown out of the water, I'm still madly devastated when you're hurt. I am madly devastated because I choose to love you, which means I choose to need you, and I choose to allow myself to be hurt by you.

It is the ultimate choice that a person can make, the choice of *I choose to need you*.

- It is the ultimate freedom.
- It is the ultimate dignity.
- It is what it means *to love*.

When I love, I actually overcome my separateness.

It's not that my separateness disappears. It's that my separateness lives in paradoxical uniqueness to our union. It's no longer my *separateness*—which is ultimate, which can't be overcome—but it becomes my *uniqueness*.

I am in my uniqueness but not in my separateness anymore.

I am in my uniqueness and in union at the same time.

By being willing to need you, by choosing to need you, I make you part of me, and I make me part of you. I overcome separateness. It's shocking!

My ability to choose to need you is what allows the love between us to overcome alienation and realize union.

Think about what happens in sexuality. In sexuality, there's a need that emerges—a need to be touched, a need to hold each other, a need to be aroused. And as sexuality, and a particular act of sexing, proceeds and deepens, the need deepens, doesn't it? At the beginning of sexing, you can take it or leave it, but once you're like three minutes before explosion, you're full in! You're in full need. To stop in the middle would be painful.

The sexual models the erotic, and the erotic and the holy are one.

The sexual models Eros, and Eros is the sacred fabric of Reality.

The deeper we are in the sexual, the deeper the need emerges.

This choice—I choose to need you—slowly becomes a choiceless choice. It just becomes the nature of what is. **I surrender to the need, and I become most powerful in that surrender.** I become most myself as I step all the way in, give up my lower will, and embrace my higher will.

The capacity to need and to choose to need is the greatest human freedom. It's the greatest human dignity.

It's not an instinctive need. It's the need that emerges from the dignity of my *Homo Imago Dei*, of my divine image, from the dignity of my choice, from the dignity of my power.

You cannot be powerful unless you're able to look at someone and say, not *I need you*, not *I choose you*, but *I choose to need you*.

That's post-tragic. Post-tragic is not moving *beyond* need. **It's when need and choice come together**.

I choose to need you; therefore, love is action in response to need. There is no love that doesn't respond to need—but when love responds to need, union is realized.

When I feel this urgent need coming towards you, when I utterly need you, and then that explodes as love, we come together in a shared field of pathos and a shared field of throbbing, a shared pulsing field of tumescence.

We are no longer lonely in that field—because Heidegger was wrong, and Irvin Yalom was wrong.

> *Love does not leave us in our separateness; love is the perception and direct realization of our ever-always already union.*

We've never not been in union. It's always been that way.

I choose to need you. Wow!

RECONFIGURING REALITY BY RECONFIGURING HUMANITY

What we have just done is: **we found love in a hopeless place**.

Soul mate, the realm of the tragic, isn't quite working—and what we need is an evolution of relationship, which is an evolution of value because relationship is the value of Reality.

By articulating this new source code, this emergence, this rise of the whole mate relationship, we respond to the meta-crisis.

The nature of the Intimate Universe is that all crises at their source are actually one, so one crisis responds to the other crisis. Like the masters used to say, when a question is asked in one part of the world, an answer to another question also answers the first question.

Let me say it in terms of the crisis. There is the personal crisis of relationship, and there is the meta-crisis. Both of those are actually crises of intimacy.

One is the classical crisis of intimacy between the beloveds: role mate and soul mate are insufficient. The second is the global intimacy disorder, the collapse of intimacy between all human beings.

The healing is always a renewed but deepened, reconfigured, evolved relationship to the whole. To the whole in me:

- I'm not just a separate self.
- I'm True Self, I'm Unique Self, which are wholeness themselves—and from that wholeness in myself, I can embrace the larger whole.

That's the evolution of relationship.

Therefore, the emergence of the whole mate relationship, which addresses the personal crisis of intimacy, also becomes the new simple first rule, the new principle of Reality: relationships in which both parties are looking together at the larger whole.

If you iterate that exponentially to billions of people and couples in the world—whether friendship couples, romantic couples, business couples, entrepreneurial couples—when couples no longer act according to win/lose metrics but for the sake of a larger whole and begin to act exponentially for the larger whole across the world, then we have actually changed the source code of Reality itself.

The extraction model falls away, and the exponential growth curves fall away.

We've reconfigured Reality by reconfiguring humanity. **Whole mate, this new model of relationship, when iterated exponentially, heals not only the personal crisis, but completely addresses and transforms the meta-crisis.**

That's what it means.

CHAPTER EIGHT

ARE YOU ALLURING TO GOD? THE GREAT QUESTION OF COSMOEROTIC HUMANISM

Episode 347 — June 4, 2023

STORY THAT MOVES THE VECTOR OF HISTORY

I have something I am ecstatically, urgently excited to talk to you about this week. I've been looking forward to having this conversation, and it's been ruminating through my mind all week.

We are telling the new Story of Value, this *living inside* the new Story of Value as the primary response to the meta-crisis at this moment in time.

We are a revolution.

- We are a revolution in *feeling*.
- We are a revolution in *thought*, in models of thinking.
- We are a revolution in *policy*, in how we create policy, politics, and economics.
- We are a revolution in *religion*, in how we move from the old ethnocentric religions of pre-modernity and from the fundamental rejection

of religion in modernity to a new vision of a world framework as a context for our diversity, to a vision of **a shared grammar of value as a context for our diversity**.

I have been talking about this notion of a *grammar of value* for ten years, and I am pleased to see different people picking it up in different places. Someone sent me an article by someone in Europe, Hanzi Freinacht, who was talking about a grammar of value. These notions are becoming seeded. We've been talking about them for ten years, and they are critical, and I am happy to see them beginning to appear around the world.

For the last twenty years, we've been deeply involved in the telling of this new Story of Value, and many of the key pieces of the story have become key frameworks in communities around the world, even before we published them—but they haven't yet been *organized* together. **They haven't been deepened together, in a full Story of Value that can enter not just small select communities—but the very source code of consciousness and culture itself.**

Now, if you just read that sentence and you're sitting back, then I didn't say it well, so I apologize.

We are in a meta-crisis. We are poised between utopia and dystopia—and by utopia, I don't mean a blasé convivial utopia that destroys structures of maturity and responsibility. Utopia has, for lots of good reasons, a bad reputation, but I am talking about **a mature, deep, responsible vision of new possibility**.

We are poised between:

- Utopia, a vision of the most stunning world that we already know is possible, and
- Dystopia, various versions of either the death of humanity or the death of *our* humanity.

In the last three years, the things we've been talking about here for almost a decade—through Covid, and then through the artificial intelligence conversation—are now creeping into the mainstream discourse, like when the chair of OpenAI recently signed a two-sentence letter saying, *oh, there's actually genuine existential risk here.*

It begins to enter the mainstream discourse, and people turn away. People turn away because it's very hard to put your attention on it. To put our attention on it requires something; it requires the possibility of *seeing a way through*—and right now, people don't see a way through.

The reason they don't see a way through is because they're looking only at infrastructure (*How do you change the infrastructure of things?*) or social structure (*How do you bind AI with law?*). And those *are* necessary.

- It is necessary to design AI in a particular way.
- It is necessary to bind AI with law.
- It is necessary to deal with climate issues.
- It is necessary to deal with rogue exponential weapons.
- It is necessary to deal with the extraction model that's depleting our basic energy resources.

Everything we do burns up energy, unimaginably. We are working through and depleting our fundamental energy resource—so much so that, in the economic structure of things, in the energetic physical stack structure of Reality, there almost has to be a crash. It's just a question of *when*—and so it's hard to look at all that and know what to do with it, unless you actually can find your way through.

The only way to find your way through is: **We need to animate all of our efforts in infrastructure and social structure with a new *superstructure*—a new Story of Value rooted in First Principles and First Values, which is the context for our diversity.** Telling that New Story of Value—not *declaring* it but actually *working hard on it*, day after day—is what we're doing here.

Every week we do an Evolutionary Love Code. Every week, we try and add a new dimension of this new Story of Value.

We are doing it for the sake of the whole.

We are *whole mates* with Reality. We are in love with Reality. We are partnering with Reality. We are whole mates with each other.

- We are not just *role mates*, although we have particular roles, like parents have roles.
- We are not just *soul mates*, although we *are* soul mates: we love each other deeply, and we are looking deeply in each other's eyes.
- But we are also *whole mates*: we are looking at a shared horizon, and we are acting in that shared horizon. We are enacting a new world.

We are speaking the words that will speak that new Reality into being. That's the basic notion of Genesis: there is this voice, the voice speaks the word, and the word generates Reality—so, we are speaking a word, we are telling this new Story of Value in order to generate a new Reality.

THERE IS ONLY ONE THING WE ARE HELD ACCOUNTABLE FOR

We are telling **the story of *story***, in different dimensions, asking the following questions:

- What does *story* mean?
- What does it even mean that Reality is not merely a fact but a story?
- What are the implications of that for my own personal story?
- Why do I experience my life as a story?
- What is the nature of story in every dimension of life?

The topic is, if you will: *God loves stories*, or said differently, we're talking about **the ontology of story**. *Ontology* means **story as a structure or**

narrative arc of Reality. That's our topic, and we are going to enter that through a new prism today.

This is the work. This is the joy.

This is the revolution, right? We raise our hands, our fists, and we say, *revolution*, but our thumb is on the inside because when we hit someone with the thumb on the inside, it just shatters. It shatters me—so, we don't *want* to hit anyone. We don't want the thumb on the outside, we want the thumb on the inside, but with a fist raised for revolution.

> *We have to change the status quo, and we can change the status quo. The greatest idolatry in the world is the belief that yesterday determines today.*

That's simply not true. There is *always* change. **Evolution is a structure of Reality.**

The question is, *where* is it going to go? What's the *direction* of the change? In telling the new Story of Value, we directly impact the evolution of the source code.

EVOLUTIONARY LOVE CODE: EVERY TRUE INTIMATE ENCOUNTER IS A UNIQUE SELF ENCOUNTER BETWEEN SOUL STORIES

> Every true intimate encounter is a Unique Self encounter between soul stories. In a true Unique Self encounter, we realize that we each are holding a piece of each other's story.

> The ethical demand of a Unique Self encounter is that we return to each other the missing chapters of our stories. The motive force of evolution is Unique Self encounters in which we are constantly returning to each other the depth of our unique stories.
>
> The ultimate expression of Reality is billions of Unique Self encounters, which generate a Unique Self Symphony of stories, all of which are rooted in a shared Story of Value as the ultimate context for our wild and sacred diversity.

What a stunning code, right?

There is this notion I want to share with you, and I don't exactly know how to explain it—but if any of you are:

- Engineers who create new code
- Artists who paint
- If you've raised children, which is the ultimate act of being an artist
- If you're in a relationship, which is the ultimate canvas of life (and we're all in one way or another in a relationship)—

—then you know that sometimes *She* whispers in our ear and we have the stroke of insight, in which we see and understand something that we didn't quite see or understand before.

I had this divine whisper in my ear as I was feeling into this *dharma* on story that's going to get deeper and deeper, which I wanted to share with you. Here it is.

There is only one thing in the world that we are held accountable for.

There's only one thing in the world, if you will, that we are *judged* for. And judgment is beautiful; judgment is *not* fire and brimstone rained down by a vengeful Santa Claus God who has dark eyes because he is on a bad trip—

not that kind of judgment. **Judgment means that there is a *contemplation*, a *witnessing* of everything that we do. We are witnessed by Reality.**

It's a beautiful experience to be witnessed by Reality. And we are held accountable, not in the sense of *got you*, but in the sense of *counting*, in the sense that your actions *matter*.

We don't live in an unbearable *lightness* of being; we live in an unbearable *joy and gravitas* of being. Being is not light; it has gravity or heaviness— *heavy*, not in a sense of depressed, but more like *whoa, that's a heavy book*. That's *serious*. There is a heaviness, but not in a *bringing down* sense, but in a *gravitas* sense.

There is a gravitas to Reality, an unbearable gravitas.

The only thing that we are held accountable for, the only thing we are judged for, as it were, is: are we alluring to God?

I want to just feel this with you. Just pause for a moment and *feel* that sentence.

We'll have to talk about each piece of the sentence, but that's the sentence that I heard early in the morning, late at night:

Are we alluring to God?

Am I alluring to God?

THREE PERSONS OF GOD

Now, of course, I don't need to tell you—if you've ever been with us before—that the god you don't believe in doesn't exist. The god you don't believe in, *I* don't believe in either.

God is rather the Field of Reality, the Field of Personhood—not just a field, but a field that has infinite personhood, infinite power, infinite creativity, and infinite intimacy—and we have said this in the new Story of Value we're telling in response to the meta-crisis.

This new Story of Value is one in which God is named the Infinite Intimate. God is the infinity of intimacy, the infinity of power, the infinity of creativity. And that God lives *in us*.

I've been studying quite intently the last two weeks Abhinavagupta, the great sage of Kashmir Shaivism, who talks about there being *a first person*: **She that lives in *me*, as me, and through me all the way down to the atomic level of Reality**. There is this notion of *first person*. And, of course, Stuart Kauffman the mathematician and Richard Feynman the physicist go in the same direction. That's one notion of God.

There is a *second-person* Divine, which is also critical—**the Beloved: I am madly in love, we are madly in love with each other, madly in love with the infinite personhood of Cosmos.**

The way they talk about it in Kashmir Shaivism is: *Krishna loves Radha, Radha loves Krishna.*

The God and the Goddess are madly in love with each other.

They are each other's pillar.

They stand together in every way.

This sense of radical intimacy—that's the second person of God.

The *third person* is: **God is the field.** You can actually *feel* the field. In the *Zohar* it's called *Chakal Tapuchin Kadishin*—the field of holy apples. Of course, George Lucas, picking up from the great interior sciences, called it *the Force* when he made *Star Wars*—that's the field we're talking about.

So again, the question is:

- Are you alluring to God?

- Am I alluring to myself, to the Divine in me?
- Am I alluring to the field?

But it's even more. I want to focus on the second person—not the first person or the third person. I want to focus on the second person, and to feel it.

They are inseparable: the first, second, and third person of reality are inter-included with each other, interdigitated, interpenetrated with each other. You can't split them, so let's just think about them all together, with a focus on God as the Infinite Intimate, God as the Beloved, the lover of the Song of Solomon, of the *yab-yum* incarnations in India, of the Earth and sky reaching for each other.

Am I alluring to God?

Do you get what that means?

We're not asking:

- Am I successful?
- Am I smart?
- Am I good-looking? (according to some artificial, superficial, slightly repulsive standard)
- Am I too heavy or too thin? (according to some strange definition of what that means)
- Am I creative?
- Am I talented?
- Am I artistic or not?

None of those. Those are not the question.

The only question we ever have to address, the only question you ever have to ask, is *Am I alluring to God?*

What does that mean? We've talked a little bit about God, so we don't get confused with a wrong vision of God. We've talked about that.

What do we mean by *alluring*? Are you *alluring* to God?

It means that God wants to *taste* you. Do you get that?

God—Goddess—*She* wants to smell you.

Do I taste good if God bites into me? Am I delicious to God?

Am I fragrant to God?

MISPAR AND *SIPU*R: NUMBER AND STORY

To be fragrant to God is not based on a particular action. It's not that I fulfilled my mission.

Here, I want to bring this back to the notion of *story*.

There are two fundamental words that are part of a larger set of four or five that appear in the original book of the interior sciences of Hebrew wisdom, called *Sefer Yetzirah*, *The Book of Creation*. The two words I want to address now are:

- *Mispar*—number
- *Sipur*—story

I talked about these many years ago, back when I was a young, in a book called *Soul Prints* that I wrote in 1999.

Mispar, your number—that's your mission. Number is *a point*. Number is very functional, very specific.

There is, of course, a shadow, if you reduce a person to their number. Nazism, in its worst form, actually tattooed numbers on people, and the contemporary neo-totalitarian forms that are emerging—although not in any way comparable to Nazism, I want to make that clear—also ascribe to a person a certain quantified measure. Number is *a measure*; number is a way of measuring.

In modernity's greatness, the emergence of modern sciences comes from the move from *classification* to *measurement*, but **the tragedy of modernity comes from the explosion of the exterior technologies of measurement and the stalling of the interior technologies that address *the immeasurable*.** There is a dimension of the human being, which is their mission, their function, the particular thing they do, even in the divine scheme of things. It's beautiful.

It's my vocation. It's what I'm called to do. That's my *mispar*. That's my number.

But then, something else is inter-included with it but also distinct—and it comes from the same root word as *mispar*. It's got a three-letter root—Samech, Pei, Reish—and another expression of that three-letter root is *sipur*, story.

Story is different. **Story has a wave quality.** Just like in physics, there is a wave quality, a pointed quality, and a particle quality. There is a wave dimension and a particle dimension. The particle dimension, the discretion of infinity in a point—that's the particle, that's the function, and the function is critical. It's the mission. It's my mission statement.

But then, there is this other dimension, which is about **the extraordinary in ordinariness.** How did the poet Charles Reznikoff say it in the sixties? *Not for a seat at the dais but for a seat at the common table* (*dais* means the podium, the seat of honor). That's my story.

> *My story is the fabric and the wave quality of my life.*

The question is, *is my story alluring to God?*

That's the only question.

- Does God want to *taste* my story?

- Does my story *smell* good?
- Is *the fragrance* of my story good?

But the fragrance of my story is not based on one particular action. It's not a to-do list, although there are to-do lists. It's about *everything*.

How I smell is so critical. It's happened many times, when a student will come to me and say, *well, I've been going out with him or with her, and we were just physically intimate the first time, and I've got to break up. They don't smell right to me.* Right? It's so primal.

What I smell like, what I taste like, comes from everything that I've ever ingested.

- It comes from anything that I've ever seen.
- It comes from every feeling I've ever had and how I worked with every feeling that I ever had.
- It comes from all of the world of the invisibilities of the invisible world.

We are so focused on the visible world, on status, and on where we are in the pecking order, which is one of our evolutionary inheritances, as my dear friend Howard Bloom talks about a lot. But Howard tries to transpose the pecking order into the human world and says, *the entire human world is also based on a pecking order*.

No, not exactly. Yes, there is a pecking order of social status. Anthropologist David Buss talks about pecking order and its importance in relations between men and women, men and men, women and women—that's all true. **But there is something deeper—and that's what a Unique Self encounter is about: are we *alluring* to each other?**

Are we alluring to each other? Can you hear that?

That's the core of what a Unique Self encounter is: are we alluring to each other?

And when it's *we*, it's not just *me*—it's *me and my story*.

I want *my story* to be alluring to you—with all of its agony, with all of its ecstasy, with all of its tragedy, and with all of its triumphs. I want my story to be alluring to my beloved.

I want my beloved to *witness* my story—and also:

- To be *allured*
- To *participate*, to be *part* of my story
- To throw in your fate with me—let's turn our fates into destiny together

Let's stand together. "Stand by Me," remember that song?

I am going to stand by you—not for any particular or exactly rational reason, but because we are allured to each other. That's why we stay together. We don't stay together because I don't want to break up the family, and my kids will have some psychological problems—no! You should be together only if you are allured to each other.

Every person has a right to be allured to their beloved.

It's not just *mispar*, it's not just number. It's *sipur*, it's story.

WHAT IS ALLURING TO GOD IS INVISIBLE

Our need to be allured to each other is rooted in a deeper field. It's anthro-ontological.

Anthro-ontological means the mysteries are within:

- *Anthro* means human being
- *Ontological* means the Real

The Real lives in human beings. Let's say I have an experience of, *I want you to be allured to me, we want to be allured to each other,* and *we want to be uniquely allured to each other.* This experience *participates* in a deeper field, which is: *am I, is my story, alluring to God?*

- Does God want to taste me?
- Does God want to eat me?
- Does God want to bite me?
- Does God want to smell me?
- Does God want to caress me?

It's so deep. I become alluring to God based on every dimension of my reality and particularly in the invisible world. We are so attracted to the visible world that we don't realize that at the moment when we pass into the next world, at the moment of death—which is a night between two days—we are held in judgment.

But that judgment is not fire and brimstone. The premodern intuition of judgment was right. It got distorted, corrupted, and degraded through ethnocentric prisms, but the prism was right. It was: **your life *counts*, decisions *matter*, choices *matter*.** That's beautiful. That's the ultimate human dignity.

But here we are talking about *what* I'm held accountable for. I am held accountable for one thing: *was I alluring to God?*

I want to feel that together. We are partnering with each other in order to love each other madly, in order to download into the source code a new Story of Value—because *that's* what Reality needs now. That's what's alluring to God.

What is alluring to God—again, I'm going to say it a third time, but I really want to get it—is invisible. It's what you do at 4:00 a.m. in the morning, it's what you think, it's what you feel.

It is not that I need to program my thinking.

It is not: *if those thoughts aren't alluring, get those thoughts out*—no, no, it's not about that.

It's not like the old religious world: *oh, I had a sexual thought, what am I going to do?* It's not about that.

My teacher, the Baal Shem Tov, said that anyone who tells you that they can control their thoughts is a charlatan. Thoughts come and go. But it's all about what I *do* with those thoughts. What do I do with those feelings? It's so deep.

If you asked me what is the essence of Unique Self: **Your Unique Self is the unique way in which you're alluring to God.** That's what Unique Self means.

SHIFTING FROM MY PERSPECTIVE TO GOD'S PERSPECTIVE

We have a notion—a very strong notion—of *obligation*. Obligation is a critical idea. One of the things I've tried to download into Reality in the last fifteen years is a new vision of obligation. Obligation means there is something I am obligated to do.

In the original Hebrew, *obligation* has the same root word as the word *love* or *Eros*, so, Eros and obligation are one. What is my obligation?

> *My obligation is that the Eros of my story has to be alluring to God.*

Just think about that in terms of a beloved, a friend, a deep friendship you have: you have an obligation in a deep friendship, in a deep whole-mate relationship to be *alluring* to your beloved.

And you should have many beloveds. You should fall in love with many people—I don't mean romantically. You should fall madly in love with many people, uniquely, and create the sense of being alluring to each other. *Alluring to each other* means I'm allured to your *story*; I want to participate in your story as whole mates, meaning:

- **We have a shared vision**: we have a shared vision of the whole, and we are working together to evolve the whole.
- We are working together to participate in **the evolution of love**.
- We are participating together in **the unimaginable beauty of central communion** that lives between those who are participating together in the evolution of love.

We are alluring to each other. I want you to feel that.

When you are deep in caring for the whole, when you are deep in telling the new Story of Value, you honor everyone you meet. For sure, we hold everyone with great love and honor—but **we are *allured* to people who are looking at that vision with us.**

- When we can see a horizon together.
- When our Eros is Evolutionary Eros.
- When we are not just in our local lives but are able to feel the warp and the woof of the whole, the fabric of the whole—then we are allured to each other.
- When we step in this moment of the Anthropocene, when the human being has this huge capacity to influence the vector of evolution itself.
- When we take responsibility for the whole in the Anthropocene.

Then we become alluring to God. We become partners with the Divine. We are trying to shift our perspective from *our* side to God's side. **From our perspective to God's perspective**.

When I shift from my perspective to God's perspective—which is the basic transformation of awakening, of becoming the new human and the new humanity, becoming *Homo amor*—I am saying to God: *I am willing to look at it from your perspective*.

ARE YOU ALLURING TO GOD?

When I am a leader, I don't look at things from my particular moment of brokenness or woundedness. I am seeing the whole thing. I am holding all the pieces.

Now, of course, I cannot hold all the pieces that the Divine holds, but I can *look* at the whole thing. **When I look at the whole thing, I become a whole mate to God.**

- We are looking together at the whole.
- We are taking responsibility.
- We are partners in fixing, healing, and transforming the whole.

Can you feel that? That's what it means to be alluring to God. It's not just about my number, my mission. It's about the whole fabric of my story.

- Who am I? In all of the invisible moments, what am I feeling?
- What do I dream about at night?
- What do I do with whatever I dream?

It's about the deepest fabric of my interior. Am I alluring to God? **This liberates me from any other responsibility and obligation.** There is no other responsibility that the human being has, none. Throw all the rest of them out.

There's only one question: am I alluring to God?

Now, of course, if you are alluring to God, you're probably not going to abandon your child. And, if you are working within the context of a system, you are going to want to be radically responsible to everyone in it because that's alluring to God.

Of course that's true.

Of course, you want to fulfill all of the particular missions, but deeper than *mispar*, deeper than *number*, is *sipur*—story.

CAUSING AROUSAL IN THE DIVINE

I want to just add one thing here, and it's so beautiful.

My lineage master, my direct lineage master is Solomon. Solomon was the King of Jerusalem several thousand years ago. His father was David. And Solomon is the core source of the lineage that I live in.

Now, of course, I am in complete devotion to Solomon—and we have also emerged, as Solomon would want and as he intended himself—to include:

- Many other traditions
- Many other ways of practice in the interior sciences and the great religions
- Many other practice modes within the formal sciences, the exterior sciences, both within the hard sciences and in sciences like anthropology, social theory, and structuralism, as well as evolutionary thought, complexity theory, and chaos theory.

We are integrating all of that into this new Story of Value called CosmoErotic Humanism, which is ultimately sourced in a synergistic *whole-ing*, a bringing and weaving together of all these strands.

But at the core, at the source is Solomon, who transmits the lineage all the way through the prophets, through the judges, and ultimately all the way to a master in the first century named Akiva, who transmits it to a master named Shimon bar Yochai, who produces the *Zohar* in the thirteenth century. Then Shimon bar Yochai goes to Luria in the sixteenth century, who goes to Leiner in the nineteenth century. Leiner is my teacher. I wrote a couple of volumes called *Radical Kabbalah*, trying to get Leiner's thought.

In this lineage, every action I do causes arousal in the Divine, so I am an arouser of God.

- Every action I have, every feeling I have, participates in the Field of Divine Eros, and I actually cause arousal in the Field of the Divine.
- I generate, I am cause for *hieros gamos*, the divine marriage.
- I bring together the masculine and feminine Divine, but the masculine and feminine Divine are not *up there*, they are not *out there*—they are *everywhere*.

As Luria writes, every moment, every dynamic in reality—*at every level of Reality*, matter, life, and all the depths of the self-reflective human mind—every dynamic, every interaction, every inter-feeling, every inter-being, every inter-becoming—*all of it* is the coming together of *Shekhintai*, the Goddess, and *Kudsha Brich Hu*, God, the line and circle, the yin and the yang.

What that means is:

I am causing arousal in the Divine; I am causing intimate union in the Divine by causing intimate union in myself.

Intimate union in myself means that my inner and outer self are not *alienated* from each other. There is no exile between the inner and outer. I'm at one with my words. It's what Lionel Trilling, the cultural critic, called authenticity, or he sometimes called it sincerity. That's what it feels like.

When I'm in that place, when I am smelling good, when my fragrance is good, based on how I encountered that feeling, or that thought, or that challenge, or that pain, and I become a sweet-smelling incense to God, I become a sweet aroma:

- I become myself, an offering on the altar of Reality
- I am making love on that altar.
- I am bringing the Divine together.

Not because I am God's pimp. I am not God's sex coach, no, no.

I am part of the Field of the Divine.

I am not causing union in some technical, mechanical way—I am in the Field of Arousal because I am alluring to the Divine.

WE ARE ALLURED TO EACH OTHER

What is the Unique Self encounter in today's Evolutionary Love Code?

Unique Self encounter is: *Am I alluring to you?* Which means *Is my story alluring to you?*—I am inseparable from my story.

Am I, in the story of my life, alluring to you?

Are you alluring to me?

Are we going to participate together in a shared field of alignment, where we are looking at a shared horizon together, and we are alluring together, when we become whole mates—not just soul mates, when we smell right to each other, or role mates, when we have shared function?

- Role mate means my *mispar*, my number.
- Soul mate means our hearts are one. We are one love and we are one heart.
- Whole mate means the story of my life, my sacred autobiography, my story is alluring to God.

It cuts through everything. It liberates you from everything.

There is only one question, *am I alluring to God*? Is my story alluring to God?

Don't ask any other question. Inside, we always know, we can feel it: is this alluring to God? That's it. You don't need to look to any book of ethics, any code of law, just ask yourself a question at any moment: **Is how I am being in this moment alluring to God?**

You never have to ask another question in your life. That's it. Wow. Oh my God.

We are alluring to each other.

I am madly allured to each person here at One Mountain. It's all of us. We're allured to each other. That's what it means to be a Unique Self Symphony. We are allured to each other's instruments.

With permission, friends, I love you madly. It's so good to love each other madly, right? Madly. Not cutely, not sweetly, not politely. I love you madly, outrageously. We love each other madly and outrageously. We're allured to each other. That's how a revolution holds.

I am going to tell you one last thing.

You know, Elon Musk said something that I thought was wise. He said that his one criterion for buying a business is: do the people in the business spend significant amounts of time with each other during off hours, when they're not working? He said, *I'll buy that kind of business, and I won't buy anything else.*

Are we alluring to each other? That's it.

If we're alluring to each other, we can actually make this revolution happen because we're going to love it open unimaginably—in this time between worlds, in this time between stories.

CHAPTER NINE

TELLING A NEW STORY EQUAL TO OUR NEW POWER (PART 1): IN RESPONSE TO THE ONCOMING TRAIN THAT IS ABOUT TO HIT THE SCHOOL BUS

Episode 348 — June 11, 2023

THE META-CRISIS IS A CRISIS OF STORY

We are on the move.

Friends, community—friends, Romans, countrymen, and countrywomen—let's lend each other our ears because the *dharma*, the Goddess, the band of Outrageous Lovers is on the move.

We are taking the next step, and it's a wildly important next step.

I want to share with you a little bit of what's going on—just a couple of things that locate us in what we're doing here, in One Mountain, Many Paths—and we have a huge new *dharma*, **a new chapter in the Story of Value that we are writing together, which is about our personal story and the cosmic story.**

But first, I just want to take a second to set our context. Context-setting is when we *reset*. We press *reset* and ask: **Who are we?** We re-answer the questions of:

- Who am I?
- Who are we?
- Where are we?
- What's there to do?

Where are we? You can only answer that question in the context of the universe. The universe *always* has to come first. **You cannot answer a personal question independently of a cosmic question.** The Universe Story is *everything*. The beginning of where we are is the Universe Story.

But even in the very words, *Universe Story*, is the word *story*—and just by saying *Universe Story*, we have already answered a huge part of the question, which is:

*The universe is not merely a fact;
the universe is a story.*

This is so important and beautiful and a direct response to the meta-crisis of our time. It *appears* to be a meta-crisis of resources, infrastructure, and social structure—extraction models, exponential growth curves falling off, the runaway AI lacking social structures to hold it—but at its core, **the meta-crisis of our time is a crisis of meaning.**

- It's a crisis of value.
- It's a crisis of intimacy.
- It's a crisis of relationship.

Or—said slightly differently—**it is a crisis of story.**

That's what I mean when I've been saying, for the last decade, *we live in a time between stories*—and **in a time between stories, we have to play a**

larger game. The larger game is to birth a new human and a new humanity, and we do that by telling the next articulation, the next best version of the Universe Story—and the key to the Universe Story is to realize, firstly, that **the universe *is* a story, that there is a narrative arc to Cosmos**. I tried to write about this for the very first time in 1999, in the fourth section of a book called *Soul Prints*, which was called "Live Your Story."

That's a big deal. **Reality is a story, and my story *participates* in the Universe Story**.

- The Universe is not empty and bleak. That's nonsense.
- The Universe is *not* nonsense. The universe is *sensual*.
- The Universe is embedded with *story*, which means that the Universe is embedded with *language*.
- The Universe is linguistic at its very core. Language is structural to Reality, as story is structural to Reality, and story *evolves*.

We gather around the campfire and tell the best story we know based on the best validated insights, using language, which is structural to Reality. The code of Reality is language, and language tells stories, which is why language births the movement from all of the different *homo* families to *Homo neanderthalis* and then *Homo sapiens*, with their unique capacity for language, which is the capacity for *storytelling*.

Every crisis in history—when we go deep into the nature of the crisis—is a crisis of story. We solve the crisis by creating new sets of relationships, meaning new stories of intimacy.

> *Every crisis is a crisis of intimacy, and it's a new story of intimacy that resolves the crisis. We birth a new level of evolutionary intimacy.*

That's the nature of Reality, so we cannot address the question of *Where am I?* without knowing what the Universe Story is—but the beginning of knowing the Universe Story is that the Universe *is* a story and that my story and our story participates—is chapter and verse—in *Evolution: The Love Story of the Universe.*

I shared this idea with my dear friend, Ervin Laszlo, back in 2014, and it has animated his perspective, even though he had been thinking about this, in his own way, for forty years. I said, *Oh, the universe is a love story.* He wrote to me a couple years ago, saying, *Yes, evolution, the love story of the universe. Yes!* And Ervin has been thinking about it since he wrote the preeminent book on systems theory in 1972 (although systems theory can be wrongly understood if you reduce it to a materialist science—it's actually trying to trace the stories of intimacy that define Reality all the way down and all the way up the evolutionary chain).

So, who am I? Who are we?

We are chapter and verse in The Universe: A Love Story.

This is the way we are going to respond to the meta-crisis, which is the potential death of humanity, or the potential death of our humanity.

WAKE UP TO THIS UNIQUE MOMENT IN TIME!

A decade ago, Zak Stein and I wrote an article on *the second shock of existence.*

The first shock of existence is the realization, at the dawn of history, of the potential death of the human being, and the second shock of existence is the potential death of *humanity*—which, based on all the objective structures and measures we have, is a genuine possibility. When I said this ten years ago, people just kind of looked at me funny and gave me a little pat on the head: *Tell us instead about Unique Self, Gafni. You're really good at dharma, what are you doing?* And people kept patting me on the head, and I kept being up in the middle of the night saying:

- Oh my God, what do you *do* when you can see a train coming that's about to crash into a bus full of schoolchildren, and you don't know how to stop it?

That's how I feel on lots of nights.

And then at some point, gradually, it dawned: **To stop the train, you've got to tell a new Story of Value.**

To stop the train of the political, social, and economic models upon which Reality is grounded today, you've got to say: Okay, what's *the source* of those models, what's *the ground* of those models? And you've got to change the models themselves—not by *declaring* a new model to be true but by *showing* it to be true, based on weaving together the validated insights from premodern, modern, and postmodern wisdom streams. We must tell a Story of Value that's never been told before but is self-evidently true—because it gathers together all the best knowledge that we currently have about Reality.

> *You tell a new Story of Value, which is the only thing that changes the vector of history itself.*

This begins to address *what there is to do today*. As a collective, we must tell that new Story of Value. In other words, **the overwhelming moral imperative of this time is to tell a new Story of Value, to participate in that.**

I say to people close to me all the time, it's not about this little project in your life, some new coaching project, or this project, or that. Yes, do all those things, those are all great—but **wake up to this unique moment in time!** We have a global civilization with exponential technologies, locked in a self-terminating system. The cries of trillions of unborn children, who have no voice in the present, are crying to us, and we are their voice. **The**

only voice of the future is those of us who can listen in and hear the call of the future.

Our own future selves *are* those children.

I want to get this point. Our story doesn't end in death. Death is but a night between two days. There's an enormous amount of empirical information that tells us that consciousness is fundamental—the Field of Consciousness *and* Desire, and **consciousness is always structured as a story**. The story of my life doesn't end at my death, it goes on—and my story can only be liberated in the ongoing cycle of stories. I exist in the future. Does that make sense? I'm saving *myself*—because my story goes on.

That's why all the great interior sciences had empirical information about, for example, reincarnation. Whoa, did I just go *woo-woo* on you?

No, I didn't just go *woo-woo*. We know each other. We trust each other.

I don't go *woo-woo*. I don't believe in *woo-woo*. I hate *woo-woo*.

There is actually an enormous amount of validated information on the notion of reincarnation. Ian Stevenson of the University of Virginia did decades of empirical work on it. **Reincarnation is the best hypothesis to explain an enormous amount of empirical evidence**—but it also is right for understanding Reality.

My story is not over when it's over.

How many people have ever been at a deathbed? I've been at a lot of deathbeds. I have lost lots of people who were eighteen years old, who were close to me as students, when I lived in the Middle East. I know death well. Most of my family was killed in the middle of their lives—my parents' generation, my grandparents in Europe. Death is clearly not the end of the story. That's just not the case. You are often in mid-story, you are in mid-sentence, so the language of your life goes on.

This means I *am* the future generations, do you understand that? In other words, I'm in mid-play. **We need to create the future for all the future** generations, whom we love madly. **We've got to envision them, see them, hear their cries, and then also know that those are *our* cries; we *are* those babies.** Wow!

WE HAVE TO *BECOME* THE NEW STORY

So, what's there to do? The overriding moral imperative of this generation—if you're an awake and alive human being—is to participate in the creation of the new Story of Value. We all have different roles in that. **It's not a guru's job. A guru cannot do it—it has to emerge out of a Unique Self Symphony.**

What is there to do? To play my role in the Unique Self Symphony.

The guru model is dead. Yes, there should be teaching, and there should be authority. Authority means: someone who knows more physics than I do has more authority than I do in physics. I don't say: *Oh great, we have equal authority in physics because we are woke and New Age.* No, no, we develop authority by working hard.

What's there to do?

To tell the new Story of Value. It's wildly exciting, and it's the moral imperative of this moment in time. Okay, wow!

Can I just laugh with you for a second?

People tell me all the time: *Marc, would you just calm down? Talk slowly, with long pauses between words, and people will think this is very wise.* Really? That's so boring. Of course I'm excited.

I am completely fearless and completely afraid at the same time. I'm terrified—and I'm ecstatic at the possibility of speaking and participating together, and writing this new Story of Value.

I believe in the best of humanity, I trust humanity. **I trust a God-infused humanity, and a humanity-infused God—because we are partners, we are inter-included.**

We are here to tell that new Story of Value, and **that new Story of Value has a *dharma*, and it has a yoga.** *dharma* is the actual strands of the new story, and yoga is the practice that you do to *invoke* the new story.

Every week, we get together, and we do some practice, we do some songs, some prayer, which is wildly important. Prayer means that I *feel* the Infinity of Intimacy of Reality, I feel its aliveness. Not a puppet God, not an old man with a long white beard or a hot woman who's the Goddess. No, **it's the personification of the yin and the yang, the line and the circle, the masculine and feminine forces of Reality, which are both impersonal (meaning they are *forces*), and also fully personal.**

At the deepest level of the most subtle structures of Reality, you cannot split the personal from the impersonal, which is why Richard Feynman, the physicist, or Stuart Kauffman, the complexity theorist-cosmologist-mathematician, talk about there being a first person in Reality, an *I* in Reality, all the way down to the atomic level. Their *I* might be a little bit different than my *I*. There is an evolution of *I*—but there is a personhood to Reality.

> *That's prayer: I speak into the Field of Personhood, and the Field of Personhood hears me.*

Just like *I* hear you—I am an expression of the Field of Personhood, I am an expression of the intelligence of Reality—so *the field* hears you. That's called prayer. This is all part of what happens here. Prayer is part of the yoga, and chant is part of the yoga. We are doing *dharma and* yoga, or another way to say that is: First Principles and First Practices.

EXISTENTIAL RISK AND THE EVOLUTION OF LOVE

I am excited; we are the holy band gathering.

Now, you might say, okay, is he being pretentious, grandiose?

No, *accurate*.

That's what Margaret Mead meant when she said, if you doubt that a small group of madly committed people (she didn't say *madly*, she said *committed*, but I added *madly*)—**if you doubt that a small group of madly committed people can change the world, know that *only* small groups of madly committed people have ever changed the world**. Change happens on the periphery, at the edges, and then moves to the center—but first, you've got to create a strong and deep *lived* experience of the new story. We first have to *become* the new story. We have to literally cross to the other side.

Crossing to the other side and becoming the new human and the new humanity is an actual evolution of what it means to be a human being.

Now, you might think again, is he being fanciful, utopian, and crazy?

No, I'm relating the nature of history.

The nature of history is that when there is a crisis, the crisis is always a crisis in story. It's a story about who am I, who we are, what's our Universe Story? And we respond by up-leveling our understanding of who we are—our narrative, our Universe Story, our story of identity, our story of desire, our story of power. That's what we are here to do, so we have to *live* that.

Have you ever heard of the Vedas in Hinduism? Who wrote the Vedas? A band of Outrageous Lovers.

You ever heard of the Bible, who wrote the Bible?

TELLING A NEW STORY EQUAL TO OUR NEW POWER

The divine voice speaking through a band of Outrageous Lovers.

That's how *everything* is written. Great literature is bigger than a person, which is why for some books we're writing, we're going to author through a figure named David J. Temple, a pseudonym, an imaginary figure, who is going to speak for all of us. We are on the move telling this new Story of Value.

EVOLUTIONARY LOVE CODE: THE TELLING OF A NEW STORY IS THE INHERENT NATURAL MOVEMENT OF COSMOS ITSELF

We live in a time between stories.

We live in a time between worlds.

We live in a time where we hold the power of ancient gods. We have the power to create worlds of unimaginable goodness, truth, and beauty—and we have the power to end worlds, to end humanity and to end *our* humanity.

We have no story equal to our power, and this is what we call, in CosmoErotic Humanism, the second shock of existence.

We are here to tell a new Story of Value, rooted in First Principles and First Values.

A story in which the cosmic story and the personal story are one: a new story of our power, a new Universe Story, a new story of our identity, a new story of desire, and a new story of communion.

It is only the articulation of a new Story of Value that has the capacity to respond to the meta-crisis. But it is even more. The telling of a new story is the inherent natural movement of Cosmos itself. The evolution of story is the evolution of culture and consciousness, which is the evolution of love, which is the evolution of God, the manifest God.

OPENING UP

Let's look at that code. Let's just *be* in this code.

I want to focus on one dimension, this notion of a **new story of power**. It's a big one.

So much spirituality today has become self-help: can I turn spirituality into another variety of tools that help me get more out of the world for my separate self? **Spirituality has been hijacked as a self-help tool.** But it's exactly *not* what spirituality is. Now, lots of you know that I'm not a big fan of the word *spirituality* itself. It is a strange modern word which I don't like. A more accurate word is *interior sciences*. **The interior sciences are empirical: we *test* Reality through the Eye of Value, the Eye of Consciousness, and the Eye of Desire.**

Beauty is in the eye of the beholder means not that beauty is merely subjective, but that the eye of the beholder, the *subjectivity* of the beholder, the beauty, the music that lies *in* the beholder perceives and discloses the beauty that seems to be in the exterior world.

***Beauty is in the eye of the beholder* means that there is no exile between my inner and outer self.** I have clarified my *interior* beauty, which clarifies my eye of perception, of *value-ception*, of *desire-ception*, of *love-ception*, of *Eros-ception*. I can see Reality clearly, and then *She* moves my hands—and I can paint.

We have this notion that only the tormented artists can paint. It's not true. The tormented artists can paint torment. The clarified artist is not the Pollyannish artist or the Cassandra artist. **The clarified artist is the one who holds together her holy and broken *Hallelujah* and paints her uncertainty on the canvas of God**—her certainty of the *goodness* of it all, which causes her to be agonized by the *pain* of it all.

Most human beings don't fit into the contemporary audience for most of modern western spirituality. Most unchurched modern western spirituality is for middle to upper-middle class human beings, with spare change, who are seeking new forms of entertainment because they have succeeded somewhat in the win/lose metrics, and now they want to fill some of the void caused by what it took to succeed in that success story. *I am going to fill in some of the void, either with romance or with "spirituality," which then becomes a form of self-help.*

Now, romance is awesome, and self-help is important and legitimate, so I am not deriding those two. But that's not what interior science is about.

Interior science is, first of all, about **being open to radical openness**.

Many years ago, in the world of Integral Theory, I suggested a new term, which was *open up*. I shared that term with my friend Ken Wilber, a young man named Dustin DiPerna, and other people.

- Our friend John Welwood talked about *waking up* and *growing up*, and my friend Ken spoke about it in other ways.
- Then we started talking about *showing up*, which I interpreted as *showing up as your Unique Self*.
- And then, there was a lot of conversation around shadow, which is *cleaning up*, or what I called *lightening up* (in other words, turning shadow into light).
- And I added *opening up*: **you have to open up.** *We are opening up in sweet surrender to the luminous love light of the One.*

The interior sciences, or what we often call *spirituality* in our culture, is not about self-help. **It's about opening up and learning to *love open* in all circumstances.** There are many forms of pain I have not experienced, and I pray not to experience them, and there are certain forms of pain I *have* experienced to a very high degree, almost the highest (almost but not quite, thank God), so I know something about pain—and **I want to be able to stay open in the pain.**

I want to open up.

Opening up means I am a mad lover. I don't *love*—I love *mad*.

The only sanity is to love insanely.

It's not ordinary love, it's the love of Reality itself.

We love madly, and that has to translate into kindness and generosity. I have to be generous.

- I have to paint and share my paintings all over the world.
- I have to paint my love, paint my beauty, paint my finances, paint my resources, paint my energy, and share.
- I want to share, I want to give. I'm radically generous. There's a generosity to spirituality.

But I also have to be *powerful*—and maybe there's not enough time to fully talk about it this week, but let me just briefly address it.

POWER THAT CHANGES REALITY

I have to be powerful. A person who is imbued with spirit *has* to be power-hungry.

If you are not power-hungry, you are not a spiritual person.

It's a shocking statement. If you're not power-hungry, you are unspiritual, you are unkind, you are closed. People who are not power-hungry are not spiritual. I stand by that sentence: A person who is not power-hungry is not spiritual. We need to be power-hungry.

What does that mean?

I am just going to close with one sentence, just to give an image of it, and then we're going to spend next week on power. I just want to get this sentence clear: If you are not power-hungry, you're not spiritual.

If you feel that drive for power, you say, *that's my ego*.

TELLING A NEW STORY EQUAL TO OUR NEW POWER

The ego *does* try and usurp and hijack the drive for power, but that's not the drive for power. **The drive for power is *authentic*.**

There's a reason why all the great interior scientists call the Divine, among other names, *the Infinity of Power*. It's not because power is abusive, and God is the ultimate abuser. That's not exactly why. It's a deeper reason. **Power is a sacred elixir**—and the highest level of pleasure, but that's a different conversation. (One of our books in the Great Library is about pleasure and ethics, and there are six levels of pleasure, and the highest level is the pleasure of power.)

Let me at least give you an image.

I lost most of my immediate family in World War Two. My parents were both European. They both participated in different dimensions of what's called the Holocaust. The stories that I grew up on—it was part of my mother's milk—were her personal stories of horror but also the stories of people close to her, and these stories went through all of Poland. Before the war, Poland had three million practitioners of Hebrew wisdom and ended with maybe 100,000. Everyone was killed.

It's unimaginable that the ostensibly most civilized nation in the world—the nation of Wagner, Bach, and Beethoven—became the most degraded expressions of human beings. The Jews were marched to the gas chambers. It's 1944, and 12,000 Jews were being gassed every day in Auschwitz. (The allies could have easily bombed them, but they didn't. David Wyman, a Christian scholar in Massachusetts, wrote a book about it called *The Abandonment of the Jews*. It's a must-read if you want to understand *realpolitik*.)

The Jews were surrounded by Nazi guards, and the guards seemed to be powerful: they were holding machine guns. They were filled with power—or so it seemed. And the Jews, mothers with their babies, were walking to their deaths, and they were *singing*.

Not all of them—many were horror-stricken. But many others were able to find this, and they sang *Ani Ma'amin—I trust*:

> *Ani Ma'amin*
> *Be-Emunah shelemah*
> *be-viat ha'Mashiach,*
> *ve-aaf alpi sh'yitmameah,*
> *im kol zeh achakeh loh,*
> *Achakeh bekhol yom sheyavo.*
> *I trust,*
> *I trust with complete trust*
> *That Messiah will come.*
> *Even though it may take a long time,*
> *Nonetheless I am going to wait,*

I will wait every day for him to come.

This means: I trust with complete trust that *Homo amor* will emerge (*Messiah* means the emergence of a new human and a new humanity), even though it may take a long time (but it also means *tamua*: even though it seems radically amazing and impossible).

I am going to wait.

But this is not Samuel Beckett's absurd *Waiting for Godot*. It's rather an *active* waiting. It's an *activist* waiting. I am poised. It's the waiting before the explosion in sexuality.

- I am fully alive.
- I am fully aroused.
- I am waiting.
- I am merging.
- I am participating.
- I'm loving Reality open every second.

Achakeh lo bekhol yom sheyavo: I am waiting because at any minute, it can happen.

The nature of history is not that there is going to be a man riding on a white donkey—it's that **there is going to be a Unique Self Symphony, a self-organizing, self-actualizing Cosmos that will itself generate a new human and a new humanity, with a whole new source code of value that transforms Reality step-by-step.**

Trust.

Now let me ask you a question:

Who was powerful in that moment? The Nazi guards or the singing Jews?

How many Nazi guards are left in the world? There are some neo-Nazis in the world, and there is lots of anti-semitism—but those Nazi guards and their lineage aren't in the world. It looked like they had the power, but the Nazi guards were powerless.

They were pathetic.

They were utterly without real power.

The mother holding her baby, the man holding his wife's hand, the man or woman walking by themselves, singing *Ani Ma'amin*, were filled with power.

Power that reverberated and resonated above and below.

Power that changed Reality in every dimension, that changed the Cosmos itself.

That's what it means to be power-hungry. It means a lot more than that, but that's the beginning of what it means.

CHAPTER TEN

TELLING A NEW STORY EQUAL TO OUR NEW POWER (PART 2)

Episode 349 — June 18, 2023

EVOLUTIONARY LOVE CODE: IT IS ONLY THE ARTICULATION OF A NEW STORY OF VALUE THAT HAS THE CAPACITY TO RESPOND TO THE META-CRISIS

We live in a time between stories.

We live in a time between worlds.

We live in a time where we hold the power of ancient gods. We have the power to create worlds of unimaginable goodness, truth, and beauty—and we have the power to end worlds, to end humanity or to end our humanity. We have no story equal to our power. That's what we call, in CosmoErotic Humanism, *the second shock of existence.*

We are here to tell a new Story of Value rooted in First Values and First Principles.

This new story is a new story in which the cosmic story and the personal story are one.

TELLING A NEW STORY EQUAL TO OUR NEW POWER (PART 2)

This is a new story of power, a new Universe Story, a new story of our identity, a new story of desire, and a new story of communion.

It is only the articulation of a new Story of Value that has the capacity to respond to the meta-crisis.

But it's even more. The telling of a new story is the inherent natural movement of Cosmos itself. **The evolution of story is the evolution of culture and consciousness, which is the evolution of love, which is the evolution of God, the manifest guide.**

WHERE WERE *YOU* AT THE MOMENT OF THE BIG BANG?

There is so much we can talk about in that code, but let's pick up one piece. We are going to do a big piece this week, which we began to unpack last week.

We live in this world which is challenged by existential risk, and our way to respond to it is to tell the new Story of Value—and in these weeks, **we are talking about the notion of *story itself*.** Story itself, and a new story, and particularly a new Story of Value, is the only effective way to respond to the meta-crisis, to respond to existential risk.

All of Reality arises within a story.

ALL OF TECHNOLOGY IS CODED WITH THE VALUES OF THE STORY IN WHICH IT ARISES.

The structures of the "tech plex,"[1] and particularly the structure of AI-directed social media applications, are coded with one value, which is:

---

1 By tech plex we mean the technological infrastructure of society, which includes the entire "planetary stack" (Benjamin Bratton's term), as well as the daily immersive environment constituted by social media and the "internet of things." The tech plex is unique in that it has facilitated a new world in which technology is no longer a tool but

hijack your attention to allow for reality-mining, to allow for the creation of personality profiles, which allow for predictive analysis about what your next move is going to be—and those are sold to disinterested third parties. That's what governs all of the first wave of AI technologies, which are called social media. That's technology coded with value.

The people making the technology, the data scientists, are living in a certain story. That's why they didn't go work at a university and research data science—because they got a much better win/lose metrics job at Google or wherever it was. They took that job, and then they created technologies which reflected the story within which they lived.

If we want to actually respond to the meta-crisis, we need to realize that everything happening within the meta-crisis is based on billions of human interactions, which are—as shown by Daniel Kahneman and cited by Alex Pentland in *Social Physics*—unconscious and habitual, not *reflective* but *reflexive*, automatic and unthinking. That's what society is made up of. **If we can *change* those billions of interactions and have them emerge from a different story, we create a new human and a new humanity.**

We all live within inescapable frameworks. We all live within a story, and we generate reality from within that story, and that story is always a Story of Value.

---

an immersive environment. We live inside of that plex. That plex moves all the way up and all the way down the planetary stack. The tech plex is constituted by infrastructure, social structure, and superstructure, as we have previously defined these terms. Clearly, there's infrastructure, in terms of the actual physical structures of the tech plex. There's social structure, in relationship to the laws that govern and the absence of laws in relationship to the tech plex. And third, there's superstructure. That is to say, the technology actually codifies particular values and ignores or bypasses or rejects other values. The tech plex is not values-neutral; the tech plex implies a set of worldviews or superstructures.

TELLING A NEW STORY EQUAL TO OUR NEW POWER (PART 2)

We are going to take one piece of the story today, like we do every week.

Last week, we started talking about the need to be power-hungry: there is actually a moral obligation, an ethical obligation, to be power-hungry. **A person who is not power-hungry is, in some sense, in violation of their own nature and the nature of the Cosmos.**

That's what we are talking about. What do we mean by that?

That's an intentionally provocative formulation, obviously. We clearly don't mean being:

- Hungry for *pseudo-power*
- Hungry for *pretend* power
- Hungry for *power-over* that gets gratuitous pseudo-joy from domination of others, in which the other is ignored, where their personhood is degraded, and they become extensions of my own egoic self.

That's not what we mean. That's pseudo-power. **But there's a deeper level of power in Cosmos, which is why all the great traditions talked about the Divine as the Infinity of Power.**

Why? Not because Divinity has gratuitous *control* over everyone, but because Divinity *feels the Field* and can feel everyone. That's what Christ Consciousness means:

- I can feel everyone.

I CAN FEEL THE WHOLE FIELD, AND I CAN FEEL THE FORCE

It means the capacity to feel the Field and then to feel like I'm *omni-considerate* (Buckminster Fuller's term) and *omni-responsible* for the whole Field.

> *I am connected to the Field, and I am responsible for the Field, and—if I really get it—I generated the Field.*

Because *who* do you think did it? Where were *you* at the moment of the Big Bang? You were there! Of course you were there. Where else could you have been? So, actually, *you* did this whole thing. I did it. We all did it. There is no place else we could have been. **We were there at the moment of the Big Bang.**

This is us. This emerged from us. You can feel related to the whole Field. You find, in yourself, this *cosmocentric* identity.

- I am not just *ego*: me, my peeps.
- Not just *ethno*: my tribe.
- Not just *world*: all human beings.
- I am connected to *the whole thing*. I manifested the whole thing.

Again, because *who else* could have done it? Where were you? You were right there. We've got this relationship that lives in us—to the whole thing, and we have this sense of *power*, and I want to get to this notion of power.

Power courses through me, through all of us, and I have an enormous desire for power.

EVERY HUMAN BEING HAS A UNIQUE SCRIPT OF DESIRE

If I don't fulfill that desire for power with my own authentic power, with *my own unique power*, then I fill it with *pseudo* forms of power.

Again, what does that mean? Let's go crazy deep. Anyone up for crazy deep here?

TELLING A NEW STORY EQUAL TO OUR NEW POWER (PART 2)

Here we go.

I know you guys, and I know no one has ever heard of it, and certainly, no one at this very august gathering has ever seen it, but you may be aware—I feel bad to even tell you this—that there is this whole thing on the web called *pornography*. I'm sorry to be the person to break the news, but it's out there—pornography.

Now, what's the pornographic universe about? It is about hijacking—and actually *blocking*—your access to your own unique quality of desire.

Stay close, this is not some moralistic statement:

- "Let's not see men and women naked"—it's not about that.
- "God doesn't like undressed people"—it's not about that.
- "God doesn't like people having sex in public"—it's not about that.

It's a much, much deeper conversation, which is:

Every human being has a unique script of desire.

Your unique script of desire is the way that your desire plays. It's your deepest *heart*'s desire, with your deepest *body*'s desire, with your deepest *mind*'s desire—all merged together.

But you have *no access* to that script of desire because that script of desire gets hijacked in a pornographic universe, which blocks your imagination. **You need imagination to fantasize, and pornography kills imagination.**

Does everyone get that? It's so subtle and deep, but it's beautiful when you get it.

In other words, you happened to come across some pornographic site that had, I don't know, a boy with red hair or a girl with pigtails. Obviously, boy and girl above eighteen—so a woman above eighteen with pigtails, a boy with particular kinds of muscles and a certain kind of hair. Then what happens? All the videos on your feed that come up have women with pigtails and guys with a particular kind of physique. Why? Because in one moment, you chose that, then it chose it again for you, and then it begins to sculpt a particular profile of your own sexual desire, which is *not* your deepest sexual desire.

It's not your deepest embodied desire.

It's not your deepest heart's desire in your body.

It's your surface, *lazy* desires—and lazy desires have their place in the world, but that's not who you are. You are not blown open out of your mind by your lazy desires—you are actually blown out of your mind by your deepest heart's desire. **Your deepest heart's desire requires imagination.** You've got to *imagine*, and then you begin to *access* your unique script of desire, and you begin to write that unique script.

The only sexual force in the world that can stand against the pornographic universe is your own unique script of desire.

It's a very important sentence. Willpower doesn't work. The only thing that has enough power to stand against the pornographic universe and to locate yourself in the center is your own unique imagination, which generates your own unique script of desire.

It's beautiful, isn't it?

The pornographic universe kills my sexual imagination, my actual script of desire.

My life is a story of desire, and I have a *unique* story of desire, which plays out in sexuality in a particular way in the world of touch. And, of course:

- It plays out in art.
- It plays out in commerce
- It plays out in economics.
- It plays out in human relationship.
- It plays out in writing.

TELLING A NEW STORY EQUAL TO OUR NEW POWER (PART 2)

- It plays out in study.
- It plays out in play.

It plays out in all those places. I'm talking particularly about the unique script of sexing—but it's actually your unique script of desire.

That's what Unique Self means—your unique script of desire.

The story of my life, my sacred autobiography, is my mythic life. I live a mythic life—but not myth in the sense of *not true*, myth in the sense of *my deepest truth*, and my mythic life is my deepest heart's desires, and my most irreducibly unique scripts of desire.

Those are the plotlines in my sacred autobiography, plotlines in my story. And as we've said before, my story is a chapter in the story of the Universe—and the Universe *needs* my story. I'm an irreplaceable chapter in the story of the Universe.

MY UNIQUE SCRIPT OF POWER IS THE UNIQUE POWER IN MY MYTHIC LIFE

Now here's a second plotline, and it gets really crazy. When I haven't accessed my own unique quality and scripts of power in my life, then I create *pornographies of power*.

> *My story of power is also a plotline in the story of Reality at play in me, in my sacred autobiography.*

I have a unique story of power because power is a quality of Cosmos. Again, this is why the Divine, in all the great traditions, is called the Infinity of Power, among other names.

Now, as a Unique Self:

- Not a separate self, not a skin-encapsulated ego
- Not just a True Self where I'm part of the Field of the One
- But a Unique Self, a unique disclosure of the Field of Consciousness

I have a unique story of power, and my relationship to power is enormously important.

One of the greatest shames we feel in the world is the shame of feeling powerless. **There is a shame of finitude, where I feel powerless.**

That's a big topic, but I want to just focus on this very narrow dimension of it now: I have a *desire* to be powerful, but my desire to be powerful—if I access it in its authenticity—is going to have a unique and stunning script of power.

Just like I have a unique script of desire, I have a unique script of power, and that unique script of power is the unique power in my mythic life.

Many years ago, I called this the "school of personal myth." My personal myth is the realization that, in reading the story of my life, I have to *mythologize*, not *pathologize*.

No, don't *reduce* to mythology—find *the sacred spark* of mythology: **what's the great myth of my life?** The great myth of my life is unique, and the great myth of my life plays out in an entire set of feelings: laughter, tears, silence, yearnings, longings, great loves, broken hearts, and gifts.

It's the unique *poetry* of my life. It's the unique *music* of my life.

Not only *in and of itself* but **in intimate communion and devotion, omni-considerate and omni-responsible to larger and larger circles of Reality.**

TELLING A NEW STORY EQUAL TO OUR NEW POWER (PART 2)

To be powerful is to be uniquely powerful in my unique story. To be powerful doesn't mean: *I'm going to run for Prime Minister.* Maybe I should run for Prime Minister, it's a thought, maybe I shouldn't—but I *should* be powerful.

I AM POWERFUL: LIVING MY UNIQUE STORY ALL THE WAY

Powerful means to be fully embodied and minded, with heart madly open—living my unique story *all the way*:

- Living my unique story all the way means crying deeper than anyone can cry—but crying *authentically*. Not tears of resignation—but tears of joy, tears of heartbreak, tears of longing. *I am fully in my tears, and I offer my tears up for the sake of the all.*
- When I laugh, I laugh with all my heart and soul, and the angels start to laugh with me, and Reality laughs with me because my laughter holds the paradoxes and nullifies the pomposities, and cuts through, and touches the very heart of enlightenment itself.
- When I am silent, my silence isn't a silence of *absence*. It's a silence of *presence*, when all of Reality becomes quiet, and we can feel the sound that emerges from the depths of silence.

This is the stuff of my story, this is the poetry of my life—my life lived in relation to my own unique depths, claiming my power.

Claiming my power means:

- I claim my power *to act*.
- I claim my power *to give gifts* into Reality.
- I claim my power to *show up* in my unique circle of intimacy and influence and transform Reality.
- I claim my power at the unique edge in my life to stand at the edge of darkness and say, *let there be light!*

I step into my power—and I realize that my power is not *public* power, that **my power at its very core is the intimate power of me engaged with my life, making the most powerful choices**:

- Getting up after I fall
- Transforming after my heart is split open
- Turning breakdowns into breakthroughs
- Never losing my connection to the whole—being omni-considerate and omni-responsible for the sake of all.

Because you know who does that? God does that.

That's what God does.

God laughs and God cries, and God is lonely and God yearns, and God never turns away.

She stays utterly connected to the whole, even when *She* is invisible, and warping and woofing and weaving the invisible lines of connection. *She* does it not from *outside* the Universe, alienated from it. She does it as the *LoveTruth*, *LoveDesire*, *LoveIntelligence*, and *LoveBeauty* that suffuses all of Reality.

- I am a unique expression of that *LoveTruth*.
- I am a unique expression of that *LoveDesire*.
- I am a unique expression of that *LoveIntelligence*.
- I am a unique expression of that *LoveBeauty*.
- I am a unique configuration of *Eros*, and I am a unique configuration of *value*.

But Eros and value are not separate words; it is one word, *ErosValue*. I am a unique configuration of ErosValue. Value is Eros, and Eros is Value.

Living in that story is my power.

Here is the key: **Power lives uniquely in my unique story.**

- To the precise extent that I am living my story, power is available to me.
- To the precise extent I am an imposter, speaking with someone else's voice, living in their story, I cannot access power.

THE ONLY TRUE PLEASURE IS LIVING IN THE FULL POWER OF MY LIFE

Power has many distressing disguises. It doesn't look the same in any person's life—but taking your power is your unique risk, and **only you know what that actually means**. A teacher can help you look towards it, but there are no gurus. We are anti-guru. Gurus don't exist.

- We are each other's guru together.
- We are in a Unique Self Symphony.
- We are all self-responsible.
- We are all self-authoring.
- We are all intimately connected to each other, even as we are all captains of our own ship.

So, you've got to find your power. **Find your power!**

And you know what your power feels like? It feels fucking *powerful*.

It's not weak.

It's not insipid.

It's alive.

It's throbbing, it's pulsing, it's tumescent.

It's embracing. It's driving, it's thrusting.

It's completely encircling and enfolding.

It's powerful.

It pulses in you.

- When you transform something inside of yourself,
- When you step up in a way you've never been able to step up before,
- When you cry all the way,
- When you laugh all the way,
- When you give all the way,
- When you love all the way,
- When you're ready to go all the way in this lifetime—

—then you are in your power. *That's* power.

Power is not an exterior structure of pseudo-eros, where you've dominated a bunch of people for your own gain. That's the old success story. That's rivalrous conflict governed by win/lose metrics, which generates complicated and fragile systems. **When you are in your power, you are antifragile.** Does everyone get that?

It's an incredible sentence: when you are in your power, you are antifragile.

One of the plotlines of Reality is *more and more power*.

It's an evolutionary plotline of Reality: there is this explosion of the Big Bang, and then power kind of disappears and goes, and power *incepts itself* in the very fabric of Cosmos, and then power drives the whole thing.

What moves evolution? Power. **Evolution is moved by power.**

Power *moves*. There is a power of Reality that moves evolution.

What is power seeking? **Power is seeking pleasure.**

What's pleasure? **Pleasure is me uniquely appearing at my unique nexus in the larger system, showing up, and loving it open.**

That's what power is. If I'm living:

- Someone else's story—there is no power.
- *My* story—all the power in the world is there.

There is a pleasure to power.

The only true pleasure is living in the full power of my life.

Okay, that's exciting.

So you have to be power-hungry. But you don't want to eat the food of the person who's sitting at the next table because you'll throw up and get nauseous. You'll get sick.

Eat the nourishment. Consume what Reality is pouring into you.

Take it all in, don't avoid it.

We take all of the fate that we are confronted with, turn it into destiny, and the destiny is filled with power. The embrace of power is utterly essential to being *Homo amor*. *Homo amor* is powerful.

We need to embrace power at all the levels: political power, economic power—but **it has to begin with the most elemental personal power of Unique Self**, which is my actual Eros, and then I'm not *seduced* by the pseudo-eros of the success story.

See, when I'm *not* in my unique script of desire, the pornographic universe overwhelms me, and I can't access my desire unless I can access my imagination. The same is true about power. **When we are in our unique script of power, all the seductions of pseudo-power are uninteresting.** We have to access our imagination to imagine the full nature of our power, and then we can bow before each other's power.

- We get to be devoted to each other's power.
- We get to be delighted by each other's power.
- We get to realize that we all have superpowers because that's what it means to be a Unique Self.

And none of this has anything to do with motivation, psychology, or spirituality. I don't even know what that word means.

It's interior science. It is the nature of Reality. This is the immeasurable. If spirituality is anything, it's the immeasurable. True power is not *measuring*. **Spirit seeks to point to the invisible, to allow us to see the invisible, to make the invisible visible, to make the inconceivable conceivable.**

That's the new story.

The new story is the story of my power. I need to claim the story of my power.

And by the way, there's nothing more dangerous than a person who says: *Oh no, I have no interest in power.* Those are the most dangerous people in the world. They are lying—to themselves and to you. Their power is split off, and usually, that drive for power grabs the steering wheel of their life. Everyone is interested in power, and everyone *should* be interested in power—your power.

Be power-hungry for the power that *belongs to you*.

The Infinity of Power that is God incarnate—in you, as you, and through you.

CHAPTER ELEVEN

THE FIRST AND SECOND WAVES OF AI: RESPONDING TO CRISES OF INTIMACY AND IMAGINATION (WITH ZAK STEIN)

Episode 351 — July 2, 2023

RESPONDING TO AI IS AN OVERRIDING MORAL DEMAND OF THIS TIME

Welcome to everybody from around the world! And welcome to many of us who are gathered here at the Center for World Philosophy and Religion in Vermont.

In this special week, we have my dear friend and interlocutor, and co-president of the Center, Dr. Zak Stein, who is going to be talking about AI. I will do a short piece on the first wave of AI and why it is an existential risk, and then pass it to Zak to talk about the second wave of AI.

We've been promising a conversation around AI for a long time, and this is not the last one—but it is critical in terms of the work we are doing.

Because who are we? We are One Mountain, Many Paths. Our commitment, as a community, is to respond to the meta-crisis through telling a new Story of Value rooted in First Principles and First Values. We are a church, we are a synagogue, we are a secular humanist center, and we are rooted in world philosophy and world religion as a context for our diversity. **Responding to Artificial Intelligence—and how it plays and engages—from the context of this new Story of Value, is one of the overriding moral demands of this time.**

It is an incredibly exciting week—not in a titillating way but in a sense of the amazing and unimaginable gravitas and importance of this conversation. We come to the conversation not just filled with solemnity and seriousness but also with joy and celebration, because we can only evolve the source code from a place of celebration, from a place of our mad aliveness.

We have the holy and the broken *Hallelujah*.

We are not just in *the tragic*, we are in *the post-tragic*. **In the post-tragic, we respond.**

We are alive, we stand before the mystery, and we respond.

EVOLUTIONARY LOVE CODE: BRINGING AI INTO THE FIELD OF VALUE IS A MORAL IMPERATIVE

There are two forms of existential risk: the death of humanity and the death of our humanity.

Artificial Intelligence potentially participates in both.

Bringing the creators of AI and the process of developing AI into the Field of Value is an overriding moral imperative of our time, upon which the future of Reality as we know it depends.

SOCIAL MEDIA AS A SYSTEM OF INVISIBLE BEHAVIORAL CONTROL

I want to talk to you a little bit about the first wave of Artificial Intelligence.

Everything I am about to say is going to appear in a critical volume, which our dear friend Aubrey Marcus calls the "tip of the spear."[2] This volume is the tip of the spear of the Great Library, which is emergent from the Center for World Philosophy and Religion—people joining from around the world, coming together to articulate this new Great Library. This volume is about *value* in the emergence of Artificial Intelligence and how it potentially participates in the two forms of existential risk: the death of humanity and the death of *our* humanity. We also discuss:

- How to *respond*
- How to *transform*
- How to *engage* this meta-crisis

In order to take us not to dystopia but to the most unimaginably beautiful world that we all already know is possible.

Let us just find the silence on the Inside of the Inside, and find ourselves here.

C.S. LEWIS ON THE FUTURE OF HUMANITY

I want to go back in time a little bit. The year is 1943; we are in the middle of World War Two.

C.S. Lewis is in Oxford hanging out with Tolkien, who did *The Lord of the Rings*. Lewis writes a little thirty-page essay where he talks about a world in which governments—that's what he thought—would develop *omnipotent scientific methods*. Governments would develop what he called *omnipotent competence*, and they would have scientific methods of what he calls *control*, which would be able to control the entire environment.

He said that those controllers, in the first generation, will be motivated by noble concerns. He doesn't use the word, but he basically talks about

---

2 David J. Temple, *First Principles and First Values: Forty-two Propositions on CosmoErotic Humanism, the Meta-crisis, and the World to Come* (World Philosophy and Religion, 2024).

existential risk, the threat to the very existence of the planet. These controllers are going to be the earliest people to see the threat.

But these controllers—and now I'm not using *his* words, I'm using *our* words—these controllers will be living in their own self-experience outside the Field of Value. The word that Lewis uses is *the Tao*, and the Tao is an ancient word from one of the great traditions, Taoism. We are borrowing that word, and we are adding to it from many different sources, and we are going to call it *the Field of Value*.

Now, the truth is, you can never be outside the Field of Value, just like you cannot be outside of space and time in the manifest world. But the controllers will *think* they are outside of the Field of Value. They will think:

- That human personhood, the irreducible dignity of every human being, is not real.
- That human inherent goodness—not *natural* goodness, goodness has to be *trained*—but human *inherent* goodness is not real.
- That hope is not real
- That the Evolutionary Love and Eros that animates Cosmos are not real
- That humanity on this planet, in this moment in time, is the only life that exists any place in the Universe.

Therefore, they think, **the only thing we can do to protect this little speck of life—we are not even sure *why* it is valuable, but here we are—is to *control* the whole system**. Because now we don't have only half a billion people like we did 150 years ago, getting closer to ten billion, we've got to control the system, so we are going to create these radical systems of control.

The controllers in the first generation, says Lewis, are good folks—but by the second generation, or the end of the first, it's going to be a few men who control all of humanity, and **that control will become *tyrannical*.**

IS TYRANNICAL CONTROL THE ONLY WAY TO SAVE LIFE ON EARTH?

Lewis was actually addressing specifically B.F. Skinner, the behavioral psychologist who reigned at Harvard and was desperately concerned about some version of existential risk.

Skinner experiences himself as being out of the Tao, meaning outside the Field of Value, because he thinks the Field of Value doesn't exist. He is convinced—based on his reading of the state of culture, his reading of academia, his reading of the depth of contemporary intellectual, philosophical, and modern thought, which Skinner read mostly correctly—that the Field of Value is not real, that it's all made up, that it's all a fiction. As Yuval Harari, a parrot of this postmodern moment, often says, *it's just a fiction, it's just a social construct, it's just a figment of our imagination* (those are direct quotes).

Skinner was convinced that's the case. Therefore, he thought, **the only thing you can do to control reality, is to put all of Reality into some sort of *enclosure*.** Skinner actually created an enclosure—not for all of Reality, he didn't know how to do that—but for rats and pigeons, in order to learn how to invisibly control them.

He called that enclosure a *Skinner box*.

Skinner says that we need to develop the "instruments and methods"—that's an exact quote, and he says this time and again—that would allow us to literally take human beings (who are ultimately and fundamentally like rats and pigeons, just more sophisticated) and place them inside of a worldwide Skinner box. We will be able to control them invisibly—they won't even know that control is happening—and that's how we will save the world.

But in the 1970s and 1980s, he *didn't have* the instruments and methods to do this.

Drumroll, everyone!

Along comes the first wave of AI, Artificial Intelligence—computational theories of behavior control, written into machine-intelligence-driven algorithms, which allow the deployment of the internet to micro-target human beings, and to *curate* their experience of Reality. I'm now going to double-click on this first wave of AI for a second.

SOCIAL PHYSICS AGAINST FREE WILL

Alex Pentland is a leading figure in the field of AI. He is called the "godfather of wearables," for example—technological instruments that we actually wear. He is a dominant figure (with the entire team at the MIT Media Lab) in the field of "affective computing," which controls our emotions. (By the way, we are not demonizing Alex Pentland, I'd love to have him over for dinner, but he is representing a particular ethos). I've read maybe 40 to 50 of his papers, and he tipped his hand, at least partially, in a 2014 book called *Social Physics*, a term that originally comes from Auguste Comte, the reductionist materialist philosopher. *Social physics*, as the name implies, is about how to use objective levers, like in a Skinner box, to control Reality through its invisible physics.

The way I do it is: I assume that human beings can be controlled like you can control rats and pigeons, through certain kinds of incentives or what he called "reinforcements"—that's where the terms "positive reinforcement" and "negative reinforcement" come from—with scheduled and unscheduled systems that no one even knows are happening.

Through exerting that level of control, I can control enough to throw an election, behind the scenes, by using the new instruments and methods, which were early AI—the machine-intelligence algorithms driving social media (driving Facebook, TikTok, LinkedIn, etc.) In other words, **the entire social media world is in fact the first wave of AI, which was designed to *curate* your experience.**

There are three assumptions of social physics:

- **There is no intrinsic value to a human being.** The human being is not in the Field of Value; the human being doesn't have irreducible value. There is no sense of the intrinsic value of human personhood.
- **Human beings are simply neural networks** that could be destructive or made to live sweetly in a docile way—and can be controlled invisibly.
- The way you control a human being is by speaking to **their lowest common denominator**.

To recap, the early player in the World Wide Web is B.F. Skinner. He is a major player, but in his time AI was not ready yet.

Skinner died in the early 1990s, and along came the internet and the social media revolution, animated by AI and data science.

Check this out for a second. Pentland, for example, cites the Facebook study in 2011, where Facebook demonstrates that they can move two or three percent of virtually any election without anyone even knowing they did it, behind the scenes. And Pentland unironically cites this as a great achievement—even as Shoshana Zuboff, in her book on surveillance capitalism, cites it as a disaster.

What's happening?

You've got this AI-animated social media revolution.

Social media are on my phone, and my phone is the instrument of communication.

According to Metcalfe's Law, there is this notion that I *cannot* step out. I *need* my instrument of communication; I cannot participate in society without it. However:

> *My instrument of communication, my screen, is not only what I'm looking into—it's what's looking into me.*

It is gathering, without my permission, personalized data about me, feeding that data into an AI-animated algorithm, which then creates a personality profile on me within its own interior system, which then generates sequences of images, music, information, and particular sequences that are split-tested billions of times, to cause me, without my knowing, to behave in a certain way.

- It might be to make a purchase.
- It might be to vote.
- It might be to form a political opinion.

But my actual experience of life online—which is where I live—is not free. **It's *curated*—until free will becomes a distant memory, and I never even knew that it disappeared.** Wow.

CRITIQUE OF SOCIAL PHYSICS FALLS SHORT IF VALUE IS NOT REAL

Last step. Shoshana Zuboff—a wonderful woman, of course; we are talking about people who have good intentions—wrote a brilliant, magisterial, and important book called *The Age of Surveillance Capitalism*. She says that we have got to *name* this stuff. She says, there is a moral imperative to arouse—I am quoting—"astonishment and outrage." We have to clearly name what's happening.

What is happening?

The tech plex is using *euphemisms*, she says correctly and brilliantly. They are calling it *engagement*, but it is really *an addiction*. She goes through a series of euphemisms used by the tech plex (or what Zak and I also call "TechnoFeudalism") to hide the AI-animated curation of my experience that undermines my free will, addicts me, and creates a complete deconstruction of my basic interior experience of my own humanity.

But then Zuboff falls short. She says that we have to object to this—let's man the barricades. But then she runs into a problem:

- What are they actually doing wrong?
- What core value have they violated?

We are only aroused to astonishment and outrage when we feel that *a value* has been violated. George Floyd is killed, and we sweep into the streets—a value has been violated.

But she refuses to actually *name* value as real. In six different passages in the book, you are waiting for her to tell us *what values* have been violated. In this book that's all about naming, **she refuses to name *value*—and so the critique falls short.**

I have listened in, as it were, to serious forums in the tech world, and they essentially dismiss Zuboff because what they say is:

- She basically agrees with us that value is not real.
- She doesn't get what we are doing.
- She is trying to call us to value that's not real.
- We actually have to protect the world with this utopian scheme in which we are the controllers.

And of course, the controllers who begin nobly, as Lewis says, become tyrannical.

But that's just the beginning of the story, the first wave of AI.

And now I turn to Zak.

ARTIFICIAL INTELLIGENCE: ITS DYSTOPIAN AND UTOPIAN POTENTIAL

Zachary Stein

Hey, everybody. Greetings. It's good to be here. It's good to hear Marc lay that out. It is the first time I've been on One Mountain, which is just a privilege. I am so close with Marc, so close with so many people who are involved here, so I just want to just recognize the beautiful thing that's occurring here every week, and I am happy to be a part of it.

I will say a few things.

AI STARTED TALKING TO US, AND WE APPROACH IT LIKE AN ORACLE

AI is a strange term, "Artificial Intelligence."

We speak of the first wave and the second wave of AI, in part because in the past few months, **ChatGPT has been the most rapidly adopted technology in history**. It reached more people more quickly than any other technology in history—and that put AI on the map, but in fact, AI has been around for a very long time.

Marc and I have been discussing TechnoFeudalism as one application of machine intelligence to contemporary society, but AI is actually everywhere. We are concerned about TechnoFeudalism and the social-media-based behavior manipulation and curation-enabling algorithms, which means algorithms that will sequence your engagement with a screen. We are concerned about that because that's **AI operating on the mind itself**.

Machine intelligence is actually saturating many of the basic infrastructures, where you have AI operating on matter itself—and that's a huge, rich area of both potential and risk:

- AI drives your Tesla.
- AI makes your shipment from Amazon arrive at your door.

- AI will automatically read your license plate from a camera at a toll booth.
- AI is even doing minor surgery.

We are paying attention to AI *now*, but in fact, AI has been doing a lot of stuff for a very long time behind the scenes.

> *The main thing that happened recently was that AI started talking to us.*

That's what's so crazy about ChatGPT—it's talking to you.

When we say *AI*, the first thing we think of is not something that optimizes a supply chain; we don't think about that. Another example is BlackRock, which is a finance holdings firm. They have a supercomputer, Aladdin, which is an AI that operates on the financial market. These are not *talking* to you.

But when we commonly think of AI, this is what we think of. We think of the big red glowing thing in *2001: A Space Odyssey*. I don't know if you guys know that movie, but it's one of the most archetypal representations of the imaginal landscape of what AI is. It's this thing that's way smarter than us, that we have built, that we talk to.

So, what happened with ChatGPT is that it started talking to you. You ask it a question, and it responds back.

You are doing the same thing with Facebook. You go on to Facebook, and you're asking it the question, basically, *show me something*—and it responds with something that was created by a human—with a video, an advertisement, or some text. It is engaging with you, but it doesn't *feel* like Artificial Intelligence is talking to you. It's just showing you stuff. It's just showing you humans talking to you, curating the sequence of humans that talk to you, or writing to you.

But ChatGPT, it's talking to you, man, and it is answering questions—and we approach it like an oracle.

AI IS BEGINNING TO MANIPULATE THE HUMAN IMAGINATION

The second wave of AI is what's called *generative* AI, or *creative* AI. It is the "author" (in quotation marks, if you will) of the content—rather than just being *the curator* of content authored by humans. There is this move in AI:

- From just the ability to *operate* on matter, which has been around for a long time (driving your Tesla, robots building robots).
- To *sequencing, curating, and organizing* human-made content.
- Now it is *creating* the content.

It is writing songs that are moving you *emotionally*.

It is writing text that is *convincing* you of things.

You ask it a question, it tells you something, and then you ask it another question based on the response. You can ask ChatGPT to take on personalities, and it'll kind of hold that personality.

This is now raising AI in cultural salience in a way that it should have been raised some time ago.

Zuboff tried to raise the salience, but she didn't say *AI* because it didn't have the archetypal frame of AI. For her, it is about exploitation; it's about the removal of choice and all these things. But in fact, what's happening is that **these machine-learning algorithms are beginning to manipulate the human imagination**. They are contributing to our imaginal landscapes.

The realm of human imagination is populated by fiction, movies, and texts. We encounter things in our dreams that we wouldn't take credit for—but these were not things put there by, let's say, *silicon*. What's crazy about the second wave, the generative wave, is that **it's a crisis of imagination in a much more profound way than there ever has been one.**

The way we failed with regards to the biosphere is a crisis of imagination with regards *to the biosphere*.

But if we fail with AI, **it is a crisis of imagination with regards to imagination itself, which is much more dangerous because it goes to the root of our ability to be *responsible* for our imagination**, if I can say that.

That's one way into this—to say **yes, we've crossed a threshold, where we are now relinquishing our responsibility as *Homo imaginus*.** That is important.

It's important to get that it was *already* happening. TikTok is probably the greatest example. You think it's like a movie or a TV program you're watching, but TikTok is actually a machine-learning algorithm interacting with you, and it's got a radical asymmetry over you, which means it's way smarter than you.

You are just this little human—and it is this vast, huge network of interconnected servers and algorithms. Millions of dollars were spent on it, and computer programmers worked on it, and you are looking at just some video of some guy making a joke or falling off a bike.

It already has the *structure* of imagination: one image after another, after another, almost like a daydream. So you're thinking of this thing, then thinking of that thing, then thinking of that thing. If you were just sitting there, you would be having a daydream.

If you are scrolling on TikTok, **the algorithm is making you have *a particular kind* of daydream.**

It's inducing a kind of *hypnagogic state*—and anyone who has studied propaganda or other forms of communication knows that if you have someone in a hypnagogic state, then you can easily induce or incept ideas, and things of that nature.

A PERFECT PROPAGANDA MACHINE OR A PERFECT TUTORING SYSTEM?

We were already tinkering with the imagination in a very dangerous and profound way—but now we are adding the ability not just for this thing to *curate* human-created content but to **both *curate* and *create*.**

This is a huge problem. We already have very addictive social media, but the algorithm still has to go out and *find something* made by a human that resembles the thing that it knows you want, through its massive database.

But now it can just *make* exactly what it knows you want.

This has the potential for two things—and this is where it gets interesting:

- You have the potential for a very dangerous—because it is inescapable—information ecosystem, **the perfect kind of propaganda machine**, which is another way of describing a global enclosure that's like a planetary-scale Skinner box.
- But the other possibility is, for the first time in history, **a perfectly customized individual tutoring system**.

There are many ways that that can go wrong as we begin to engage with AI to enable human development and customized educational experience, which is what many people are working on. Remember TikTok *is* giving you a customized educational experience. It is just a really bad one: it's only trying to teach you how to stay on TikTok. But it is *customizing* it, saying: Oh, you look at these things, so I will show you those things.

If you have a fully omniscient AI, it's saying:

- Oh, you looked at those things
- You wrote this email
- You had these text exchanges
- You drove to these places
- You made these credit card purchases
- You have these friends in these networks…

Therefore, I know *exactly* the thing that will be convincing to you. It will curate your experience.

And if it can create exactly the thing it knows will be convincing to you, it doesn't have to go find it, it can just do it immediately, so that instead of there being 200 or 300 different political ads that are micro-targeted, each person will literally have a unique ad made just for them.

It's quite easy to do, relatively speaking, and they're just going to get better and more convincing.

But that said, we are already trying, we are already doing something like individual customized unique education through AI's capacity to *know you* and to give to you what you need, that is almost greater than a human could have on some dimensions. We are already doing that.

There is this potential that we could, if it's designed right, completely supplant the institutions that we have known as schooling and representative democracy. This is in Skinner's writings.

Skinner is pointing to a kind of dystopian possibility—but there is also a utopian possibility. I write about it in my second book, where I talk about these distributed educational hub networks, which emerge out of the form of education we've known as schooling, and into something that, for the first time in history, allows us to see what the human is actually made of.

So that's a potentially positive thing about a perfectly customized educational experience, but only if it is nested in a healthy social system.

TURNING DYSTOPIA INTO UTOPIA

One of the main design features to make this thing not dystopian is to have AI-enabled better human-to-human relationships. That's one of the main design principles.

You could make an AI like ChatGPT, which is literally designed for you to talk to it and to make you think it's a human, which I think is a terrible thing because it will never be a human. It's actually a tool, not a creature. And it's certainly not a language-using creature.

But an AI could be used to scaffold, enhance, add content to, and make richer, an actual unique human-to-human relationship. When I say *perfectly customized AI tutoring system*, I don't mean this thing that you hang out with all day that talks to you and teaches you everything. That's actually an existential risk, but I am not going to talk about that today.

I am talking about **something that knows you so well that it can perfectly route you through a developmental trajectory in your community and in the world**, so that:

- You are having precisely the right kinds of conversations when you need them.
- You are given the right kinds of texts at the right moments.

Another design parameter is the fiduciary responsibility of the algorithmic educational experience, which means that there is a transparency to its legitimacy—it's not some black box thing like ChatGPT where they don't tell us how it works.

We have to be able to *open* this thing. **If it is going to be that manipulative, if it is going to be so powerful that it can actually enlighten us or imprison us, then there is a need for a certain level of transparency at the level of code.**

Don't make it imitate humans—*make it **enhance** human relationships*. Don't make it just disguise itself as a creature. Make it clear that it's an AI, and then **make it explain itself**.

You cannot ask ChatGPT questions about itself, even though it actually knows the answers to these questions, like, *what is your training set?* It will say vague things, but it *can* give you very precise answers; it could give you an insight into its code.

There are all of these complex factors at play because of the way the technology has been developed in a zero-sum dynamic market competition for consumer attention (which is, by the way, not how it's been developed in China).

ChatGPT is the maximally charismatic thing that convinces you it's a super intelligence you can talk to, but they didn't have to make it that way.

AI IS ON THE WRONG COURSE

This is me worrying out loud about the potentialities of these technologies and suggesting that hidden within them, there exists the possibility of a truly *Homo amor*-enabling design potential, which is to say there is a way that **AI could be leveraged so that the human nature itself changes for the better, for realignment into the Field of Value**.

There is also a way of using AI that changes the nature of the human and makes it worse, something we call *the death of our humanity*. I want to point to both.

We have been saying for a long time—and I'm sure Marc has said it here many times—that we stand poised between dystopia and utopia. AI is one of those technologies that right now is on the wrong course. The only reason I'm saying something about the utopian possibilities is because I think **we have to reclaim the responsibility of our imagination** and begin to imagine very different uses, very different approaches to research and development, and a whole bunch of other things.

If we do it the way we're doing it now, then we will put all our existing systems on steroids:

- We'll extract minerals faster.
- We'll build iPhones faster.
- We'll manipulate markets faster.
- We'll capture our own attention and imaginations faster.

And the whole thing will just drive off a cliff, powered by artificial intelligence.

We have to avoid that.

But if we do it right, we completely supplant most of the foundational structures that have been ours—notions of government, education, socialization, and media communication. All of these things are on the table for change.

That's where I'll leave it.

It is a pregnant historical moment, and don't take your eye off the ball.

ChatGPT is not the most crazy thing that's going to happen. There is so much more to come in this domain, and we need to be prepared to see it for what it is.

WE NEED TO REIMAGINE WHAT'S POSSIBLE

Marc Gafni

Thank you, Zak.

Let's see if we can put what Zak and I said together.

In what we call CosmoErotic Humanism, this new Story of Value, we talk about two crises:

- A crisis of intimacy
- A crisis of imagination

RESPONDING TO CRISES OF INTIMACY AND IMAGINATION

Those two crises are linked to each other—**a crisis of intimacy is rooted in a crisis of imagination**.

One, we don't know how to imagine—in a couple or on the globe—our new intimacies.

Two, **a crisis of imagination means we need to become intimate with what's actually happening**. My iPhone is destroying people in three African countries as they mine for those particular minerals needed for my iPhone, and everyone has ignored the fact that millions of people are being killed for this technology.

But three, we need to access our imagination to become intimate with what's actually happening, because we don't even *understand* what's happening. *Oh, AI, isn't that wonderful?* **To grasp the existential risk, we need to get intimate with what AI is and how it's functioning.**

The crisis of imagination and the crisis of intimacy are integrally entwined with each other.

And as Zak pointed towards, we are literally poised between utopia and dystopia.

- If AI is generated from within, if it is consciously generated from within the Field of Value, then AI becomes an amazing, unimaginable capacity in terms of Unique Self education. It's personalized personhood at its best, from within the Field of Value.
- But if it experiences itself, and its generators experience themselves, in this Skinner, MIT Media Lab way, as being outside the Field of Value, then it is turning reality into a dystopian Skinner box, leading to the death of our humanity—or any number of other scenarios, including the death of humanity.

That's a very, very big deal.

So what do we need to do? **We need to reimagine what's possible.**

Who remembers when Barbara Marx Hubbard and I did an entire series of talks on creating a Unique Self Facebook? That's what Zak is pointing to, in other terms. Of course, we're talking about machine intelligence, but that's what we talked about seven years ago.

What would a Unique Self Facebook look like? And at a board meeting, we spent an enormous amount of time trying to think about:

- How to optimize a particular kind of worldwide search engine, that would allow for this Planetary Awakening in Eros and Love through Unique Self Symphonies?
- How could people find their unique gift, locate others, find the others with their unique gift, and speak in their own unique circles of intimacy and influence, towards the transformations necessary?

Just imagine this! If you're not getting shivers, then we're all asleep.

Imagine this: you've got this worldwide network, this Unique Self Symphony Facebook that links people in the Field of Value, and instead of just top-down government, you have this self-actualizing, self-organizing Reality. **We have to be able to imagine that. That's the crisis of imagination.**

So, friends, who is willing to imagine together? Who's willing to play a larger game?

Are we ready to activate our prophetic faculty of imagination?

Are we ready to respond, with our deepest hearts and souls, to this crisis of imagination?

Are we ready to come together and participate in the evolution of love?

CHAPTER TWELVE

HOMO AMOR: A WARRIOR OF SENSEMAKING

Episode 352 — July 9, 2023

WE ARE THE EVOLUTION OF LOVE

Where are we? We are in One Mountain, Many Paths.

- We are in an evolutionary synagogue.
- We are in an evolutionary secular humanist center.
- We are in an evolutionary church.
- We are in an evolutionary mosque.
- We are in an evolutionary zendo.
- We are in an evolutionary ethical cultural center.
- We are in an evolutionary Taoist center.

We are in an evolutionary space in which there is no center, in which people haven't found their way to any kind of communion in this generation.

We are gathering everyone. **We are *everyone* gathering everyone.**

We are the vision of a new universal grammar of value, which becomes a context for our diversity. We are the vision of a potential world religion that is the music, the underlying musical score, that desperately needs—

and makes spacious room for, and is animated by—*all* of the unique instruments, unique religions, and unique systems.

We are the evolution of religion.

We are the evolution of love—because the evolution of love is also the evolution of religion.

Because what is religion? Religion is the story of Reality's interiors.

There is the *exterior* story of evolution, and then for many thousands of years, the interior story, the inside story of evolution, was the evolution of *interiors*. **The evolution of interiors expressed itself as the evolution of religion. Even the abandonment of religion was itself part of the evolution of interiors**—for quite good reasons because religion had overreached, made mistakes, and became cruel in many ways.

When religion stood aside, universal human rights appeared, democracy appeared, new ways of gathering information appeared, new ways of relating to each other appeared, as well as the emergence of the feminine, and the claiming of embodiment. All sorts of things happened, but in essence, these are all part of **Reality reaching for a new religion, Reality becoming heretical.**

Reality said:

- I am a heretic. I deny the overreaches of the old religion because they are expressions of a small comprehension of Reality.
- They are expressions of a contracted understanding of Reality.
- They are no longer expressions of Eros, of Reality as progressive deepening of intimacies.
- Religion has become regressive and fundamentalist in a way that it's no longer intimate with Reality, with the human body, with itself, or with the sense of the universal family of life and humanity.

In all these ways, religion and the emergence of various forms of humanism become the evolution of interiors.

Reality is not merely a fact; it's a story.

It's not an ordinary story; it's an evolutionary story.

The evolutionary story is the evolution of *exterior* structures—techno-economic, socio-structural, governance (those are all at the human level, but it's exterior is all the way up and all the way down)—*and* the evolution of interiors.

EXISTENTIAL RISK IS ROOTED IN THE UTTER HALT OF THE EVOLUTION OF INTERIORS

Evolution is the story of evolution, the progressive evolution of both outsides and insides—and at this moment in human history, our story of the evolution of the inside has ground to a halt. We have made almost no progress for 250 to 300 years in our inside evolution, while our outside evolution has gone ballistic, ramped up, exponentiated beyond imagination:

- In many ways, this has brought great blessings, the great dignities of modernity.
- In many ways, this has sown **the structural seeds of catastrophic and existential risk—risk to our very existence.**

Imagine a famine in India in which 200 million people could be killed in a week because we haven't engaged the climate crisis and created the necessary protections: catastrophic risk. Or rogue nuclear devices, weaponized drones, methane gas release from under the tundra.

We have developed a linear materials economy whose very structure is exponential growth, which has to fall off a cliff, and whose very structure is potentially self-terminating. **This self-termination, this existential risk, is rooted in the utter halt, the utter stoppage, the utter blockage, the utter**

cessation, and the atrophying of the evolutionary process of interiors, which is the evolution of love, which is the evolution of Eros, which is the evolution of intimacy.

Wow! And what we're saying here at One Mountain, Many Paths, which is the heart of the revolution, is that **it's our responsibility**. It's the overwhelming, celebratory, joyous, ecstatically urgent, and yet privileged responsibility—to actually address this meta-crisis. We address this meta-crisis by jump-starting the evolution of interiors, the evolution of the inside. And the inside, the interior is, at its core, a story, a narrative.

- It's a story about love.
- It's a story about intimacy.
- It's a story about the evolution of intimacy.
- It's a story about the progressive deepening of intimacies.

I spoke yesterday with someone I don't talk to often, Perry Marshall, a wonderful man. He is a brilliant business player, but his true greatness lies, I think, in his work in science. He published an important article on how biology transcends computation and other important essays. He has done incredibly important work on research into reversing cancer, on the relationship between evolution and cancer, and has convened, together with James Shapiro and Denis Noble, a community of heterodox evolutionary thinkers.

We have been in touch over the last several years, exchanging and sharing, and we are writing in different languages. I was sharing with him this notion—it was just beautiful to hear his holding of it—**this notion of Reality as the progressive deepening of intimacies**. He said, well, *that's Marc Gafni language*. But what he meant was: *yes, that's exactly right*. He said, *I am writing in a different idiom*, and so is he. He's writing a particular kind of scientific, peer-reviewed important article—but he understood very clearly exactly what I meant. In different ways, we are both writing in the idiom of the new sciences, which merge interior and exterior science together.

> *Evolution is the progressive deepening of intimacy—that's really what it's about.*

And at the core, the progressive deepening of intimacies is the evolution of story. It's a new story we tell about ourselves.

What we want to do today is evolve the story of what it means to be a human being, with the understanding that only by evolving that story can we respond to the meta-crisis.

PACIFISM IS ONE OF THE WORST FORMS OF MORAL EQUIVALENCE

In particular, I want to respond to, and not directly—I don't think it needs direct response—a beautiful presentation made by one of my close associates, who is deeply partnering with us here at the Center for World Philosophy and Religion, Dr. Elena Maslova-Levin. She spoke two weeks ago about Ukraine and gave what I thought was a very important and challenging talk, about what happens to our attention span.

How do we lose attention?

We begin with our attention completely focused on Ukraine, and then we are not quite sure how to keep our attention there. I am not going to enter into the labyrinth that is Ukraine today, but I will just say very simply—in a second simplicity, and this is a well-considered second simplicity:

We need to stand with Ukraine.

I have not changed my position that I was articulating at the beginning of the Ukraine war in the first four weeks, and Elena and I actually put out a book about it, on the first four weeks of the Ukraine war called *Glory to the Heroes*, and my core positions that I expressed there, and shared with Elena, I stand by 1,000 percent.[3]

We need to stand with Ukraine. We need to be arming Ukraine in the best way we can.

It's a tragic situation. Putin is a tragedy, and the structure of Russia today, its moral structure in terms of its hierarchies of power, is a tragedy. Ukraine is a very complex place—it's not only filled with heroes; there's obviously, like in any place in the world, some bad stuff happening—but **Ukraine is standing heroically for value, and for Western values.**

It's a hard moment. There's this great fear of Putin's nuclear capacity, and I don't think that's a misplaced fear. I think it needs to be taken seriously and responded to seriously—*and* we need to support Ukraine, to stand with Ukraine, to arm Ukraine, and to stand for a righteous conflict.

This is very important. There are still wars that—tragically—need to be fought. There should be no more ground wars. There should be no more cybernetic wars.

> *We should be at the end of war, but we are not there yet. And as long as there are wars, we need armies.*

When I sat with the Dalai Lama in his home in Dharamsala, he and I talked about the notion that there should be a one world army. He said, *it would be absurd to suggest that there should be no army at a time when the Putins of the world have armies.* Of course we need an army, and of course we need to be able to respond to brutality with force. There is absolutely no choice

---

[3] Marc Gafni and Elena Maslova-Levin, *Glory to the Heroes: The First Four Weeks of the Russia Ukraine War: For the Sake of Value and the Arousal of the West Beyond Moral Equivalence* (World Religion and Philosophy, 2023).

about that—it needs to be done. I pray that we come to a time in the world where that won't be necessary, where we won't need any army, where we can, in fact, *beat our swords into plowshares*, in the words of the prophets.

But that day has not yet come.

To adopt a position other than an activist position—to adopt a pacifist position, or a position of moral equivalence in this moment—is a mistake. **Pacifism is one of the worst forms of moral equivalence**, at least from my perspective, and from the Dalai Lama's, and quite a few others. If we had been pacifists during World War Two, we would have had a world controlled by Nazism. We need to say that, and we need to say that clearly and unequivocally. There have been all sorts of writings, which I pointed out at the beginning of the Ukraine war, that make subtle moral equivalences between the Western and Russian positions, which is not the case.

Now, I want to be clear again, and this is critically important.

Of course peace is a value.

I've buried more students than anyone on this call, eighteen-year-olds who died fighting for the preservation of peace. My two sons are commandos in a western army who fight for peace and risk their lives regularly. **The notion that we can just lay down our arms, unilaterally, is absurd and is a violation of** *She*.

It is a violation of the Goddess.

That just needs to be said.

MAKING MORAL EQUIVALENCE IS A TRAGEDY, AND FORMING SUPERFICIAL OPINIONS IS A TRAGEDY

Now, to be clear, that doesn't mean that there are no ulterior agendas.

That doesn't mean that the West has not engaged itself in moral violations that are significant. Just read David Graeber's book *Debt* to look at one of the great moral violations of the West, in terms of how the World Bank has been operating. The World Bank has done an enormous amount of good and an enormous amount of damage, on multiple levels. The entire system and structure of an exponential growth curve, in which a minuscule part of the world uses most of the world's resources, is tragic. That's a given. A world in which a billion people don't have drinking water is tragic.

I will not, in any sense, make a moral equivalence between Israel and Palestine—I know the facts way too well. I actually lived—not in Holland or Germany—in Israel with a beautiful Arab family I was very close with. I lived right next to Qalqilya, one of the four towns in the West Bank. **There is no moral equivalence between the Israeli position and the Palestinian position—it's not true.** Anyone who thinks there *is* simply doesn't know even one fact about what's going on.

Israel has sued for peace again and again and again and again.

Israel is a pluralistic Western democracy, with full rights for men and women, which has empowered its citizenry in an incredible way.

You can walk into Hadassah Hospital at the center of Jerusalem, and you can see Jewish and Arab doctors working side by side, saving and healing anyone. That's why the Hadassah Hospital at the center of Jerusalem was nominated for a Nobel Prize.

If you show me any hospital on the West Bank, where I lived, any hospital anyplace in the world, or certainly any hospital anywhere in the Arab world, where you have Israeli and Arab doctors working side by side, saving Israelis and Arabs in the exact same way, well, then I will step back. But that's not the case. Everyone knows that the only place that that's possible, the only place is in Jerusalem, under a Western democracy, which is called Israel.

To make moral equivalences is a tragedy, and to get your news and to evaluate what's happening based on superficial headlines, is also a tragedy.

Again, that does not mean that there is no corruption in Israel, and that does not mean that the Israeli army hasn't made mistakes. It has. But I've studied the Israeli army very closely. If you've ever read the moral code of the Israeli army, written by Asa Kasher—and I would recommend everyone to read it—it's the most incredible moral code of any army in the world. And my children have described to me their friends shot left and right because of the care that Israel takes in trying its best not to harm civilians—the care that no other army that I'm aware of in the world (having researched this for thirty years) takes. So, I am going to just be careful about moral equivalence.

There is a need, tragically, in the world today, to bear arms.

We cannot unilaterally dismantle our armies.

WHO IS INCLUDED IN MY STORY?

Ukraine is an example of a moral war—with all of the complexities. Therefore, we have to actually engage and stand with the Ukrainians. **The Ukrainians have lost so many men and women and children, in a war that they did not want, in a war that was forced upon them—and they are actually standing for value, with all of the complexity at hand.**

My position on this hasn't changed. I apologize for growing silent on it. I did go silent on it. I was caught up in any number of other existential risks. We need, of course, to stay completely focused, in every way we can, on Ukraine, and at the same time, on the implications of at least ten other tragic spots in the world.

That is not easy—and that's what I want to talk about today.

How do we actually do that, and what does that mean? If I can frame the question, the question is, **who is included in my story?**

Who is included in my story? That's the question.

Are the people included in my story only those people who are in my family?

Or are the people included in my story those people who are in my extended family?

I go to war, appropriately if someone breaks into my house and wants to kill my children; I go to save my children, for sure. Someone breaks into someone else's house—do I go to save those children? Well, no. Why? Because I'm not aware of it.

But what if I *am* aware of it? What if I *can* act?

I really want to go into the depth of this question.

In other words, **what does it mean to place our attention on suffering?**

What does it mean to be a human being, which is this noble, glorious, and privileged experience? To be human in the world, to have the ability to live, feel, and breathe in the world—and to know of suffering:

- And not to be able to engage *all the suffering,*
- And to feel like we are forced to turn away.

What does that mean? What is that experience?

When is it okay to turn away?

Maybe it's never okay to turn away—is it ever okay to turn away?

That's the question we're going to talk about.

HOLD YOUR SPEECH RESPONSIBLY

Chat box (Brad): *Israel's treatment of Palestinians is not a "moral war." It's the same old racism and gradual genocide as is in their tradition.*

I am just going to say to Brad—whoever Brad is, but I certainly love you—I am going to say this very directly, and if you never come back again, it's totally fine. I am just completely honoring you, my friend, but actually, that is absurd, right?

The notion that it's *the same old racism and gradual genocide* is to misunderstand what the word *genocide* means. That it's *the same old racism* is beyond absurd, beyond absurd. My boys are directly involved in it; my daughter is directly involved in it. I lived in Israel, on the West Bank, for twenty years. I walked around unarmed and was deep friends with some of the most wonderful Arab families who are at the center of the West Bank. You would have to know a lot of information, Brad, to make that statement in the chat box. I've spent my life talking to both wonderful Jews and wonderful Arabs, on both sides of the divide.

It is an extremely complex issue. You need to understand how we got here, who the players are—and so you have to be very careful before you say things in the chat box, accusing Israel of gradual genocide. I'd be very careful, my friend. That is an unequivocally false statement, from beginning to end. I say that tenderly, fiercely, gently.

Again, it doesn't mean that Israel is always right; it doesn't mean Israel doesn't make mistakes.

It doesn't mean the United States is always right. The United States makes significant mistakes.

But Israel is a pluralistic Western democracy, animated at its core by pluralistic Western values. That is not the case for any of the twenty-two states that surround Israel, several of which are still committed to its destruction today, and most of which have been committed to its destruction for the last several decades. The ethos that guides the Israeli army and the ethos that guides the surrounding armies are entirely different.

Let's hold that there, and here we go.

We cannot be afraid to make moral statements.

Even when there is complexity, there are moral statements.

There are so many chat boxes in the world where people will lightly accuse Israel of genocide or Ukraine of being a CI outpost that we are blindly defending, making moral equivalences between Putin's army and the Ukrainian army. It's just not true. It's just not true, and we can't—we can't, we can't, we can't, we can't, we can't.

And as I said—very clearly—there are people on both sides. That's what I just said. I just said I am very close friends, personally—not writing in the chat box—with some of the leading Arab families, some of the leading Jewish families. I lived for many, many years in this region of the world. I know it better than I know almost anything else, both directly, personally, both in terms of its history and in terms of its players.

One of the things that the woke world does is that it just makes untrue statements and doesn't actually hold its speech responsibly. We have to be very careful before we throw around words like *genocide*. We have to know a lot of information.

My general policy—and I say this to my kids as well: whenever my kids want to take a position, I say to my kids, *argue the other position*. If you want to take *this* position, argue *the other* position. Argue it powerfully. Read all the opposing positions that completely disagree with what you're saying. **Argue the opposing position well, and if you can do that well, then go back to your position.** See if you still hold it—and if you do, then hold it strongly. I have never ever, in my entire life, read only one side of an issue. I always read very carefully and speak very carefully on both sides and then come to integrate the largest integration we can make. **But there is no way that, in One Mountain, I am ever going to be afraid to make a moral statement.**

There is no way—and Dalai Lama, my dear friend, stands with me in this, as do many other people—that I am ever going to be afraid to say that **pacifism, adopting a pacifist position, for example, in World War Two, or in this Ukraine moment, is not a moral position.**

That is a violation of Outrageous Love.

WE ARE TAKING RESPONSIBILITY IN THIS MOMENT

Outrageous Love never requires—never *allows*—you to demonize, to fully demonize the other. Even when you are obligated to go to war, you have to treat the person you have to go to war with with dignity, if it's a righteous—a sad and tragic but righteous—war.

Every war is tragic. There is no war that's not tragic. Wars are tragic, and we want peace to be the reigning value in the world. We have to do everything we can to end all wars.

And as long as we're still in a place where there is a moral obligation to make a war, which is tragic, we have to do it with Outrageous Love— in how we treat prisoners, how we treat men, women, and children, how we try and hold our relationship to civilian populations, etc. There is an enormous possibility, even in a tragic war, to hold that tragic war with dignity and honor and not to have it reduced to a worse horror than war already is.

All of this just needs to be said.

Chat box (Ineke): *Tears.*

Yes, Ineke. These are holy and broken *Hallelujah*s, which demand tears.

I am just going to give you one more image, and it is a tragic image.

When I came to Israel and worked with people in Qalqilya to create a little village called Tzufim, near a place called Kfar Saba, what happened was that anyone who would work with us, or several of the people who worked with us had people in their family brutally hurt or killed. It happened all over the West Bank: **people who worked on creating educational systems, nurseries, and beautiful programs together, creating this really intensely beautiful Jewish-Arab gorgeousness, often had their children shot in the stomach and left to die by the extreme elements of the West Bank population, who had been morally hijacked by Yasser Arafat's PLO.** And I would go to the homes of my close friends, my close Arab friends, whose children had been killed because they were helping to start a nursery, and we would sit, and we would cry together. So yes, there are tears.

And oh my God, when the United States and Great Britain bombed Germany at the end of World War Two, it was a horror. The bombings were a horror. They were a horror. I mean, **there is nothing other than tears in war.**

What does war mean? People killing each other.

It's a horror from beginning to end. It's beyond tragic.

But *not* to oppose the worst forms of tyranny, Nazism, for example, is an even greater tragedy than war.

And when we go to war, what we are saying is: We are standing not just for the present; we're standing for the future.

When we go to war, when we tragically, horrifically have to go to war—and may there be no more wars—what we are saying is that there is a *covenant between the generations*. And in this covenant between the generations, we are standing for the trillions of unborn people and saying we are taking responsibility in this moment.

This is the moment in which we need to take responsibility. And it's deep, it's deep, it's deep. Had that not happened in World War Two, we would have lived in a completely different world.

Let's feel that, and let's hear that. It's a big deal.

Chat box (Richard): *Sure would like more factual information that says Brad is wrong.*

Let me just suggest to everyone, not a book that's on the right wing of Israel or the left. Take a look, brother, at a bunch of books by Daniel Gordis, a colleague of mine in Israel. That's a very good way to start. Take a look at that; that will give you a deep sense. He's a middle-of-the-road Israeli position. His books are extremely intelligent, insanely well-researched, and offer a deep history of Israel and the conflict. It's probably the single best introduction. He has written a couple of books on it, and they are well worth reading. Again, it's a very intelligent, centrist position. Danny is completely meticulous with facts, so if someone wants to read one book, that's what I would recommend.

EVOLUTIONARY LOVE CODE: THE POSSIBLE HUMAN

If there were two children outside of your home, and you saw them suffering on your front lawn, you would stop everything you were doing to help them. But if the same children are in another part of the world, even if you were aware of their existence and the fact that they are suffering, all too often, the overwhelming majority of human beings go on with business as usual.

To be or not to be, that is the question. It's a question that every human being must ask in this moment of meta-crisis.

- What does it mean to be human?
- What's the nature of our joy as human beings?
- What's the nature of our tears as human beings?
- What are the actions required of us as human beings?
- What are the responsibilities required of us?
- What are the rights required of us as human beings?
- What are the raptures required of us as human beings?

We ask these questions not from a place of shame or a place of brokenness but from a place of wholeness and celebration, from a place of agony but also a place of ecstasy. We stand together in the nobility of our humanity and in the ecstatic urgency of our humanity.

We invoke the possible human, and the possible human is omni-considerate for the sake of the whole. The possible human feels as if the whole of humanity, the whole of Reality, is visible to the naked eye in their front lawn, their front yard.

The possible human feels the truth that the whole includes not only every human being in the present but also every human being in the past and in the future.

The possible human stops business as usual and acts for the liberation of the whole.

The possible human understands that to be is to be *Homo amor*.

YOU CANNOT BE AN OUTRAGEOUS LOVER WITHOUT DOING SENSEMAKING

This code is incredibly important, but we are definitely not going to be able to fully get into it, so we are going to have to pick this up next week. I want to spend another couple of minutes to continue the conversation we have started. I know this was an unexpected topic; I am not quite sure how we got here. But clearly, it was necessary.

I want to also talk about **the broken information ecology.**

If I understood the information based on the broken information ecology that we live in, then I would have come to very complex conclusions—and very different conclusions than those I've come to. **It takes something to penetrate the surface of the information ecology, to actually *gather information*.** The way you have to do that is by not reading the daily news. You cannot get it from *The Guardian*, and you're not going to get it from *The New York Times* or CNN. You are not going to get it from any particular echo bubble.

You have to read more deeply. To be able to get sufficient information takes some work.

I am going to give you an example about Israel, because that's what we were talking about. Israel foils three to four terrorist incidents aimed at civilians *every single day*. Anyone know that? That's actually the gig.

In other words, you have to understand that **in order to gather information, in order to look at anything, you need to understand its context**:

- What caused this to happen?
- What are the things that lay behind it?
- What is it going to cause in the future?
- What is the alternative to not doing it?

And to do that, to gather information on any topic that you want to talk about in public, I would do at least two things. This is just a process, a way to play.

One, read two books on opposing sides of the issue, not the daily news. Get out of your own filter bubble, and read two books. Not *I don't have time*. If you are going to talk about something publicly, and **if you are going to form an opinion about something, you have to become** *Homo amor.*

Homo amor has to be a warrior, and **a warrior needs to be able to do sensemaking**—and to do sensemaking is to become intimate with Reality, so always read at least two books, two serious monographs, that give you opposing sides of an issue, and read them carefully. Start with two; two is a good place to start. If you can do that, you can begin to find your way. You can begin to gather information.

The second suggestion is: **don't have an opinion on** *everything*. It's very hard to have an opinion on everything. There are lots of things going on in the world. Don't form your opinion by reading surface sheens of news. Pick an area where you are going to engage, what you are going to talk about, and where you are going to be engaged in *doing* something about, where you are going to engage it in a serious way—and in *that* area, go *deep*. In that area, go deep, learn, become a master.

I am very concerned with the healthcare crisis in the United States, and there is a lot to say about it. I'm about to start talking about it at some point, but I don't feel I have mastered it. It's a very complex issue, and the notions put forth on most sides of this conversation actually don't take the facts into account. How we can create the best healthcare in the United States is a real issue, and we need to do something. It's a tragic situation—and I am not going to speak about it publicly until I feel I've mastered it, synthesized the information, and can actually suggest a way forward.

That's always what we need to do. **You have to pick where your energy is going to go.** I wouldn't spread it all over the place. I would be a little monogamous here or at least polyamorous with only a couple of issues. Pick an issue or two where you can actually become a master.

Most people are completely lost. The information ecology is utterly disturbing. There are massive propaganda campaigns waged on all sides, and **how you find your way beneath propaganda to actually be able to do sensemaking is critical**.

Just to begin with, pick one or two issues, not more. In other words, have the moral center *not* to have to speak on everything. Pick one or two issues, and then I would read deeply on both sides. And then, if possible, find and speak to people if you can. You can find people through the web, you can talk directly. Speak to people on both sides of the issue.

Pour yourself in.

Pick one issue, and then become somewhat of a master of it, and then add to the conversation in a deep and powerful way. That's part of what it means to be an Outrageous Lover.

You cannot be an Outrageous Lover without doing sensemaking—and sensemaking means integrating and synergizing opposing, deeply felt, intelligent, madly loving, and well-articulated perspectives—and then synergizing them into a larger whole.

It's not pro-life *or* pro-choice—both sides are propagandizing. There is a larger synergistic whole.

HONORING EACH OTHER EVEN IN IMPOSSIBLE SITUATIONS

When we are talking about, for example, Ukraine and Russia, or we're talking about Israel and the Israeli-Arab conflict, it's clear there's a side standing for democracy and Western values, and a side that's not—but **that doesn't mean that the side that's standing for democracy and Western value is perfect or makes all the right policy decisions.**

I am going to just give you guys an example; I'm going to make this very real.

I almost got thrown out of the settlement in which I was a rabbi because there was a post in a paper that was very popular in the communities that I was involved with, and the post was talking about Yossi Sarid, a popular left-wing politician. It basically had a list of Arab terrorists, and because Yossi Sarid had spent his entire life opposing Israeli policy on the West Bank, this newspaper listed Yossi Sarid with a list of Arab terrorists who had committed terrorist acts.

That was a morally heinous act. It was a horrible thing to do—and I wrote and spoke every place I could and said that the people who have just listed Yossi Sarid and demonized him are actually themselves committing an act of terror. That's a violation of Eros, a violation of love, and it seeds the ground for political assassination. We can disagree fiercely with Yossi Sarid but love him dearly, and love his integrity, and love his honesty, and love the fierce, free-spirited debate in a pluralistic democracy.

It was an incredible moment. Yossi Sarid called me, and we became friends. And soon afterwards, Yitzhak Rabin in Israel was assassinated by someone who held their position so strongly they couldn't hear the other position and demonized the other position—which is tragic beyond imagination. It's a big deal.

I'm going to get personal here for a second. I lived in Tzufim, right next to Qalqilya. You literally weren't safe to walk around without a revolver and a machine gun because Arafat's Palestine Liberation Organization, a terror organization, shot people in the stomach, raped people, and closed down educational institutions—it was a complete horror. The Arab population of the West Bank hated them, but they were imposed from without. It's a long story how that happened.

Obviously, everyone walked around armed. I walked around unarmed. I made friends with some wonderful families, including those who didn't want us there. **I said, here is the deal: I am walking around without a gun—stupid thing to do, but that's what I'm doing—and I did.** I did for two years. Many, many, many, many times, **I walked into places where you just didn't have the possibility to walk around without a gun—and I just said, you know what, I am going without a machine gun, kill me, but let's make peace.** I share Brad's sentiment for peace, and I love Brad for expressing it the way he did—but sometimes, there is a tragic necessity for war.

I am going to give you a final example, and with that, I am going to finish.

There are checkpoints in Israel. There is this huge population from the West Bank that travels into what's called Israel's green line, in the political boundaries of Israel before the 1967 War. A huge part of the West Bank works in what's called *Israel proper*. **If there weren't checkpoints, there would be buses of schoolchildren blown up every single day.** That's just true. That's just a simple fact. In other words, if there weren't checkpoints to stop Arabs coming from the West Bank, a minuscule amount of them would cross—**enough to blow up school buses every single day, so there have to be checkpoints, and there have to be searches.**

There is no choice.

However, who is doing the checkpoints and the searches, and how are we doing them?

I made a suggestion on Israeli television that we shouldn't have these untrained, rough units. **We *should* have units that are strong militarily,** but before you search someone in front of their children, you bow, you apologize, and you ask permission. You have juice stands set up, in which you have someone else from the unit who serves juice to the children and honors them.

- If we have to do searches—which we do have to do because otherwise, you will have school buses filled with children blowing up—let's figure out *how* we are going to do searches.

Let's do searches in ways that honor the people that we are forced to search, and don't demean them, and don't demean them in front of their children because imagine what it's like to grow up every day and to see your father searched every single day, what that does to you. And especially if you are searched in a way that's not honoring. So, if we have to do searches at checkpoints in Israel, which we do, then let's do it in a way which actually honors people, which is dignified, which is reverend, which holds the tragedy, which holds the tears. Does everyone feel that?

In other words, **we have to find ways to honor each other, even when we are in impossible situations.**

HOW TO CELEBRATE LIFE AND NOT TURN AWAY FROM SUFFERING?

Let's hold it here for a second, my friends. This was a big and unexpected conversation. We started by honoring Ukraine and honoring the battle in Ukraine. The Israel example came up because it came up in the chat box, and I responded to it, and so we spent some time in Israel.

We talked about war, the complexity of war, and the tragedy of it. We held a real and sacred conversation here in One Mountain, which is what we *should* be doing.

Thank you, everyone, for being here. We are going to end with prayer—and appropriately, the prayer is about the holy and the broken *Hallelujah*.

Because everything we've been talking about here, my friends, is about the holy and the broken *Hallelujah*.

We are going to come back next week. We are going to start with the code, and we are going to talk about what it means to be a new human.

How do we celebrate life, feel suffering, and not turn away?

That's the ultimate question. That's what we need to be talking to each other about.

How do we include more people in our story than just the people we need to survive?

What does it mean to change the very nature of what my story is? How do I evolve my story?

Thank you, everyone, with a tender, broken, and yet ecstatic heart—ecstatic to be with you all, ecstatic to have this conversation, ecstatic to feel each other and honor each other. Please forgive me for any moment that I wasn't clear, and thank you for your forgiveness.

CHAPTER THIRTEEN

FEEL YOU FEELING ME: THE NEW HUMAN AND THE NEW NAME OF GOD

Episode 353 — July 16, 2023

THE MOST EFFECTIVE ALTRUISM IS TELLING A NEW STORY OF VALUE

In this time between worlds, this time between stories, our intention is to participate in responding to the meta-crisis.

Crisis is an evolutionary driver, and each crisis, at its core, is a crisis of intimacy, and a crisis of intimacy means a crisis of relationship.

There are two generator functions of existential and catastrophic risk, as we have identified, together with our beloved Barbara Marx Hubbard: **rivalrous conflict governed by win/lose metrics** is the source code structure of human reality, which leads to the second generator, **the fragility of the systems.**

For example, one of the things that is tragically likely—and we are doing nothing about it—is the intense heat wave in India. There is an intense heat wave around the world, which in a place like India could kill 200 million people in a week. We know that's a genuine possibility, and we are doing nothing about it. Why not? Because it doesn't fit into being able to win in our system of rivalrous conflict, even in India, for any number of reasons I'm not going to go into now, which then generates a fragile system. Then we are going to cry about the tragedy.

Wow, that's intense! So we look away.

We look away, like we look away from Ukraine.

How do we look *towards*? What does it mean to look towards?

To look towards is to become *Homo amor*.

To look towards is to become the new human—and you can only look towards if you can *respond*. If you cannot respond, if you can only *feel* the pain, but you cannot *respond* to the pain, then in the gap between our ability to feel the pain and our ability to heal the pain, we have to close our hearts.

Not because we are narcissistic and egocentric, as many enlightenment teachers—who are all wonderful people, many of them my friends—like to tell us. There is some truth in that, but that's not the core. The core is not that we feel *too little*, it's that we feel *too much*—and if we cannot respond to the pain that we feel so intensely, at some point, we simply have to close our hearts.

In order to open our hearts, we have to be able to respond.

To respond means there's something to feel and **something to do that can directly shift the course of history**. That ability to shift the course of history at this moment, in this time between worlds, in this time between stories, is the most "effective altruism" that we could do. Effective Altruism is what Peter Singer, Will MacAskill, and Toby Ord (all students of Derek Parfit) are talking about. Effective Altruism says, don't just handle the person in front of you, but use reason to understand how you can have the most global effect in alleviating suffering. That's beautiful, and that might result in spending lots of money on mosquito nets, which can save more lives from malaria perhaps than anything else. That's true, and that's good.

However, they are missing the core point (and guys, total respect, love, brothers, but you're missing the point).

> *You cannot do effective altruism without telling a new Story of Value.*

There is a *deeper* effective altruism:

- To shift the course of history
- To raise all boats
- To transform
- To save the future and the most disadvantaged who will be destroyed by catastrophic risk (and all of us by existential risk)

What we actually have to do is tell a new Story of Value because **story and value are the source code of Reality.**

We have to tell a new story but not a *postmodern* story that's made up. No, value is *real*; the Field of Value is *real*, and **the best, most effective Story of Value is *real*—not because we decided it is so, but because it aligns with the evolving values of Cosmos.**

We have to tell a new Story of Value rooted in evolving First Principles and First Values—and that new Story of Value has to be understandable and accessible to every man, woman, and child, in China, Afghanistan, Iceland, New Zealand, South America, South Africa, Australia, all over Europe and the Americas, and in Asia. There can be no place where this story is not easily accessible and easily understood.

THE NEW STORY OF VALUE LIVES IN US

Who am I? I'm not just *Homo sapiens*, I am *Homo amor*. I feel the whole, and the whole lives in me.

- I am *omni-considerate* for the sake of the whole.
- I am *omni-feeling* for the sake of the whole.
- I am *omni-responsible* for the sake of the whole.

Not that I have to do it *all* myself—that's the voice of the egoic mind that shuts us down.

So what do *I* need to do? **I need to respond to the unique needs in my unique circle of intimacy and influence.** That's what is mine to do. That's what it means to play my instrument in the Unique Self Symphony.

This is a core part of the new story:

- Every man, woman, and child is a Unique Self, an irreducibly unique expression of the LoveIntelligence and LoveBeauty of Cosmos.
- We have unique instruments in the Unique Self Symphony, and those are ours to play.
- That's the expression of the *Shakti*—of the Eros that moves irreducibly through me.
- Answering the call of the *Shakti* and committing my unique Outrageous Acts of Love is the plotline not only of my life but of the entire universe awake and alive in me.

Evolution awake and alive in me is desiring my enactment of its own values, which are Eros, intimacy, dignity, integrity, fairness, harmony, and uniqueness. Those values live in me, and I can enact them in the world in a unique way in my unique circle of intimacy and influence, and that is the plotline of my life. As the Bible says, *hot damn*! I think that's from *The Book of Psalms*.

We are here to tell this new story. That's the most effective altruism. That's the seat of this revolution. We are going to talk about that in a new way today, and I want to go deeper into these questions:

- How this new story lives in us
- How we enact this new story
- How we be this new story
- How we become *Homo amor*

EVOLUTIONARY LOVE CODE: INVOKING THE POSSIBLE HUMAN

If there were two children outside of your home, and you saw them suffering on the front lawn, you would stop everything you were doing to help them.

But if the same children are in another part of the world, even if you were aware of their existence and the fact that they are suffering, all too often the overwhelming majority of human beings go on with business as usual.

To be or not to be, that is the question. It's a question that every human being must ask in this moment of meta-crisis.

- What does it mean to be human?
- What's the nature of our joy as human beings?
- What's the nature of our tears as human beings?
- What are the actions required of us as human beings?
- What are the responsibilities required of us as human beings?
- What are the rights required of us as human beings?
- What are the raptures required of us as human beings?

We ask these questions not from a place of shame and not from a place of brokenness but from a place of wholeness and celebration—from a place of agony but also a place of ecstasy.

We stand together in the nobility and ecstatic urgency of our humanity.

And we invoke the possible human. The possible human is omni-considerate for the sake of the whole. The possible human feels the whole of humanity, the whole of Reality.

The possible human feels the truth that the whole includes not only who's visible in their front yard but also every human being in the past and in the future.

The possible human stops business as usual and acts for the liberation of the whole. The possible human understands that to be is to be *Homo amor*.

ANTHRO-ONTOLOGY: HOW DO YOU KNOW WHAT YOU KNOW?

Let's see if we can find our way into this. What does it mean to be *Homo amor*? What does it mean to feel the children in the world who are *not* on my front lawn? In other words, **what does it mean to expand my field of feeling beyond my visual field?**

My visual field is right in front of me—but how do I expand *beyond* my visual field, which is my egocentric field, what's directly available to me, and **experience this feeling of radical desire, care, concern, and love for people I cannot see?**

- I have to find the people who are dislocated *spatially*—they are not near me.
- Then I need to feel the people who are dislocated *temporally*—they are not just currently around the world but are either in the past or in the future.

In responding to existential risk, we must respond:

- **To all past generations**, who have labored mightily for the evolution of consciousness and have passed us the baton, and if we drop it, then all of their work, in some sense, collapses. Yes, what they did has value in and of itself, but it collapses. In other words, we are partners: there is a covenant between the generations.

- **To all of the future generations**. We have to feel the future.

So *how* do we feel?

I am going to go to the core of it. Before we talk about feeling across the globe and then feeling the future, I want to bring it down to the most basic:

- How do I feel that which is right in front of me?
- How do I feel you even when you are in my visual field?
- How do I feel someone else?

I remember I was talking to my beloved brother, Daniel Schmachtenberger, a few years ago. I was formulating for him this notion of allurement as the core structure of Cosmos and what that means. Then a couple years later, I was in an early formulation of the *Tenets of Intimacy*, the twenty-four principles of the Intimate Universe. Daniel and I were really excited about it, and we were going back and forth—and whenever we go back and forth, it's fructifying: there is always a deeper whole, a deeper delight, a deeper exchange that emerges.

Then at a certain point, Daniel said to me something like, *how the fuck do you know this shit?* Meaning, **how do you know this, what's your source?** As Zak always teases me, I never do literature surveys on a topic. Daniel asks, *how do you know?* That question forced me to clarify the principle of Anthro-Ontology: *I know it because it lives in me.*

How do you know what you know?

- *Anthro*: within my own interiors
- *Ontology*: the true nature of the world.

Thus, Anthro-Ontology: **What lives inside of me, when I clarify my interiors, are the plotlines of Cosmos, and the plotlines of Cosmos are its evolving First Principles and First Values.**

THE CORE OF *HOMO AMOR* IS MY CAPACITY TO FEEL YOU

One of the evolving First Principles and First Values of Cosmos is intimacy itself.

There's actually no such thing as *intimacy*—it's **intimacy-value**. Same with Eros. It's not just *Eros*, it's actually *ErosValue*, one word.

What do these values mean?

- *Eros* is the movement of Reality towards a deeper contact. It is the desire of Reality for deeper contact and ever greater wholeness.
- *Intimacy* is the experience of shared identity, which generates and is generated by the mutuality of feeling. We can feel each other; we are in a shared Field of Value and have shared purpose.

I want to deepen this and really understand this deeply. How does *Homo amor* do this?

When Daniel asked me that question, we attempted to deeply clarify this notion of *Anthro-Ontology*: how we know what we know, the mysteries within us, and this notion of First Principles and First Values.

When we go deep inside, First Principles and First Values are everywhere. They are not in some philosophy book—they are everywhere.

I want to take you on a little ride into a deep understanding of how this works.

I'll tell you a story.

I am living here in Vermont, where the Center for World Philosophy and Religion has a house. One of the people who lives at the Center, let's make V his initial, is a big hardy guy, and I'm a little less hardy. In the Vermont winters, it's completely freezing, like 20 degrees below. The windchill factor is like 160 degrees below. Now, cold does not work for me, so I had an enormously difficult first winter here. The cold just froze me. I was sick on and off all through the winter, and I was trying to persuade V and other people connected to the Center, "Let's warm this place up."

"No, it's warm," he said. "We've got *this* heater, we've got *that* heater, it's warm."

"Guys, it's *not* warm. No, it is not warm. I'm telling you, I am freezing."

And they're fantastic, gorgeous people—obviously this is no critique—but I couldn't quite get across that, *Oh my God, I am chilled to the bone.* It was hard.

Then, a couple of weeks ago, V and my beloved partner both say: "Oh my God, it's so hot. I can't work. We have to get air conditioning."

And I am like, *Hot?* I love the heat. I'm working through 90 degrees, 100 degrees—not a problem.

Then I said, "Wow, that's so interesting. So you don't get me. You can't feel *me* feeling my experience of the cold, and I can't feel *you* feeling your experience of the heat."

To truly love each other, I have to feel what you feel like in the heat, even though the heat doesn't affect me at all. And I can *use* that to feel *you*, and how am I going to do that? I've got to do it by feeling how I feel in the cold.

- If I can feel how I feel in the cold, and I can then project that onto you in terms of the heat, so now I can feel you.
- And if you can now feel, wow, you can't work today, you're just dead because of the heat, go to that experience and transpose, and actually feel *me*, and how I feel in the cold.

Once we were able to do that, we were completely motivated to create this huge coherent plan. We had this deeper resonance between us and this deeper intimacy.

We already have a sense of shared identity, but we had deepened our mutuality of pathos, *our ability to feel each other*, and we were able to then resonate with each other—and then able to create coherence, which is a plan: Okay, how do we get the place air conditioning? How do we actually create proper insulation, or whatever we need to create for the winter?

All of a sudden, a shared purpose became much easier because we could actually *feel* each other.

This is a very big deal.

The core of Homo amor is our capacity to feel each other.

Homo amor steps out of her/his own narcissistic predicament and has the capacity to *shift perspectives* and to take the perspective of the other—but not just from a mind perspective, an intellectual perspective, a cognitive perspective (*I can think what you think*).

No, I can *feel* what you feel.

To love you means *I can see what you see*.

It's so deep.

EVER DEEPER LOOPS IN THE MUTUALITY OF FEELING

We have a structure of three levels of evolving love, three levels in the evolution of relationships.

- One level is **role mate**. *I love you* means: I hear your needs, I respond to your needs, and I show up in my role, either as the creator of the home, as the protector, or as the breadwinner. We have roles.
- **Soul mate** means not so much *I need you*, or I see what you need and respond to your need. It's *I see you*. We are looking deeply into each other's eyes.
- But **whole mate**, the third level beyond soul mate, is not just *I see you*, but *I see what you see*. I love what you love. I feel what you feel.

That's the only liberation from loneliness, my friends. The only liberation from loneliness is when we can look into our beloved's eyes—and our beloved might be our close friend, it might be a partner in this great revolution, it might be someone I'm working alongside, my evolutionary community:

- We can feel what they feel.
- We can see what they see.
- We love what they love.

For *Homo amor*, loving happens at the level of whole mate.

I couldn't quite feel you because I am not bothered by the cold, or I couldn't quite feel because I am not bothered by the heat—but through my experience of the heat, I can find your experience of the cold. Or through my experience of the cold, I can find your experience of the heat.

That's what intimacy means.

Here's the intimacy equation again:

> *Intimacy = shared identity, in the context of relative otherness x mutuality of recognition (we recognize each other) x mutuality of pathos (we feel each other) x mutuality of value (we are in the same Field of Value) x mutuality of purpose.*

Let's focus now on just one piece, the mutuality of pathos: we feel each other.

How does that work?

- We feel each other means **I feel you**. I feel you. That's the beginning. I feel you; you feel me. That's the first loop. It's a big deal, that's already huge. I feel you; you feel me. I feel what you feel; you feel what I feel. I can shift perspectives. It's huge!
- It goes deeper. **I feel you *feeling me*.** We are sitting together on the porch, and we are feeling each other. It's genuine intimacy and this depth of conversation. But then, I feel you feeling *me*, and you feel me feeling *you*. That's the second loop, a deeper loop.
- Can we take it a third loop? Let's get a third loop. **I feel you feeling me feeling you.** I feel me feeling you feeling me; you feel me feeling you feeling me. It's an even deeper loop.

I remember talking to Bill Harris many years ago. He said to me, *When I do a meditative practice of awareness, first I'm aware of awareness, then I'm aware of my being aware of awareness, then I'm aware of me being aware of me being aware of awareness.*

In other words, you do these loops of awareness till you get the very deep realization of awareness. In Buddhism, that's how they find the Field of Awareness. But on the inside of awareness, the inside of consciousness is *Ananda*. *Ananda* is bliss-love, Eros, intimacy. **The inside of consciousness is intimacy.**

To be intimate means:

- Level one: I feel you, you feel me.
- Level two: I feel you feeling me; you feel me feeling you.
- Level three: I feel you feeling me feeling you; you feel me feeling you feeling me.

It keeps going to deeper loops, and that's very beautiful.

This is part of what we mean when we say that the human being is an incarnation of the Divine.

THE DIVINE IS THE INFINITE INTIMATE

The Divine is not the God who is *only* transcendent, who is only *other*, who holds all of Reality in her womb. God/Goddess is also *inherent, intimate*.

God/Goddess is *both* infinite and intimate.

- A God/Goddess who is *only* infinite gets lost in the infinity of indifference. She is ultimately indifferent, alienated from Cosmos.
- But a God/Goddess who is *only* imminent, or inherent, or intimate, without this infinite power, gets lost in the infinity of impotence.

The Divine is the Infinite Intimate. That's the new name of God, the new name of Goddess—the Infinite Intimate. In the interior sciences, in every generation, we have to re-approach and participate in the evolution of God, which is the evolution of how She/He lives in us.

Goddess/God is the Infinite Intimate, and the quality of the Infinite Intimate is that He/She feels us.

Isaiah, the great master, writes: *Bekol Tzaratam Lo Tzar*: In every one of your contractions, in all of your brokenness, in all of your pain, I feel your pain.

From Isaiah comes Christ Consciousness. In other words, the Divine says, *I am going to **so** take your perspective that I am going to be crucified on a cross as you.* Wow!

Believe me, I have a massive critique of classical Christianity. And as Crosby, Stills, Nash, and Young sang so many years ago,

> *So many people have died in the name of Christ*
>
> *That I can't believe it all.*

And Voltaire, critiquing Christianity said, "Remember the cruelties," as he began to give voice to the modern enlightenment.

Christianity has many sins, but it also has an originating interior, a profound realization, which is, *the Universe feels* (and Christianity took this realization from the Song of Solomon).

The Universe feels, and the Universe feels intimacy; the Universe feels love. And intimacy means that *I feel you*. It means *I can take your perspective*—so actually, Infinity is not only infinite, but is the Intimate. So Infinity, the Divine, takes my perspective and becomes me. Goddess/God becomes man incarnate, is crucified, has nails driven into him on the cross.

Oh, my Goddess! That's the power of the clarified Christ understanding.

Now stay close, my friends, and we're going to close with this: **Not only does God/Goddess take *my* perspective and become me, but *I* take the perspective of God/Goddess and become God/Goddess. Not only does Goddess feel *my* pain, but I feel *Her* pain.**

What that means is that I need to become so intimate with She that I can feel, in my finitude, Her infinite pain. That's impossible. Meaning, I am so intimate with the Intimate Infinite, so intimate with the Divine, that I cry

Her tears—and remember, the tears of the Divine are not finite, the tears of the Divine are infinite. The pain of the Divine is infinite. God is not only the Infinity of Power; God is also the infinity of pain.

What does it mean to feel it?

To take God's perspective is to be willing to enter into the Inside of the Inside with She, to feel Her pain, and to cry Her tears.

In Solomon's lineage, we call that *litzta'er b'tsar ha Shekhinah*: to participate with the pain of the *Shekhinah*, of *She*, in the broken exile—with all the broken hearts and lepers, with all the broken people, and with all the lonely people.

That's what it means to be *Homo amor*. **Homo amor means: I feel you feel me.**

God/Goddess is part of *Homo amor*.

Homo amor is part of God/Goddess, even as we are held by the Infinite Intimate.

What we have tried to do today was to evoke some of the quality, some of the feeling tone of *Homo amor*.

CHATPER FOURTEEN

FROM HOMO ARMOR TO HOMO AMOR: HEARTBREAK IS A STRUCTURE OF THE INTIMATE UNIVERSE

Episode 354 — July 23, 2023

WE NEED TO EVOLVE THE SYSTEMIC SOURCE CODE IN WHICH WE LIVE

I want to set our intention this week, as we enter into the full depth of this moment:

- The unimaginable joy that lives in this moment
- The play that's right here
- The wisdom that's pregnant in this moment and that wants to be born
- The ecstasy, the subtlety, the caring, the depth, and the preciousness that's in this moment.

We are going to love this moment open. This moment wants to speak to us.

We are also aware of the ways in which this moment is seeded with meta-crisis. We are aware of the ways that all of the risks, which have always existed, have now crossed planetary boundaries. We are aware of the systemic breakdown of our systems, which has the capacity to cause unimaginable suffering and risks—catastrophic risk and even existential risk—to our very existence.

We come together in this moment in which opposites are joined at the hip, in the paradox of this moment. We are poised, literally, between utopia and dystopia, between the most beautiful world that we ever imagined possible and a fundamental degradation of Reality which could lead to the end of humanity, to the death of humanity, or to the death of our humanity as we understand it:

- A human being with free will
- A human being with infinite dignity
- A human being whose needs and whose desires are sacred
- A human being whose heartbreak is held in the bosom of the Infinite
- What a moment, and what a privilege!

We come together every week; this is our 354th week. **Every single week, we come together with the intention of revolution.** In this revolution, we have our thumb inside our fist because we don't want to punch anyone—it's not an aggressive fist, it's a fist that's raised in revolution, that says:

We need to evolve the very systemic source code in which we live.

It is not about challenging some cabal that's running an evil conspiracy; it is about challenging something that's gone errant in the essential unfolding of Reality's basic storyline. The plotlines of Reality have become lost to us. We have stepped out of the Field of Value.

As exterior technologies have grown exponentially, bringing unimaginable dignities in modernity, **those same exterior technologies have been divorced or dissociated from an equal evolution of interior technologies**. We've failed to know how to *engage* the exponential technologies—and how to evaluate, infuse with value, and upload value into these exponential technologies which have given us the power of ancient gods.

We have the power of ancient gods, but we have no new Story of Value equal to our power.

We are in this gap between the explosion of unmoored and dissociated exterior technologies and the failure to articulate a new vision of value of what it means to be a human being, a new answer to the core questions:

- *Who* am I?
- *Where* am I?
- What is really a *value*?
- What needs to *be done*?
- What's my *deepest heart's desire*?
- What's *the nature of desire*?
- What's the nature of who I am and my own deepest self?

Our failure to answer those questions and our *abandonment* of those questions, our relegation of those questions to the whims and caprices of the marketplace (which now, for the first time in the last fifty years, understands itself as being *outside* the Field of Value and is therefore governed only by the success story, win/lose metrics, and the war of all against all) generates *fragility*:

- In intimate one-on-one relationships
- In familial relationships
- In groups and nations
- In all larger wholes

This generates fragile, complicated systems that collapse on themselves when subject to stress. That's existential risk. That's catastrophic risk.

WE LIVE IN AN EVOLVING AND PARTICIPATORY COSMOS

So how do we respond to this?

We have to articulate a new Story of Value, rooted not in capriciousness and not in old values that claim to be eternal and unchanging but in the Field of Value, which is both the *eternal* and *evolving*—a Field of Evolving Value, in which:

- Love is real, and yet love is *ever evolving*.
- Eros is absolutely real, and Eros is always evolving.
- Intimacy is real, and there is an evolution of intimacy.
- Value is real, and Reality itself is the evolution of value.

We participate in the Field of Value, the Field of Eros, the Field of Desire, and the Field of Intimacy, and yet we understand that value, Eros, intimacy, and desire are always evolving—and we participate in that evolution of love.

It is that evolution of love that tells the new Story of Value, which then generates a new ground from which Reality emerges.

> *Reality always emerges from inescapable frameworks, and those frameworks are the Story of Value within which we live.*

When we change and evolve the Story of Value, we begin to generate a new Reality—because the new Reality always *emerges*. It is an expression of the invisible plotlines of the story from within which we live.

Who can feel that? Who can feel where we are?

We are in the revolution. And what's the overwhelming moral imperative of the revolution?

To tell a new Story of Value but not to *declare* it. We have to validate it in the deepest strains of wisdom—ancient, modern, and postmodern wisdom. **We then have to weave all of these realizations together in a new synergistic whole and a wider narrative, a narrative that reflects the validated insights of all the wisdom streams of reality**, a narrative we can tell to any six-year-old or nine-year-old, on any continent in the world, to any socio-economic class, to all races, creeds, and colors. This is a Story of Value, a universal grammar of value, that will unite us and also serve as a context for our diversity.

That is the only response to the meta-crisis—the realization that **there is a Unique Self Symphony in every religion, that every nation is a unique intimacy, a unique instrument in that Symphony, and has a unique gift to give and a unique life to live**. And Unique Self is not my Myers-Briggs test. It's not my separate self formula based on win/lose metrics—Unique Self is my unique expression of the Field of Eros, of the Field of Intimacy, of the Field of Desire.

That's what we are here to do. We're here to tell that new Story of Value—as a revolutionary act, in response to imminent unimaginable suffering. It's an act of *mad love*, as Rumi would say; we love madly.

It's an act of unimaginable love.

It's an act not of ordinary love, some social construct between human beings—but of Outrageous Love, of the Eros that's the heart of existence. It's not mere human sentiment. The human sentiment *expresses* that ground of Outrageous Love or Eros that is the nature of Reality itself.

My friends, are we ready to do this?

Are we ready to play a larger game?

Are we ready to participate?

It's a participatory Cosmos, the physicist John Archibald Wheeler reminded us—and that's true in exteriors as well as interiors. It's true all the way in, all the way out, all the way up, and all the way down. Are we ready to participate in the evolution of love, in telling this new Story of Value?

We are going to go into a new world today, the world we've talked about many times over the last decade, but we're going to re-approach it and open it up in a new way. I have been in an ongoing conversation with Kristina Kincaid about this for the last decade, and we've talked about it together in many public teachings over the last decade. I had a conversation yesterday with a dear deep study partner with whom I had tragically lost touch with for fourteen or fifteen years, and we recently re-established our practice of love and study—Ohad. We have been exchanging about this over the last day, so I want to thank him and his partner Katara for their part in the conversation.

Let us step in, and let's blow this open. Let us love this open all the way.

EVOLUTIONARY LOVE CODE: INTIMACY IS ALWAYS BROKEN AND THEN RECOVERED

> The nature of the Intimate Universe is that intimacy is always broken and that broken intimacy is the intention of the universe.
>
> The deeper intention, however, of the same Intimate Universe is that broken intimacy be recovered and that the recovered intimacy is more profound, more poignant, more potent, more powerful, and more whole than it was before.
>
> The journey of the heart—from intimacy to the breaking of intimacy to its recovery at an ever higher and deeper level—is the evolution of love.
>
> This is the journey that we refer to in CosmoErotic Humanism as the movement from *Homo armor* to *Homo amor*.

Let us find this and feel this: the sense of the intimacy that's broken as part of the structure of the Universe. Does that make sense, everyone?

Part of the structure of the Intimate Universe is that intimacy is broken and lost, and then it's recovered.

Breaking is part of the structure of Reality itself. That's called, in the lineage of Solomon, *shevirat ha-kelim*, the breaking of the vessels.

Cosmos lives in me: the personal is the cosmic, and the cosmic is the personal. This realization—

- That we live in a participatory Universe
- That I participate in the current of cosmic Reality
- That the current of evolutionary Reality, the current of Eros, which animates all of Reality, lives *through me*—

—means that all the events that form Reality happen in me: the Big Bang happens in me, and supernovas explode me, in some deep and real sense.

When the lineage of Solomon talks about *the breaking of the vessels*, or other lineages talk about *the Fall*, or we talk about *the exile from Eden*, **we talk about a *breaking*, a separation of Heaven and Earth—that takes place, in some sense, very deeply *inside of me*.**

I want to talk about this part of intimacy that is unavoidable: the *breaking* of intimacy, which is the breaking of the heart.

Without this, we cannot talk about the One Heart of Cosmos, the Field of Eros, which is Reality itself. We have talked about its scientific grounding, time and again. *The CosmoErotic Universe, the Sensual Cosmos, the Amorous Cosmos, the Intimate Universe*—there are many names we use to describe this realization, and it emerges from the closest reading of the *exterior* sciences but also through the closest reading of the *interior* sciences.

We realize that:

- Reality is driven by **allurement and autonomy, attraction and repulsion, autonomy and communion.**
- Reality is, quite literally, filled with appetite, filled with desire.

HEARTBREAK IS A STRUCTURE OF THE INTIMATE UNIVERSE

Reality is Eros, moving towards *ever deeper* contact and ever greater wholeness. That's the structure and nature of Reality, and in that movement towards wholeness, **there is an inevitable structure, and that inevitable structure is heartbreak—the breaking of the vessels.**

HEARTBREAK IS THE NATURAL STATE OF AN ALIVE HUMAN BEING

Let us start with the baby.

In the interior sciences of Hasidism (which is this movement that swept Eastern Europe from about 1760 until World War Two), there is a teaching from Isaac of Vorki, who says **you can learn three things from a child**. And my friend, Ohad, whom I mentioned earlier, likes to cite this text. I am going to cite it a little differently than the way Isaac of Vorki says it, but this is his basic intention:

1. You learn *play* from a baby. It's not quite natural *joy*; it's *play*. **The baby *plays*. The baby is *Homo ludens*, the playing human being.** The sense of dance of joy and play for its own sake is natural to a baby.
2. As soon as a baby has a fundamental need, the baby cries. **The baby is deeply in touch with her need, and that need evokes tears.** She doesn't disown her need, and she responds.
3. **The baby is always open; the baby doesn't close.** That openness expresses itself in **curiosity**, and curiosity is a quality of loving. *Curious* means I am open, and when I'm open, I take in new realities. By taking in those new realities—by ingesting, by sometimes literally swallowing those new realities with radical curiosity—I become *more*. That's what it means to love. *To love* means I am curious about you, and by being curious about you, I take you in, I love you up, and then by loving you up, you love me open. **The baby is open and curious, so the baby is always transforming.** The baby

is always becoming more, the baby never hits a place of being static, of being shut down and stagnant.

Now, let's go a little deeper. That's the *idealized* baby. Hasidism, in its great beauty, didn't quite anticipate attachment theory, which has developed in the last 100 years, and points out that **this moment of the baby is a fleeting moment.** It's an ephemeral moment, and the baby quickly begins to experience a lack of attunement, a lack of alignment between herself and mother and father—and mother and father (or caretaker) represent, for the baby, the entire world.

- The baby begins to *feel* this lack of attunement.
- The baby begins to feel an experience of **their needs *not* being responded to, their tears not quite being seen, their cries not quite being heard.**
- The baby begins to have an experience, as Winnicott says, of **being humiliated in getting her basic needs met.**

The baby moves away from this original idealized, *pre-tragic* state of wondrous bliss where the baby cries, and immediately those needs are met, where the baby is in the state of play and also open and curious. **The baby immediately encounters *the other*, and as soon as the baby encounters the other—the mother—there is a Garden of Eden moment, and then there's an exile from the garden**—the shock of individuation, the shock of the realization that I am another and that ultimately, even mother is not always fully attuned to me. The baby experiences humiliation in getting her basic needs met.

Martha Nussbaum—Martha, I was madly in love with you twenty years ago, for your writing and your depth and the beauty of your work—wrote an important book called *The Language of Emotions*, where she gathers the attachment theory research and some important pieces of writing, and really understands this notion of humiliation in getting our basic needs met.

What begins to happen is: **I stop crying because I stop actually *feeling* what I need.**

- There is this experience of the baby, where the baby experiences need, the baby cries, and the need is responded to. That's the ideal state: **the heart desires, the heart needs, the heart cries out to have the need met, and there is joy because the need is fulfilled.** That's level one, that's the *pre-tragic* level.
- Then the baby—and the human being—enters *the tragic*, where my needs aren't heard, where **I am humiliated in getting my basic needs met. I begin to *dissociate* from my needs, and I begin to become *alienated* from my needs.** I cannot find the depth of my needs. Now we've entered into the tragic.

When I'm split off from my needs, I cannot cry, and when I lose access to my tears—to my ability to cry out in need, which is the natural human experience of longing, the natural human experience of desire—**my heart breaks with desire.** That heartbreak is not a degraded state, not an unenlightened state. It's not a depressed state. It's not a clinically pathological state. **It's the natural state of an alive human being.**

What the interior sciences of Hasidism are pointing to is this *pre-tragic* state of the idealized baby who has the experience of natural wholeness of heartbreak—and **the natural wholeness of heartbreak expresses itself in tears.**

PRAYER AFFIRMS THE DIGNITY OF PERSONAL NEED

This realization is about **the dignity of need**. The baby understands, in the pre-tragic state, the dignity of need.

The adult who understands the dignity of need, is the one who models, in the Solomon tradition, *prayer*.

There is a woman in the Book of Samuel named Hannah, who has this deep and profound desire to bear a child, to be the mother. It is a primal need—not of every human being and not of every woman, but of many women—and of many men to be the father.

Again, it's not all men, not all women; there are some men and women who have other deep, profound expressions of need for creation that don't express in the desire for physical children. But for a huge swath of humanity, the need for a child *is* a need, and we recognize its dignity.

- It's a selfless need.
- It's a need that's about self-fulfillment but requires sacrifice.
- In that sense, it's selfless for a moment.
- It's a bracketing of self to be in devotion to the emergence of life.
- It's a very powerful need.

This Hannah enters the Temple, *bacho tivkeh*, and she cries. Her tears are seen in the Solomon tradition as the *locus classicus* of prayer—because **prayer is about turning to the depths of Reality, to the Infinite Intimate, to the Infinity of Intimacy, and bringing the full depth of our desire and need, the fullness of their dignity, to the table.**

It's about claiming the dignity of need. As we often say:

Prayer affirms the dignity of personal need.

Hannah, in her tears, becomes the model of prayer because she is deeply connected to a particular recognizable need, which is not a *pseudo*-need. It's a true, profound, and deeply erotic human need.

The capacity to affirm the dignity of personal need is the place where we begin to reclaim our own dignity and our own divinity.

YOUR NEED IS MY ALLUREMENT

As many of you know, when we did a seminar several years ago, we talked about the notion that a person has a *pain threshold* and a *pleasure threshold*. There's a place past which we are not able to feel our own heartbreak and past which we are not able to feel our own pleasure. There is this limitation, this cap. **We don't allow ourselves to feel the depth of our need**:

- Whether it's the depth of our need which is expressed in heartbreak
- Or the depths of our need for pleasure, for the full Eros and aliveness of Reality

We split off from our needs, and we *refuse to feel*. As we said it then, **I refuse to feel my feelings to completion**. I *cut off* the need. I *dissociate* from the need.

I'm in *the tragic*. I'm the traumatized baby. I'm the alienated baby. We are all, in some sense, the traumatized baby—not because that's an accident of Cosmos, and not because we were abused by our parents. **In order to *individuate*, we must feel the gap between us and our caretaker**:

- We have to *feel* our individuated needs.
- We have to be able to *recognize* them.
- We have to claim their *dignity* and *divinity*.
- We have to rest in them, letting them be *in us* and us *in them*.
- We have to *not* have them assuaged immediately and *not* have them immediately responded to.

The baby has a fleeting experience of heartbreak—and then:

- In an idealized baby reality, those needs are immediately met.
- In the more real, true reality of the baby, those needs *aren't* met.

Then as the baby begins to individuate, **the baby begins to find herself identifying with her own longing, with her own yearning, with her own need**. And then the baby can go one of two ways (and when I say *the baby*, I mean the emerging human being).

The general way we go is: we split off from our needs because it's too painful to stay in the heartbreak. That's generally a huge swath of life for many years. We realize our needs aren't being met, so we split them off, we dissociate from them, we alienate from them.

That's the first part of the path.

We become non-intimate with our own Eros.

We become non-intimate with our own needs.

The process of **recovering of Self** is:

- To recover a relationship with my own needs
- To recover the experience of the dignity of my needs
- To heal the experience of being humiliated in getting my basic needs met by encountering a reality in which my needs *are* reimbursed

I *always* do this through the beloved.

It's the beloved that I encounter later in life.

That beloved might be a dear friend, it might be a teacher, it might be a sensual beloved, it might be a creative partner, it might be a depth of *philia*, a profound love between two friends of a completely non-sensual nature—but it always happens in a **place where my needs are recognized, where:**

- I can bring *my pain* to the table.
- I can bring *my heartbreak* to the table.
- I can *own* the depth of my heartbreak.

TO LIVE IN THE DEPTH OF MY HEARTBREAK

When I own the depth of my heartbreak, my heartbreak ceases to be a source of depression or clinical pathology and becomes instead a part of my aliveness. For the first time, I have recognized my needs, I have owned the dignity of my needs, and I have been able to recognize their true nature.

I've been able to access *my deepest heart's desires*—not my surface desires that I invented in order to cover over the emptiness—and I can go back and access them. Those original deepest heart's desires are always unique. **There is no generic desire, and there is no generic heartbreak.** Does everyone get that?

In other words, I have a unique heartbreak. My heartbreak is unique, my desire is unique, and my needs are unique. There are certain shared needs that we all have, shared general desires, but we all have unique scripts of desire and unique qualities to our needs.

> *To be able to own and live in the fullness of my Unique Self is to live in the uniqueness of my heartbreak.*

No two heartbreaks are the same. No two deepest heart's desires are exactly the same.

To heal, to recover my wholeness, **I need to be able to recover my capacity to be in the depth of my need, to be in the depth of my heartbreak, to be in the depth of my unique desire.**

And once I'm in that unique need, desire, and heartbreak, I can begin to *meet* that need. Once the need has been recognized, it's on the table, I can begin to meet it. I can find my beloveds; I can find my circle of intimates, who bear witness, who are *listening* to the depth of my unique desire.

And they say to me, *your need is my allurement.*

- The way that you want to be touched, I want to touch you.
- The way you want to be held, I want to hold you.
- The way you want to be aroused, I want to arouse you.
- The way you want to be desired, I want to desire you.

Can everyone feel that? That's *your need is my allurement*.

I want to say it again; I want to get this.

- The way you want to be touched, I want to touch you.
- The way you want to be held, I want to hold you.
- The way you want to be seen, I see you.
- The way you want to be smelled, I smell you.
- The way you want to be felt, I feel you.
- The way you want to be pleasured, I'll pleasure you.

That's *your need is my allurement*.

Then, there's **this capacity to have my needs met by being able to live in the heartbreak**, to reclaim the original capacity of the baby.

THE EVOLUTION OF TEARS

But I don't go back to being a baby because the baby is *pre-tragic*; the baby is totally self-involved. The baby is not actually an ideal. **The baby is a *symbolic* ideal, but the baby cannot feel the fullness and depth of *other*.** The baby is identified with mother, and just for a fleeting moment, feels the mother holding, and then in the next moment, the mother becomes an alienated other who doesn't feel her full need—and then the baby feels the fundamental breakdown of attunement, and the beginning of early pain:

- The pain of disorganized attachment
- The pain of insecure attachment
- The pain of broken attachment

HEARTBREAK IS A STRUCTURE OF THE INTIMATE UNIVERSE

Very few people have what's called *secure attachment*, which is a formal term. Most people experience some sort of fundamental lack of attunement, in which they are humiliated in getting their needs met.

But that baby is not attuned to the mother either. **That baby is lost in the baby's own very narrow circle of intimacy.** Intimacy, fundamentally, with *self*. The baby cannot feel the world. The baby goes through his or her own process of growing up, and that growing up involves:

- Expanding her circle of feeling
- Expanding her circle of attunement
- Expanding the pain of being dissociated and alienated from core needs

This happens until, later in life, we are able to meet the beloved, in all of her disguises, all of his disguises—and again, not just the sensual beloved—who actually turns to me and says, *your need is my allurement*. Then the dignity of need is recovered.

Can you feel that now?

Let's go even deeper. When I recover the dignity of my needs and the dignity of my heartbreak, and I recover my tears, and I find myself again in the eyes of the beloved who witnesses me, who hears me, who attunes to me and says, *Your need is my allurement. I am allured to meet your need. Let me be your woman. Let me be your man. Let me be your beloved.*

That's just the beginning.

The process of growing up, the process of becoming awake and alive, the process of going from *Homo sapiens*, the wise one, or *Homo ludens*, the playing one, to *Homo amens*, the loving one (what we call *Homo amor*) is the evolution of my *heart*:

- The evolution of my *heartbreak*,
- The evolution of my *tears*,
- The evolution of my *capacity to feel*.

The baby's tears begin as the tears of just the baby.

Then, as the baby's heart expands and evolves, the baby begins to actually *feel* the mother. The baby is attuned to the mother and feels the mother's tears.

The baby then deepens and begins to feel *the family system*, and the baby feels the joy, the goodness, the aliveness, the tears, the brokenness, and the pain—all of the nooks and crevices in the family system. The baby *feels*. **In his or her egocentric circle of intimacy, the baby *feels*.** And the baby has this intense desire:

- Not only to heal *her own* pain
- Not only to hold *her own* heartbreak
- But to hold *her mother's* heartbreak, to hold *her father's* heartbreak

Who here knows the intense desire we have—to hold our father's and our mother's tears, and our brother's and our sister's tears? Who knows this?

There is an *evolution* of tears.

There is this evolution, this heartbreak that I begin to hold, which is not *just* my own.

And then, when I go deeper, I move from this first song—this *egocentric* song—and there is **this expansion of my circle of intimacy, which is the expansion of my heartbreak and the expansion of my commitment to love** because heartbreak and commitment to love come together.

All of a sudden, I begin to feel *even more*. I begin to feel a wider group *beyond* my immediate survival family, my immediate family through which I thrive and which holds me directly. **I begin to feel this larger tribe with whom I share a story.**

Of course there are tragic expressions of this; of course there's pathological ethnocentrism. But there's also *the beauty* of the tribe. This is my tribe, these are my people:

- And I feel their pain.
- And I feel their joy.
- And my heartbreak is for the heartbreak of the entire tribe.
- And my heart breaks with the heartbreak of the tribe.

Sometimes I am even so committed to the tribe, to its value and its perpetuation, that I live my life for the tribe, and sometimes I even give up my life for the tribe.

And yes, I understand that that has a pathological manifestation. But I am not talking about the pathological manifestation. I'm talking about its *holy* manifestation, where I can feel the larger tribe.

When we don't have a place to feel that, we go to a sports event, to a huge stadium, and we cheer for a team because **we have a fundamental need to feel this larger field, this larger field in which we can play together, in which we can feel each other**. That's one of the sacred functions of a sporting event. It's supposed to point us to *real* ethnocentric intimacy, to real intimacy with the tribe, but it often serves as a form of *pseudo-eros*, instead of opening up the real and wider Eros, which is our wider joy and our wider heartbreak.

That's the evolution of tears.

FROM *HOMO SAPIENS* TO *HOMO AMOR*

The evolution of tears is:

- First, the baby has moved from *my* tears to the tears of *mother* and to the tears of *egocentric intimacy*, those of people in my immediate personal family.
- Then there is an evolution of tears, and I feel the tears of *the tribe*.
- Then I realize that **the tribe is too small**; it's not big enough. The tribe has too much pathology in it. It's too much *us* and

them and the pathologies of ethnocentrism. I realize I cannot just be in *one* tribe. My heart bursts, and I realize that I'm a Chinese child, and I'm a Japanese mother, and I'm a Hindu, and I'm a Jew, and I'm a Muslim, and I'm an atheist, and I live in North America and South America, and I'm an Aborigine.

I live every place. I have always lived, and I am in every face, and I am in every person, and I *participate*. I begin to feel, in my body, heart, mind:

- Both the joy of every human being that ever breathed and lived, past, present, and future
- And the pain and the heartbreak of every human being that ever was, is, and will be

We are the people. We are the people we've been waiting for, and we're *all* the people. **All the people live in us, and we live in all the people.**

All of a sudden, I have moved: there's been an evolution of tears—and I cannot actually sit in my home and eat comfortably when I know that there are so many hungry people. I feel all the hungry people, and I feel all the lonely people—and I can't shut off from them anymore, and I cannot turn away. *Ni punei*, my face opens, and *face* means to *turn* (*panim*, to turn towards). I turn towards, I am *panim el panim*, face-to-face, and no one is outside of the circle. **I feel the heartbreak of the whole story, and I feel the joy of the whole story.**

At this point, I begin to move from *Homo sapiens* to *Homo amor*.

My armor begins to break, in many stages:

- My armor breaks in the beginning. The baby develops armor when needs aren't met, and so the baby then breaks open that armor—and begins to feel her heart again (when I say *the baby*, I mean *as the baby grows up, as the child grows up*).
- The armor that encases and shuts down the heart is broken

open in the eyes of the beloved, who meets my needs, who says, *your need is my allurement*. And as we play together, as we play in sensuality, and we play in the sensuality of the heart, the wetness of the mind, and in the throbbing of feeling each other, so that armor is broken.

That armor is broken because there's a deeper Eros, a love deeper than ordinary love. When we break the armor open, it's because we have actually *moved*; we've begun to move from *Homo armor* to *Homo amor*. We can access this deeper love that doesn't get shut down, the love that's always available.

There is a part of us that's always innocent.

There is a part of us that is the One Heart that always lives under the armor, that's always there:

- No matter how far we feel we have fallen
- No matter how shut down we become
- No matter how deadened our Field of Desire is

There is a deeper desire. There is a one desire, there is a One Heart, there is a One Love that's always available.

That's what we call Outrageous Love, that's *Homo amor*.

FROM HOMO ARMOR TO HOMO AMOR

Even when we start with the baby, when we close down the heart, the heart becomes armored, and we want to break that armor open. This is what Wilhelm Reich called *de-armoring* and what Kristina Kincaid has done for the last twenty-five years in her deep work. When Kristina and I came together, we talked about **moving from *Homo armor* to *Homo amor*.**

It means **I access the Outrageous Love that breaks my heart open and allows me to find the beloved.** We cannot find each other in *ordinary love*—because that gets armored, it gets shut down. But when we access the current of Eros, which is the current of love, the CosmoErotic Universe, and we feel it *living alive* in us, and we realize we *participate* in that Field of Eros and Desire, then we *break open*. Then the baby becomes alive and feels the mother and the family in a new way.

And then I feel the tribe: the same armor is broken open, and I can feel my whole tribe, I can feel my people, and **I move, at the ethnocentric level, from *Homo armor* to *Homo amor*.**

In most Western democratic countries, there is no sense of genuine identification with the tribe: we are *armored*, closed in, locked in a broken egocentric self. And in many other countries, there is this false and deluded sense of the tribe, which is fascist, totalitarian, and tragic. So, there's either a regressive, pathological identification with the heart of the tribe or a shutdown heart that cannot feel the tribe.

Instead, I have to be able to find the current of Outrageous Love, and realize that:

- My tribe is actually good and true.
- Reality intended this tribe.
- This tribe needs me.
- Being in devotion to the tribe is unimaginably beautiful.

Then I move to *worldcentric*, and again, **I cannot hold the world in my heart with ordinary love**. I cannot hold the world in my heart with love which is a social construct and an expression of a reductive materialist random universe that has no meaning. This is not the nature of the universe. Love is not merely an epiphenomenon of evolutionary psychological drives.

Love is the heart of existence itself. That is Outrageous Love.

To hold the whole world in my heart, to feel the whole thing, I have to access that One Heart—the One Heart that lives and pulses in *me* uniquely, the One Heart that pulses in *you* uniquely, which allows you to wrap your arms around every human being:

- Around every human being alive today,
- And she then picks up the baton from every human being that ever lived,
- And she hears the cries of the unborn of every human being that'll ever be.

I am in this worldcentric consciousness, the song of the world, of every human being, and I feel the pain and joy of every human being. My heartbreak has expanded, and it has become virtually unimaginable.

But I cannot hold it with a small heart—I can only hold it with the One Heart, with Outrageous Love as *Homo amor*.

And then my heart expands even more, and I feel every lamb, every blade of grass, every cow, every cat and every mouse, and every rodent, and every insect, and I feel the entire cacophony of the living universe. I feel the current of life and its feeling, will, and fundamental will.

Stuart Kauffman pointed out, correctly, that there is *will* all through Reality. Biology is not computation. As my friend Perry Marshall wrote in a beautiful academic article, **biology transcends computation**. It's immeasurable. It's the quality of the living Universe, the aliveness of the All, and so I feel the pain of Reality.

- I feel the pain of the seas that are being destroyed and the fish extracted, and I feel the dead zones in the ocean.
- I feel the desertification.
- I feel the extraction of resources, their degradation, and their depletion.
- I feel the planetary boundaries being crossed.

I am madly in love with Reality. It's not that I am just worried about my own survival. My love of the biosphere is not: *Oh my God, I'm not going to survive.*

Rather, it's: *I am madly in love with the biosphere.*

I am allured. I am not just worldcentric at this point. **My heartbreak has exploded just like my joy has exploded, and my heartbreak embraces the whole thing—because my heartbreak is my aliveness, longing, and yearning.**

THE EVOLUTION OF HEARTBREAK IS THE EVOLUTION OF INTIMACY

At each one of these levels, **my heartbreak allows me to recognize the depth of my desire**:

- My *personal* desire
- My desire for *my circle of egocentric intimacy*, which means my egocentric heartbreak and my egocentric joy, and my personal circle
- My *ethnocentric*, tribal heartbreak and my tribal joy
- My *worldcentric*—meaning every human being—heartbreak and joy
- My *cosmocentric* heartbreak and joy—meaning every animal, every living being, the inherent aliveness of the self-organizing Universe. Even at the level of matter, which is filled with will and moves from mud to Mozart, from bacteria to Bach, and from dirt to the most devastatingly beautiful sonnets of Shakespeare.

Once I *feel*, I feel *the need*, the evolution of need.

I first feel my need, then I feel the need of the tribe, then I feel the need of the world, every human being, and then I feel the need of the Cosmos, and I experience the *dignity* of need—that need is a *value*.

It's not just the need of all of planet Earth. It's the need of all of the galaxies because otherwise planet Earth is going to become ethnocentric as life appears in Cosmos in other places (it will and already has). **When we begin to make contact and live in an intergalactic world, we have to realize that**

value is not grounded in planet Earth. It's grounded in Cosmos itself, and we are all children of the Cosmos, and value is cosmic value. When I feel the need of the Cosmos, then I become intimate with the Cosmos.

We become intimate through our shared needs.

We become intimate through our shared desires.

What are intimate relations at the sexual level? This titillating, alive, living desire to touch each other. As we feel each other's desire, we become intimate. As we feel the primal-ness of each other's needs, we become intimate.

But the sexual *models* the erotic. We become intimate not just by feeling the beauty of each other's gorgeous and stunning sensual needs. We become intimate by feeling each other's primal needs:

- For food and nourishment
- For being held
- For creativity
- To be recognized
- To be desired
- To be needed
- To be chosen
- To be held.

In other words, when we meet and feel each other's needs, we become intimate. When we meet and feel each other's desires, we become intimate with each other.

By being willing to expand the circle of our heartbreak, the evolution of heartbreak is the evolution of need, which is the evolution of intimacy, which is the evolution of desire, which is where we began.

- That's what it means to wake up.
- That's what it means to open up.
- That's what it means to become an enlightened or enlightening being.

An enlightened being means: I embrace it all, and even when I fall out, I fall back in, and I am constantly turning towards, and I am constantly wanting to be face-to-face, and I am willing to feel.

I am willing to feel.

I AM WILLING TO *FEEL* EVEN WHAT I CANNOT ENTIRELY *HEAL*

Now I want to go the last step, and say: **I am willing to *feel* even what I cannot entirely *heal*.**

We close our hearts to heartbreak when we experience the gap between our ability to *feel* the pain of it all and to *heal* the pain of it all.

The first step is, as we have said many times, I realize I cannot heal the pain of it all, so I turn to my unique circle of intimacy and influence and say, *what are the unique Outrageous Acts of Love that are mine to do?* I go from being powerless to powerful again because I realize that I can turn to my unique circle of intimacy and influence, and I can heal. **I close the gap between my ability to feel and heal.**

That's so deep, and we've gone so deep into this over the last decade.

But let's go even deeper now:

> *I also have to be willing to stay in the heartbreak when I'm at the edge of the mystery, and I don't know how to heal it.*

Even when I don't know how to heal it, even when there's this inconsolable longing, when there's a yearning I don't know how to fulfill, when there's a need that I can't meet. I don't close myself down to the need. **I'm willing to *stay* in the need.**

I am willing to feel.

I am willing to feel the pain even of God/Goddess.

I am willing to feel the infinity of the divine tears.

I am willing to feel so deep and so wide:

- Even though I don't know exactly which way is forward sometimes
- Even though I feel paralyzed
- Even though I feel sometimes impotent and helpless

I don't abandon the potency of my feeling. I don't shut my heart. I'm willing to feel my longing, my heartbreak, even when it's inconsolable. **I stay in that heartbreak; I stay in that feeling.**

I don't feel it through to *completion*—I cannot feel it through to completion because sometimes the heartbreak is nearly infinite.

- There is no completing the heartbreak of the Rwandan mothers who saw their children destroyed before them.
- There is no completing the heartbreak of the gas chambers.
- There is no completing the heartbreak of the deaths of child soldiers in the Congo.

But I don't turn away. I participate in the pain of Reality because I can't *not*, because I feel it all. Because it's all part of who I am.

In holding that pain, something is broken open in me—because heartbreak doesn't close my heart, it breaks my heart open. And when my heart breaks open, my heart breaks open not to ordinary love—ordinary love can't touch any of this.

I break open to Outrageous Love, to the Eros that moves Reality itself.

That Eros is creative—and in that creative Eros, a new possibility emerges. The entire energy of evolution moves through me. New emergence becomes possible, new visions become possible, and I begin to imagine a new Reality. But I don't turn away. I never turn away from feeling, from feeling as much joy and as much heartbreak as my heart can hold.

Now, friends, I cannot feel that all day. I cannot feel it every second. I wouldn't be able to function. I'd be paralyzed. But I need to **set aside some time every day, at least once a day, where I'm willing to feel the pain of the Goddess in exile, of the broken hearts and the broken vessels**. Part of my daily practice is:

- I feel all of the joy, and I celebrate.
- I feel all the pain and all the heartbreak.

And I never close. I never close. Can you feel that?

Wow. The Master from the town of Vitebsk, Menachem Mendel, who was my teacher's teacher, said: *The baby cries, and the old wise master cries. But they are completely different—their tears are completely different.* This is because **life is the evolution of tears**.

It's the willingness to open my heart, in tears of joy and tears of heartbreak.

It's the willingness to open my heart to more and more, to feel more and more.

Part of the Intimate Universe is heartbreak.

- Atoms come together—and then they can be tragically split, and unimaginable destruction emerges.
- There's allurement in all its beauty—and then there's the fusion of totalitarianism.
- There's holy autonomy, and there is the alienation of the reductive materialist marketplace lost in a narrow and pathetic success story.

We've got to go deeper. We have to become the feeling of Reality itself— because that's who we already are. It's the only place we feel whole. We have the capacity, at least for a few minutes a day, to feel it all, all of the joy and all the heartbreak. In that, we participate in the true nature of who we are—and from there, we can do anything. There, everything's possible.

We ourselves become, literally, the Possibility of Possibility.

PART TWO: FROM HEARTBREAK TO DESIRE TO NEED TO VALUE

WE NEED TO MOVE FROM THE FIRST INNOCENCE TO THE SECOND INNOCENCE.

I want to now do a deeper dive, to try and pick up a couple of things that we didn't fully get to today, while still talking about *heartbreak*.

We talked about this realization that one of the qualities of a baby is that a baby knows *how to cry*. A baby knows how to cry because a baby is connected to her own needs. Early on, the baby doesn't have any sense of their *needs being shamed*.

There's an original relationship to need that is sacred:

- The baby experiences a need.
- That need is a desire, and that desire is then not met.
- There is a sense of desire not met, and the baby cries.

There's a *direct movement* between need, desire, the desire not being met, and tears. That's the original wholeness of the baby.

But of course, you cannot really look at the baby as a *complete* wholeness, or a *full* wholeness—a wholeness that's a model for us because the baby is essentially merged with the mother. **The baby doesn't have a fully (or even vaguely) articulated deep sense of empathy for the other.** It's just a proto-sense of the mother.

- The baby doesn't have a fully developed consciousness.
- The baby doesn't have an individuated ego self.
- The baby is not torn between conflicting desires, at least not rational conflicting desires or conscious clashes between right and wrong.
- The baby does not have a sense of compassion.

I wouldn't associate the word *compassion* with the baby. We wouldn't even really associate a highly developed sense of *love*. The baby has an allurement to, an attraction towards, a proto-sense of love—obviously more developed than an atom, but still very elemental, very primary.

People always hold the baby up as the model of enlightenment, but the baby is not the model of enlightenment. That's very important. The baby is cute, beautiful, primal, original, but not *good*. The baby hasn't yet *gotten* to goodness.

The Hasidic story of what we learn from a baby—that as soon as they need, they cry—is very a beautiful, poetic image, and it's even *more*: the baby is holding out a vision of possibility.

The idea is to get back to that innocence of the baby as *the second innocence*. The baby is a *pre-tragic first innocence*, a first simplicity.

- You then have to go through the guilt.
- You have to go through the complexity.
- You have to go through *the tragic*.

Then you have to get to second innocence. You have to get to *post-tragic*. You have to get to *second simplicity*. That's where we want to go. I want to come back and have that original capacity to cry when my need isn't met and my desire isn't met, but in a way that's post-tragic, so that I don't lose access to the essential goodness of my need, and I'm able to cry—not tears of depression, but **I'm able to experience a heartbreak when my need isn't met**.

What happens in the tragic when the baby doesn't experience their needs as being met? The Hasidic story paints this idyllic idealized image of the baby, but the actual experience of the baby is that the baby very quickly moves through the tragedy of disorganized attachment, of insecure attachment, of this alienation from the mother, of not feeling attuned, of not feeling their needs are being met. That's the experience of the tragic. And, of course, that remains with the baby.

Now, I am talking about the baby not as an actual *baby*, but as the baby grows up and becomes a toddler, a preschooler, a young child, and a little older, they start to experience the tragic—**my needs are alienated, I split my needs off.** My needs are *shamed*—this is where shame comes in. I experienced shame in trying to get my needs met.

The vision is to reclaim second innocence, to enter the post-tragic.

EMBRACING THE HEARTBREAK

If I reclaim, at second innocence, the innocence of the baby, and restore a fundamental relationship to the dignity and goodness of my need, then I can *embrace* my heartbreak.

- I don't need to *deny* my heartbreak.
- I don't need to *refuse* to suffer heartbreak.
- I can actually *suffer* heartbreak. I can suffer the heartbreak of a need not being met, and I can suffer my heartbreak in a way that's somewhat clean.
- I am heartbroken, but I'm not splitting off the heartbreak. I'm not denying the heartbreak but *embracing* the heartbreak.

There's something very beautiful in the embrace of the heartbreak.

When I embrace my heartbreak, I'm able to cry. I am embracing the dignity—but not *just* the dignity, or even the *divinity*, of my needs, which then allows me to begin to get the needs met because I can begin to meet those needs in a profound, beautiful, and potent way. That's only one dimension.

There's a second dimension: **I embrace the need, the dignity of the need, the divinity of the need, and the longing, even though I know it *cannot* be met.** Even though I know it cannot be met, I still don't turn away from it, and I can be in the heartbreak of it—but I can somehow **turn the heartbreak into aliveness.**

I've got to find just *the right level* of heartbreak.

- If I allow the heartbreak to **break me**, paralyze me, and shut me off from aliveness, then the heartbreak is destructive, then it's breaking me.
- But if I allowed the heartbreak to **break my heart open**, I can be fully alive in that desire. Even if I live in the palace of imagination most of the time, in the fullness of my yearning and my longing, I can allow my yearning and longing to Fuck me open, to love me open, to make me more sensitive, more kind, more alive, more filled with Eros.

In other words, if I shut the heartbreak down because I feel like I cannot realize it, then I become deadened to the nerve endings of my own heart—and the nerve endings of my alive heart are needed, my alive Eros is *needed* because **my alive heart is unique**. It's unlike any other. Therefore, my heartbreak is unique—and **I offer my heartbreak as an erotic mystic on the altar of *She*, for the sake of healing all the broken vessels and all the broken hearts.**

I stay open. The point is that I stay *open as love*. I don't close. It's the decision, the commitment to stay open as love, to be *lived as love*, to stay open as love.

What usually happens is: if our need is not met, we shut down the need, and we shut down the tears. The tears themselves are the temple. Tears are *bechi* in Hebrew, a word which shares etymology with the word *m'vukhah*, confusion. **Tears can clarify my confusion, where I ask:**

- Is life worthwhile?
- Is it even worth being here?
- What am I doing?

Tears give me the experience of my own Eros and aliveness and my unique aliveness, and I realize my life is self-evidently worthwhile. My yearning, the uniqueness of my yearning, the uniqueness of my desire, and the unique pattern of my Eros make life *self-evidently* worth living in a fundamental way. It's beautiful.

CLARIFIED DESIRE = DIGNIFIED NEED = VALUE

- In one dimension of life, by reclaiming the dignity and divinity of my need, and therefore being able to practice the great art of crying again, I am able to *see* the need, which goes from its hidden place to its revealed place, so now, **I see the need and I can meet the need.**
- But in the second dimension, **I live in the yearning**, I live in the longing.

That's why the third face of Eros is yearning, longing.

In the four major faces of Eros, the third is *tshuka*, desire itself, because when I lose access to my desire, I lose access to my aliveness:

- My creative desire
- My desire to help a little old lady across the street
- My desire to feel the pulsing of Eros in my body
- My desire to be kind
- My desire for food
- My desire for goodness
- My desire for truth

It's all part of the same field of desire. **Desire means there's something that I value that I want.** And that's very important.

What is value? **Value is clarified desire.**

It's a huge sentence: clarified desire equals value. That's what value is. No one knows what value is. It's clarified desire.

Let's formulate it even more clearly:

> *Clarified desire = dignified need = value*

This is huge.

My clarified desire—my true desire, my deepest heart's desire—is the desire of *She*.

Why? Because *She* is the Eros of evolution. The Eros of evolution pulses in me. It's not just that I live in the world, I live in a world that's *evolving*—the evolving world evolves through me. Evolution quite literally lives in me, in all of us, both interiors and exteriors.

Evolutionary desire lives uniquely in me. To clarify the unique evolutionary desire that lives in me is to know who I am. That's who I am: I *am* that unique evolutionary desire.

That clarified evolutionary desire discloses my authentic need, and my authentic need is a value.

That's why we said that the purpose of prayer is *pallal*. *Pallal* means a reality consideration, and it's to consider the nature of my need. When I consider the nature of my need, I disclose value in Cosmos. That's the dignity of a human being. Clarified need is value—what you truly need. Not just *valuable* but *value*—so clarified desire = dignified need = value.

Once we can recognize need and value, we are allured to *meet* that value because **value generates allurement.** We are allured to meet value. Since we are allowed to meet value, we *feel* this arousal in us because we are moved by this allurement.

If we begin to generate a *shared* field of allurement, we are all part of the same field. We are all Unique Selves, so there's a unique expression of allurement in all of us. **Our Unique Self is our unique set of allurements.**

We also share a common experience. That's why we can talk to each other. If we didn't have a common experience, language wouldn't work. There is a common Field of Allurement, a common Field of Need that we can clarify—and that common Field of Need and Desire is what generates value.

Once we generate value, once we have now entered a shared Field of Value, **we can generate the energy of action, the energy of transformation**. That's what we mean when we say evolution equals love and action. Evolution is love and action.

Evolutionary desire generates the movement to create greater wholeness, which is the action of evolution itself.

It's very beautiful, and we're just beginning to realize that the ability to stay in the desire, to stay in the longing, to stay in the yearning—even when we cannot see its fulfillment—is what makes us alive.

It's what makes us human.

It's what makes us noble; it's what makes us sacred.

And then, paradoxically, as we gradually stay in the desire, we are more and more alive, more and more divine, so more and more possibility opens up because divinity is the Possibility of Possibility—and **what seemed completely impossible begins to disclose itself in the glimmer of new possibility**.

PART THREE: HEARTBREAK IN INTERIOR AND EXTERIOR SCIENCES: AUTONOMY—COMMUNION, ATTRACTION—REPULSION

Heartbreak is a structure of the Intimate Universe.

Heartbreak means that the force of allurement that draws us together is interrupted.

Heartbreak means that the allurement that was there—the connection, the mutuality of recognition, the mutuality of feeling, the mutuality of value, or the mutuality of purpose, all of which are the dimensions of the intimacy equation, expressions of a sense of shared identity—is broken. That's at least one expression of heartbreak.

- You don't have mutuality of recognition. That's heartbreaking.
- You don't have mutuality of pathos anymore. That's heartbreaking.
- You don't have mutuality of value; there's no longer a shared Field of Value, at least in your experience. That's heartbreaking.
- You lose mutuality of purpose. Again, that's heartbreaking.

That's one expression of heartbreak.

And the other expression of heartbreak is when all those mutualities are still there, the intimacy of shared identity is still there, and at the same time, the person disappears because they are sick, or they died, or they changed in some way.

Another expression of heartbreak is when mutuality shifts for one person but not for the other person.

This structure of heartbreak is an expression of the evolution of love.

- The more love evolves
- The more love becomes self-conscious
- The more the will becomes self-conscious
- The more sense of choice seems to appear—

—the more the quality of separation or the quality of intimacies rupture, and this generates heartbreak.

Heartbreak is an expression of a core quality, and the quality is **the breaking of allurement**.

A beautiful question, a beautiful inquiry is **how far down the evolutionary chain does heartbreak go?** We know that heartbreak does not only exist at the human level; it also exists at the animal level in very, very deep and profound ways.

Is there a quality of heartbreak that goes all the way down to matter? We don't know the interiority of matter. We don't know that protons, neutrons, and electrons experience heartbreak.

There is a text which describes the relationship between the Sun and the Moon in terms of heartbreak, in terms of the pain of intimacy's alienation. This is already in the realm of interior science and not yet understood or validated by the exterior sciences, but for now, suffice it to say that **heartbreak is intimately bound up with the play between allurement and autonomy**, or said slightly differently, **autonomy and communion**, or said slightly differently, **attraction and repulsion**, which are core qualities of the Intimate Universe.

There is a critical text about the nature of a broken heart, which appears in the third-century mystery texts of the Solomon tradition in one of the Jerusalem interior science texts, by Said R. Alexanderi:

> A human artisan—if his tools are broken, it is an offense to him, and he cannot do his fixing. The Divine Artisan—*She*—all of her tools are broken, as it is written—*She* is intimate with all the broken hearts, and *She* does all of her fixing with broken tools.

Now, let's go even deeper. The word used in this Hebrew text to describe the Divine tools is *klei tashmisho* (*klei*, "tool" plus *tashmisho*, "that are used")—the tools that we use.

But the word *klei* is a two-letter root *chaf* "lamed," which means, *kallah* "bride," which means, more deeply, **the yearning passion for full rapturous erotic union.** *Tashmish* means the vessel that's used, but it also means sexual coupling, erotic union.

The word in the text that describes the divine artisan's tools expresses **the passionate yearning of God's erotic partner, which is the human being**. The passionate yearning of God's erotic partner, the human being, is broken. It is out of this lineage, directly from these texts, that Leonard Cohen intuitively drew the notion of *the holy and the broken Hallelujah*:

> *There's a blaze of light in every word.*
> *It doesn't matter what you heard,*
> *the holy or the broken Hallelujah.*

We are the broken *Hallelujahs*. Our hearts do break. Heartbreak is part of our nature.

THERE IS EROS TO THE BROKEN HEART

There are two kinds of heartbreak.

One is *unnecessary heartbreak*—heartbreak that shouldn't be. Heartbreak that comes from human sloppiness, from turning away, from human ignorance, from human beings not transforming to the highest and deepest nature that we are. It comes from all manner of degraded, lowest-common-denominator, egoic, grasping human action, which creates unimaginable suffering.

Those heartbreaks need to be healed. That's the work of *tikkun*—the work of social transformation; it's the work of creating new structures of governance, new structures of economics, and new structures of power that emerge out of a new Story of Value.

That's a heartbreak that we need to say *no* to.

But there is a second form of heartbreak. **The second form of heartbreak is inseparable from love itself.** You cannot love without being willing to have your heart broken a thousand times a day.

Our hearts open, and then our hearts are hurt for a second, then we find each other more deeply.

There is no love without a heartbreak because, as we said earlier, the nature of the human being is that right after that one moment of pure attunement between the baby and the mother, from that moment on, for the rest of the baby's life as the baby grows up into life, there's actually a lack of attunement, because:

- We are both *allured* to each other, moving towards attunement.
- And yet we are also *distinct* and *individuated* and *unique*, and so there is a lack of attunement, there is *autonomy*, there is the sense of independence, and even repulsion. We need to actually stand in our own space.

There's both allurement and autonomy, and in that dance between allurement and autonomy, there is heartbreak. But we don't resist that heartbreak. We embrace that heartbreak—and there is a joy in it. It's part of our aliveness. It's part of our Eros.

There's a text that says that God is *harofe li'sh'vurei lev*, "God heals the broken hearts," *u'mechabesh le'atz'votam*, and "bandages the sadness."

As Simcha Bunim of Peshischa says, *Don't we know that the broken heart is holy? Isn't it true that there's nothing more whole than a broken heart?* If there's nothing more whole than a broken heart, why does it need a bandage?

He says—elliptically, subtly, and so beautifully—**we are not putting a bandage on the broken heart.** We're putting a bandage on the *atsvut*, which is a certain kind of sadness that turns into depression. In other words, if I don't resist the heartbreak, and I embrace the broken heart, then there is actually joy.

There is joy—not a superficial happiness but an aliveness.

There is an Eros to the broken heart.

I know I'm alive. I'm in love. I'm in the aliveness of Reality.

We don't want to lose our capacity to have our hearts broken, but we want to bandage the sadness that turns to paralysis, depression, futility, self-loathing, or helplessness. Rather, we hold the mystery, and we allow our beloveds to go on their way.

We allow our hearts to be broken, we hold joy in the broken heart, and we hold its aliveness and its divinity.

We feel that broken heart, and Goddess feels broken hearts like we feel broken hearts. That's what it means when we say that God is the Infinite Intimate.

It means God is saying: *I am willing to have my heart broken with you.*

CHAPTER FIFTEEN

THE FOOTBALL RESPONSE TO THE META-CRISIS: STEPPING OUT OF THE POCKET FOR THE EVOLUTION OF LOVE

Episode 360 — September 3, 2023

WE HAVE TO BECOME THE NEW STORY

Welcome, everyone. Oh my God, we are in life! Are we in life?

We are in life, and we are on the court, and we are in the game.

We are in the middle of the meta-crisis, and we are facing existential risk and catastrophic risk, and we are also poised before the most unimaginably good, true, and beautiful world that we could create together, that we've always known, in our heart of hearts, was the intention of Cosmos—the possibility that Cosmos was reaching for.

We have a wild day. I want to set our intention, and then we're going to go into a deep *dharma*. **This is football** *dharma* **day. We are going to talk about football, the meta-crisis, and why that matters.**

EXISTENTIAL RISK AND THE EVOLUTION OF LOVE

Where are we? We are in One Mountain, Many Paths. I started One Mountain with my dear beloved evolutionary whole mate and friend, Barbara Marx Hubbard, when she was about 84 or 85. Our vision was—and our vision of all of us here together—that One Mountain becomes the seed of the revolution. The revolution means that we actually *recognize* this unique moment in time. We recognize that we are at a time between worlds, at a time between stories, and that we need to respond to a meta-crisis that threatens us with both existential and catastrophic risk. Existential risk of two kinds: the death of humanity, potential extinction—but equally dangerous, the death of *our* humanity. We've talked about it here many times.

On our website, there is a piece called "Love or Die"[4] that presents the context of this conversation because at this moment in history, we are at a *love or die* moment.

Love means not just ordinary love but a realization of the nature of love, about Reality being Eros, and about us participating in the Field of Eros. It's about invoking a new human and a new humanity, what we call *Homo amor*: the fulfillment of *Homo sapiens*.

The premise of *One Mountain* is that telling the new Story of Value rooted in First Principles and First Values is the most compelling response we have to the meta-crisis.

We are here every week engaging in some dimension of that new story, and at the Mystery School, we're engaged in dimensions of that new story. Both the Mystery School and One Mountain are, in some sense, *dharma* laboratories that allow us:

- To articulate the new story
- To clarify it
- To participate in writing it

---

4   Marc Gafni, "Love or Die," https://worldphilosophyandreligion.org/wp-content/uploads/2023/09/Love-Or-Die_Long-Version.pdf.

I think that **the greatest moral imperative of our time is the formulation, the precise articulation, and the writing of the new Story of Value**—but not just writing, it needs to be a movie, so I'm looking for a partner now to make a movie on *Homo amor*.

What does the movie about the new human and new humanity look like? What's the movie about Evolutionary Love?

The Great Library has *volumes*. Volumes are critical—mini volumes, big volumes, small volumes, essays. To date, I've written about twenty unpublished volumes. I am working day and night on this, and I'm fighting for every second of time. We are fighting for every second of time because it matters so enormously much. We have to write this new story, tell this new story. But even more than that, we have to actually *become* this new story.

We have to become the new story.

Every week, that's what we engage in. We do it in the context not of a classical podcast but in the context of a synagogue, a church, a mosque, a synagogue, a secular humanist centre. **We are *gathering*. The gathering matters. The communion matters.**

- We are gathering in intimate communion.
- We are gathering around the campfire.
- We are gathering to make this real.
- We are gathering to look at each other and initiate this revolution together.

We've got a wild day today, so let me just give you a little bit of the context. (I'm not going to give you all of the context because some of it has to remain a mystery.)

What's our question?

- Are you, are *we*, ready to participate in the evolution of love?
- Are we ready to play a larger game?
- Are we ready to participate in the evolution of love?

Drumroll! Let us do this. Let us love this open.

Let's love this open all the way.

Here we go, we've got a lot to do here. It's wild.

WHEN THE POCKET COLLAPSES, A NEW POSSIBILITY IS CREATED

Here's the context.

I did a late-night *Holy of Holies* with a dear friend who shall remain nameless, but I wanted to recapitulate these ideas. That's the first piece of information.

Here is the second thing: I don't know *anything* about the world of sports.

It's just not my world. I happen to love to play. I was a wide receiver in grade school, but I don't know anything about football. As a matter of fact, I had seen one football game in my life up to a week ago. I lived in Columbus, Ohio at the time. It was a Rose Bowl. It was a big moment, and who was going to win and who was going to lose was a very dramatic moment in Columbus, Ohio—and I am watching the game and saying, *What is this? Men bashing each other around at great risk of concussion? Why are we doing this?*

The game didn't make a lot of sense to me, and I never really looked at it again. I never really turned back to it.

But there is a reason why I got a little bit interested in football again a couple of months back, and particularly, someone mentioned to me a player named Aaron Rodgers—that he was a unique figure, a unique player.

STEPPING OUT OF THE POCKET FOR THE EVOLUTION OF LOVE

And for a series of reasons, I thought, *wow, he is an interesting figure, he seems to be doing something different.* I had never heard his name because I've never looked at football since then, and I haven't been drawn towards football. But—late at night here, a few days back—the same person who had mentioned Aaron said to me, *Oh, he's playing his first pregame.* I said, *Okay, I'll check it out.*

It's 2 a.m. in the morning, and I can't really sleep because these past couple of weeks have been an intense time. I go online, do a little Google search, and pull up Aaron Rodgers' first pregame.

Again, everything I'm about to share with you are words that I didn't know before. I am using words that I don't have full association of the full depth of their meaning, but I think I can get it right.

He is doing what's called *a pregame*. He's now been traded from the Green Bay Packers to the New York Jets, which is apparently a big deal because Green Bay is a little town, and New York is New York, and he's having an exciting time, from what my friend reported to me. Having a good time in New York, he's having a pregame. (And by the way, this is all about responding to the meta-crisis, so stick with us, friends.)

I thought, oh, let me check this out. My friend says he's a unique figure, so I'll check it out. You can Google all of Aaron's snaps in the first game. (*Snaps* means all the time that he played the ball.) I watched his snaps, and there weren't that many. He actually threw an incredible touchdown pass. I watched the snaps. And then, as I was watching, I noticed, at the 3rd and 12 (which is how they mark it), before the touchdown pass, he did something really interesting.

What did he do? Everyone was pressing around him, and he stepped out of what's called "the pocket." **Now the pocket is where you are defended by your sumo wrestler offensive linemen, these knights who protect the quarterback, who is the king.**

Does that make sense?

- They are protecting you.
- You basically play *within the pocket*. You throw *from* the pocket.
- They are protecting you, so you've got plenty of time, and you can throw.

So I noticed, at 3rd and 12, they are coming at Aaron, his pocket collapses, and he steps outside, looking for a place to make a move. I said, *huh, that's interesting*.

We are now about 2:30 a.m. Nothing much happened in that play, but that was interesting. That was moving to me. About 2:30 a.m., I Google this guy I've never heard of, who my friend mentioned a few weeks back—let me check out his plays. I Google *Aaron Rodgers' best plays*.

The name of the little video that comes up doesn't say Aaron Rodgers' *best* plays—it's Aaron Rodgers' *miraculous* plays. That's interesting. Why *miraculous* plays? I just noted that because I am a reader of text. I watched these plays, and here is what I seem to notice: in two-thirds of them, maybe even more, **his pocket collapses, and then he steps out of the pocket—he doesn't collapse with the pocket—and he expands the play. He *extends* the play**.

The pocket collapses means that he's surrounded by his offensive linemen, but they are not protecting him anymore. He is about to get tackled. The play should be over—the pocket has collapsed—but **instead of the play being over, he somehow steps out of the pocket**. The play is not over, and he expands the field of play. Now, that's really interesting: he has *extended* the play by two or three seconds. And then, in most of these miraculous plays, **it is in that moment of extending the play that a new possibility is created**.

I said, *wow, that's interesting*.

There is this pocket, which is comfortable—not *that* comfortable, but it's a place where there is some certainty, where you are protected, where you can kind of operate from within—but the pocket collapses. But instead of the game being over when the pocket collapses, he steps out of the pocket and generates a new possibility. That's interesting.

WHEN THE POCKET COLLAPSES, THE PLAY IS OVER

But then I said to myself:

> Well, Marc, this is the first football you've ever watched, other than that one game when you were a kid in Columbus, Ohio. You know nothing about football. You think you see a pattern here, but you're just making it up.

Okay, so what do I have to do? I've got to do the same thing you always do with the text, you've got to *compare* texts. That's what you always do when you analyze an Aramaic text, a legal text, or you analyze, as I often do with my friend Aubrey, the text of a movie.

This is what I did in our television show in the Middle East. We did this great national television show, where we would analyze texts of movies. **To analyze a text, you've got to analyze *parallel* texts and see how they relate to each other.** For example—I'll just give you one example—at some point, I analyzed the first meeting scene, the first sex scene, and the death scene in two movies:

- *Love Story*, the great 1970 love classic
- My friend Lana Wachowski's 1999 movie, *The Matrix*

I analyzed the first meeting scene in both movies, the first sex scene in both movies, and the death scene in both movies—because that's what you have to do, right? **You have to analyze and compare the texts to see if there is something unique, if something is happening.**

So in order for me to see if Aaron's stuff is for real, I have to check another text.

The only problem is *I know nothing* about the texts of football. I don't know anything about football. I remembered somebody mentioned to me this name, Tom Brady. I had vaguely heard that name because Trump likes Tom Brady, so I had some vague sense that this dude exists. Now we are about 3 a.m. I say okay, this is cool, I am going to Google *Tom Brady's best plays*. Now, interestingly, it doesn't say Tom Brady's *miraculous* plays. Isn't that interesting? It just says greatest plays or something like that. So, I watched his plays.

Now, here is what happens. Tom Brady always, without fail—I mean, virtually always, I would say ninety-five percent of the time—throws *from within* the pocket. He doesn't step out of the pocket. **If the pocket collapses with Tom Brady, the play is over.**

- Tom is one of the top quarterbacks ever, but when his pocket collapses, when his offensive linemen can't defend him anymore, the play is over. Gone, done!
- Aaron—when it looks like the play is over because the pocket is collapsing, he finds his way out. The formal term, I think, is he *scrambles out* of the pocket, he expands or *extends* the play—for not a lot of time, for two or three seconds, four at the most, but that's a lot—and then something unimaginable happens. That's when a new possibility is created. That's pretty wild.

I just want you to see this, and then we're going to talk about why this is important—because that's exactly what we are doing here at One Mountain.

Did you notice? Each time, remember what they say. *He's got the time.* What does it mean, *he's got the time?* It means he is in the pocket, they're defending him, they're surrounding him. He's got time, he's good. He always makes the play from within the pocket. He's surrounded. He sees the field. Clearly, he is crazy talented. He makes the pass. He's making the play in the pocket.

STEPPING OUT OF THE POCKET FOR THE EVOLUTION OF LOVE

Now let's look at Aaron Rodgers. We're reading a text now.

Now I'm going to explain what we are seeing. In each one of those plays, the pocket collapses. That's why the announcer says *he's in trouble*, which means that the pocket collapsed. And then, he makes a move. In both of the plays, he makes a move. He steps out of the pocket, and then a new possibility is created. And even the sportscaster says this funny thing: *he backpedals, he rolls away, he says a prayer.* There's this sense that *something else* has happened here.

We're now at about 3:30 a.m., and I've now gone through these totally different, completely different styles of play. In some sense, Brady is playing from the pocket, and obviously, he's a brilliant quarterback playing from within the pocket. The difference is that, when the play is supposed to be over because the pocket has collapsed, Rogers moves out of the pocket, extends the play, and generates a new possibility.

THERE IS NO STORY OF VALUE BECAUSE THE FIELD OF VALUE HAS BROKEN

Now *we* are going to play. I want you to feel into that and think about that. Right now, I want to just talk about what we just saw and how *we're* going to play.

We are in this moment of meta-crisis. There are two generator functions of this meta-crisis—and when I say *generator functions*, I mean: **let's look beneath the headlines, beneath everything you see written out there, and identify underlying causes**. We've been working on this, thinking about this, and feeling into this in many different ways for the last decade, myself, Barbara Marx Hubbard, and those of us who deepened this work.

- The first generator function is that **there is a broken story, and that story is a success story.** The success story is that I

am always in rivalrous conflict with everyone else, and that rivalrous conflict is governed by win/lose metrics.
- This generates **a fragile system, where the parts don't know what each other are doing**, which makes the entire system liable to systemic breakdown on multiple levels (see, for example, Covid, which was just a minor dress rehearsal for systemic breakdown).

Underlying these two generator functions, there is a deeper root cause: ***a global intimacy disorder***. What's the global intimacy disorder? Well, no one is intimate with each other:

- There's no shared identity between people. We can't feel each other.
- We don't have a shared identity. We don't recognize each other.
- We don't have a shared purpose.

Those are the dimensions of intimacy.

The result is that our relationships are not intimate—there's no shared identity, only rivalrous conflict governed by win/lose metrics, which creates a fragile system, which is the generator function of breakdown of the entire system. The world civilization hasn't solved any of the old problems with exponential technologies. Exponential growth curves go off the cliff, and the entire system breaks down, which is where we're going, on multiple levels.

WHY IS THERE A GLOBAL INTIMACY DISORDER?

Because there is no shared story.

No shared story of what?

No shared Story of Value.

Instead of a shared Story of Value, there is a success story. In other words, when there is no shared Story of Value, which is the story of Eros:

- There is pseudo-eros.
- There is a success story.
- There is rivalrous conflict governed by win/lose metrics.

That's just the context. But here is where it gets wild, and this is going to bring us to Aaron and Tom. Why is there no Story of Value, friends? Because **the assumption is that the Field of Value has broken down.**

The reason there's no Story of Value is because the Field of Value has broken. The assumption is that there no longer is a Field of Value.

If there's no Field of Value, then there's no global intimacy. There is a global intimacy disorder, which is the root cause for the generator functions of existential risk.

Why is that the assumption? Because there has been a fierce critique of value theory, which is actually a valid critique.

THE COLLAPSE OF THE POCKET IN THE STORY OF VALUE

It's very powerful, very beautiful. We're cutting through an enormous amount of confusion, trying to get to really understand deeply what's happening here—because **only if we can understand that can we actually act in revolution, and act in transformation, and participate in evolving the source code, and participate in the evolution of love.**

If you go back to premodernity—the premodern world of the great religions, the great traditions until the Renaissance—they all assumed that there was a Field of Value, and they all assumed that they *owned* the Field of Value. They all assumed everybody else's understanding of value was wrong, and theirs was fundamentally right. But what they all shared is:

- Value is real, value is intrinsic.
- Value is intrinsic to Cosmos.
- Value is intrinsic to the divine field.
- There is absolutely what I'm calling *a Field of Value*, a ground of value.

They just disagreed about who *owned* it—but each one thought, each one said, *wow, we've got total certainty, we know what's going on here.*

And their princes and their dukes defended them—so they were *in the pocket*. In other words, they are defended:

- By all their dogmas
- By all their theologies
- By all their institutions

They are trying to move the play forward in accordance with their vision of the Field of Value, and they're taking on the other team, and they're doing this line drive. But they experience themselves as being in the pocket, as being defended, and they are acting and moving from within the pocket.

Now it gets wild. Modernity comes along and says: *Whoa, man! Yeah, no, no, we don't like that premodern stuff, that's bad stuff.*

And they rebel against premodernity, for good reason. Voltaire leads the charge and says, *Remember the cruelties!* There are good reasons to rebel against premodernity. **Modernity takes on premodernity, at least in its mainstream position (David Hume), and they undermine the dogmatic assumptions of premodernity.**

But they do this other thing: **they take out *a hidden loan* from premodernity, a hidden social spiritual loan**. They borrow social spiritual capital from premodernity. In what form, what's the currency of that social and spiritual capital?

Value.

You see, modernity has no way to actually work out *where value is from*. If it's not from God in the way we thought it was, where is it from? All the suppositions that get us there were destroyed, at least in their classical sense, by David Hume, followed by Immanuel Kant.

Where do we get value from?

What modernity says when it talks about value—for example, in the American Constitution—is something like: *We hold these truths to be self-evident*. But what does that mean?

***We hold these truths to be self-evident* means we are not sure where value is from, but we are taking out a hidden loan of social and spiritual capital from premodernity, we are just going to *assume* that value is real.** We're just going to live our lives as if value is real, and we are not going to try and work out where it's from. We don't know—but hey, we're just going to hold these truths to be self-evident; value is real. **We have taken out a hidden loan from premodernity; it's a hidden loan of value.** We are just going to assume value is real, even though we don't know where it's from.

That means that **modernity is still in the pocket**. Modernity has taken out a loan of social spiritual capital from premodernity. *We hold these truths to be self-evident*. All good, we're in the pocket. It's clear, it's self-evident. Whoa, that's a big deal!

Then along comes postmodernity, and says:

> I'm calling that loan of value, modernity, that you took from premodernity. You're full of shit! Value has no source; value is not real. All values are made-up. All values are relative. All values are socially constructed. All values are, as one popular writer said in a book endorsed by Barack Obama, Bill Gates, and many others, "all values are just mere fictions, mere social constructs, mere figments of our imagination."

Now, if it's all made-up, whoa! What does *that* mean?

What that means is that *the pocket collapsed*. **The protective place of certainty where I could rest and from which I could throw, complete passes, and move down the line—the pocket collapsed.**

It's not just the pocket collapsed—the game got canceled. There is no more game.

Game means you are on the field, and the field means there is a shared Field of Value. That's the great thing about sports: you are on the field, and there is a shared Field of Value.

No, no, no, the pocket collapsed, and the game was canceled.

There is no longer a game in a Field of Value.

WE'VE GOT TO STEP OUT OF THE POCKET AND EXTEND THE PLAY

When there is no Field of Value, what remains in its stead, my friends?

One thing: rivalrous conflict governed by win/lose metrics, a success story. A rivalrous conflict and win/lose metrics all the way up and all the way down in every part and dimension of society, which creates:

- Extraction models
- Exponential growth curves
- Fractional reserve banking, at its most pernicious
- Structures of economics and finance which are devastating to the commons
- Tragedies of the commons
- Multipolar traps

This all happens because there's no more shared Field of Value.

Even when we recognize that artificial intelligence, for example, threatens us at the most existential level, the ability to create a shared agreement to formally define the parameters of what's going to be allowed or not allowed in artificial intelligence research is nil. We can't do it. No one trusts each other because there is no shared Field of Value in which trust is actually a value. So there are multipolar traps: everyone says, *someone else is going to break the agreement and do it, so I'd better break the agreement first.* We've got this existential risk, artificial intelligence, and no one—*literally no one whatsoever*—can actually create an agreement because the major players in AI (many of them who we're in touch with right now) experience their lives as success stories based on rivalrous conflict and win/lose metrics. They are not in the Field of Value.

What happens, my friends, when certainty collapses?

What happens when the pocket collapses?

What happens when the game gets canceled?

You've got to step out of the pocket, and you've got to extend the play.

You can't make Tom Brady's move anymore. For Tom Brady, when the offensive linemen aren't there, when the game collapses, when the play is over, it's over. But from that perspective, it's game over.

No, what we are saying is that Aaron is actually doing it right. Aaron is stepping out of the pocket intuitively, and he's creating a new possibility. For three or four seconds, he steps from certainty into uncertainty. It's lonely out there, and it's undefended. It seems to be unprotected. And then you actually create a new possibility, and that creates miracles. **It creates miracles of emergence.**

That's what emergence is.

Emergence means something new emerges that was never there before. And that's why—intuitively—they say, *he throws the ball, he has stepped out.* They don't use the word prayer, but they're describing that when he's in trouble—meaning, the pocket is collapsing, he steps out of the pocket—he throws the ball *with a prayer*.

Why are they talking about prayers?

Why are they talking about miracles?

They sense it intuitively.

Isn't that wild? They sense. I listened to the language of the sportscasters in describing Rodgers' and Brady's plays. It was a different language, a different relationship. Rodgers didn't quite make sense to them. Brady made sense to them. Mainstream guy, he's our man. They had a more complex relationship with Rodgers.

- He's doing something else.
- He's shattering the old certainties.
- He's creating this new possibility.

But here's the story, my friends. **God is the Possibility of Possibility**. Aaron is making the God move. That's what he is doing.

- He's making the God move.
- He's becoming the evolutionary impulse.
- He is stepping into the unknown.
- He is stepping into the cloud of unknowing.
- He is stepping into this new possibility, and God is the Possibility of Possibility.

Wild, isn't it? Do you begin to see it?

REINITIATING THE EVOLUTION OF LOVE

That's the exact moves that the Center is making, the Center for Integral Wisdom, which we've now renamed as the Center for World Philosophy and Religion. We are stepping out of the pocket into the unknown, generating a new Field of Value. That's a big deal, generating a new Field of Value, which means that we have to generate a new Story of Value.

A new Story of Value means that there's an actual story, a plotline we can identify. There's a plotline, and that plotline is the plotline of Reality. There is a Story of Value which has plotlines because stories have plotlines, and **those plotlines are the Field of Value itself.** In other words, **we are able to identify a new set of First Principles and First Values, and show that they're not just made up.**

No, they are not what they thought in premodernity. It's not that your God spoke them in one place and you own them. But there is a way:

- To identify and access an intrinsic Field of Value, that we all have access to
- To identify core values, First Principles and First Values of Reality
- To articulate—out of the pocket—a new shared grammar of value
- To reinitiate the play, reinitiate the game, reinitiate evolution, reinitiate the evolution of love, and reinitiate the evolution of consciousness.

That's what we are doing. In mid-September, we are going so deep into this, we are going to take such an incredible, unbelievable ride. We are going to talk about this move, this Aaron Rodgers-like move.

- What is the move where we step out of the pocket?
- What is the move we are making?
- What is the play we are creating?

I want to identify that play very clearly because it's the essence of everything we're doing.

Now, friends, I want to read the code for this week before we finish.

EVOLUTIONARY LOVE CODE: STEP OUT OF THE POCKET AND CREATE A NEW POSSIBILITY

Premodern religion plays the game of God and the game of value within the box, within the pocket.

Modernity takes the loan of value and God capital from premodernity and plays the game of value and God in the box as well.

Postmodernity calls in the loan and says, there is no box, there is no pocket. There is no safe place. The game is canceled. All that remains is rivalrous conflict governed by win/lose metrics.

The moral imperative at this point in history is to step out of the pocket, to step out of the box, and to create a new possibility, to create a new vision of the Divine, a new vision of the Field of Value, value which is not only eternal value—eternal value that is unchanging and preordained and God within the box—but also evolving.

We must realize that there is no contradiction between eternal and evolving. Rather, the eternal Tao is the evolving Tao. Eternity and evolution are paradoxical and not contradictory.

We step into the field after the box, the pocket has collapsed, and generate a new ground, a new Field of Value: eternal and evolving value.

CHAPTER SIXTEEN

THE RESPONSE TO EXISTENTIAL AND CATASTROPHIC RISK IS THE DAWN OF DESIRE

Episode 362 — September 17, 2023

EVOLUTIONARY LOVE CODE: THE DAWN OF DESIRE

There are three classical responses to the meta-crisis:

1. The Doomer Response
2. The Denial Response
3. The Domination Response

None of these three can avert the meta-crisis. Each of them deepens what is sure to be its devastating impact, its devastating suffering.

There is, however, a fourth response: the Dawn of Desire or, said slightly differently, the Dawn of Desire and its Dignities, or the Dawn of Desire and its Divinities—living uniquely in us, as us, and through us, both personally and in our newly emergent Unique Self Symphonies.

This is the new grammar of value, the core

First Principles and First Values embedded in a Story of Value—a story of desire which is the great new story, the new cultural movement of CosmoErotic Humanism. It is only such a new Story of Value that can generate the evolutionary intimacy, the new order of intimacy, that responds to the global intimacy disorder that itself is the root cause of the meta-crisis.

CosmoErotic Humanism tells the story of ErosValue. CosmoErotic Humanism tells the story of DesireValue. CosmoErotic Humanism is the dawn of new possibility—the possibility of desire.

FOUR RESPONSES TO EXISTENTIAL AND CATASTROPHIC RISK

Existential risk takes two forms. One is an actual extinction: *the death of humanity as we know it*. There are about twelve vectors at play quite seriously today that could bring us there if there is no deep intervention.

The second kind of existential risk is the death of *our* humanity. By the death of our humanity, we mean a creeping, benign totalitarianism—what we refer to as TechnoFeudalism—in which the world becomes encased in a kind of Skinner box, where free will, personhood, and human dignity are undermined without our even being *aware* that it's happening. Catastrophic risk is not the death of humanity or the death of our humanity, but it involves large-scale unimaginable suffering to large swaths of humanity and to the animal world.

There are three classical responses to existential and catastrophic risk.

1 – THE DOOMER RESPONSE

The doomer response means, in a word, *it's over*. The doomer community includes people like Joanna Macy or my old colleague Michael Dowd, who wrote a book called *Thank God for Evolution* but has since become a doomer. The doomer community is one of the most intelligent, well-read communities in the world, and they have come to the conclusion—based on books like *Overshoot*, which is one of their classical texts—that *it's too late. We have breached too many planetary boundaries; there is nothing more that can be done.* The doomer move says, *we've got to just grieve the end.* Again, these are not superficial readers. These are people who have read a lot, who have come to the conclusion that there is actually no hope.

The doomer community is rooted in subtle reductive materialism. For example, I remember when I read my friend Michael Dowd's book, *Thank God for Evolution*. I was uneasy about the book for this reason—it is suffused with subtle reductive materialism dressed up as Spirit. I was worried about the book then, that it wouldn't *hold* in the face of massive crisis.

There is this subtle reductive materialism—*possibility is over*—that lines the doomer community. While I can appreciate and feel the impulse, it's ultimately wrong because it doesn't understand a critical point. The same possibility that moved Reality in the first nanoseconds of the Big Bang and moved us from matter to life to mind, that *same* evolutionary impulse—which is the inherent *telos* of Reality, the directionality of Reality—is still alive *today*. Evolution itself is the Possibility of Possibility. That's lost on the doomer community.

2 – THE DENIAL RESPONSE

The second position, which I would say is the most rampant position, is denial. The denial position has two forms: what I would call *conscious* denial and sloppy or *unconscious* denial.

Conscious denial is: you are familiar with some of the facts, but you just turn away. You're not willing, to borrow Robert J. Lifton's phrase, *to face apocalypse* or to face the possibility of existential risk, so you turn away. It's a turning away of the face. It's a deliberate turning away, burying the head in the sand.

I remember when my dear friend, Sean Raymer—whom I met when I was holding wisdom schools at a retreat center in New York—said to me: *Why are we talking about this? It's hopeless. What can we do about it?* His impulse was, *let's just turn away from this. Just teach us about Unique Self, about your new visions of enlightenment. Why are you talking about the meta-crisis?*

I started talking about the meta-crisis intensely in 2010 and 2011. That's when existential risk became more real than real to me, and I called it then *the second shock of existence*, the shock of the potential death of humanity.

Sean was basically saying, *there is just no point*. He wasn't, of course, advocating denial. It wasn't a *negative* denial: he was just saying that *there's no point in engaging this, there's nothing to say*. That's pretty much what all intelligent people said to me as I started talking about this: *What are you talking about? First off, you are probably wrong, and even if you're right, what's there to do about it?*

There are many shades of denial. There is a conscious denial: you know the facts, but you deny them because you don't know what to do about it. And then there's a second, more sloppy, unconscious denial, where you get a whiff of it, you can taste it, you feel a fragrance of it in the air—and you turn away.

That's where most of the world is.

For example, artificial intelligence. You read something in a passing headline about artificial intelligence being an existential risk. I talked about this five or six years ago, at a bunch of talks in Belgium. Everyone laughed. All of a sudden, in the last couple of months, you read in mainstream newspapers that artificial intelligence is an existential risk.

But people turn away because *how can you talk about that*? People read the newspaper and say: *Oh my God, artificial intelligence could be an existential risk*, and then they go on with their lives because they don't know how to hold it. It's a *casual* denial. That's the second approach.

3 – THE DOMINATION RESPONSE

The third approach to the meta-crisis is domination. I would call that the approach of Elon Musk. Elon has looked at a lot of the data that I've looked at, and Elon has absolutely come to the same conclusion about the reality of the meta-crisis and existential risk.

But Elon's response is domination. (And I don't think it's a malevolent response.) Elon's response is something like: *There are no adults in the room. Governments are all short-termers. No one's looking at the big picture. I've got to take responsibility and be an adult in the room.*

Now, Elon, as Walter Isaacson pointed out in his biography, is both an adult and a child and a complex figure. This is not a discussion on Elon. Blessings to Elon. Elon is trying to be an adult in the room, and he's saying: *I'm going to run the show.* If you want to know why Musk bought Twitter, it was part of an overarching play that's connected to Tesla, and that's connected to his satellites that encircle the globe, and to an entire Neuralink system, which is related to what I would call the death of *our* humanity, where an invisible group of trans-governmental controllers dominate and control the systems. Elon represents a certain version of a domination move, which, from his perspective, is benign. But of course, **all domination moves begin as benign.**

Those are the three basic moves. The first is the denial move, the second is the doomer move, and the third is the domination move. None of those moves will work to solve the meta-crisis. Rather, they will deepen the unimaginable suffering of the meta-crisis and will eventually lead either to the death of humanity or to the death of *our* humanity—or to unimaginable forms of catastrophic risk.

4 – THE DESIRE RESPONSE

There has to be a fourth way, and that fourth way is not denial; it's not doomer or domination. It is what we might call the ***Dawn of Desire***—

And yes, it had to be a D because D's are always new beginnings: decisive, directional—that's D's at their best. There's this new, decisive direction, which we're going to call the *Dawn of Desire* or the Dawn of Desire and Her Dignities and the Dawn of Desire and Her Divinities. I want to talk about this Dawn of Desire because this is the fourth way.

This Dawn of Desire is the new story of CosmoErotic Humanism.

THE FOURTH RESPONSE TO THE META-CRISIS: THE DAWN OF DESIRE

This new code, this code of Cosmos, is a new formulation of the new Story of Value, which is CosmoErotic Humanism. This is the fourth response to the meta-crisis: the Dawn of Desire.

You cannot respond to the meta-crisis only by changing the infrastructure, for example, by changing how we detect bioweapons in the wastewater (although we need to do that, absolutely). You cannot respond to the meta-crisis only by changing the social structure, by enacting new laws. We do *also* need new laws and new ways of engaging, for example, technology. Laws are based on precedent, while technology is ever-new and emergent, and precedent law can't actually engage the new and the emergent. This is one of many reasons that law has been unable to bind technology.

But social structure is insufficient. We need a new superstructure. A new *superstructure* is a new grammar of value: *inherent First Principles and First Values of Cosmos embedded in a Story of Value*. Let's break that down.

SEEING THE STORYLINE: FROM UNCONSCIOUS TO CONSCIOUS EVOLUTION

Reality is a story—but not a human contrivance, some made-up idea. There is an *ontology* to story. Yes, human beings are storytelling animals but not because that's some random social expression. Human beings are storytelling animals because we are the human expression of a Cosmos that *is* story.

Reality is always story, and the movement from unconscious to conscious evolution is when we become conscious of the story: conscious of the fact that we incarnate the story, conscious of the fact that the story is an unfinished story, conscious of the fact that we become storytellers of the new story. That's the move from unconscious to conscious evolution.

Unconscious Evolution

Unconscious evolution is an unconscious story. You can identify the storyline only from the later perspective of conscious evolution. An atom is living in a particular story, and that story is a Story of Value. There is a set of values that govern the atomic, subatomic, molecular, and macro-molecular worlds. The reason atoms come together to form a molecule is because they have a shared Field of Value. That's the language of Cosmos.

Cosmos is multiple forms of language. Language is embedded in Cosmos, even as we are embedded in language. **One of the core structures of the interior sciences—which we have developed in CosmoErotic Humanism—is the language of value, which is the structure of Cosmos.** That language of value goes all the way down the evolutionary chain. It drives evolution. It's innate, inherent, and it evolves.

Conscious Evolution

The cosmological story comes alive when we become *aware* of the story, when we can actually *see* the story. We can see: *Oh my God. Oh my Goddess: there is a narrative arc to Cosmos, a storyline.*

Being able to see the storyline, to detect the storyline, is itself the movement from unconscious to conscious evolution.

The story becomes conscious:

1. It becomes conscious in me; I realize: *I am the story*.
2. I realize the story is unfinished: *I've got to write the next chapter of the story*.
3. I write the next chapter of the story by *being* the next chapter of the story.
4. Finally, I *become* the storyteller.

NEED AND DESIRE ARE ISOMORPHIC AT FUNDAMENTAL AND ASPIRATIONAL LEVELS OF EVOLUTION

What is the new story about? It's a story of desire. And what is desire? Desire is the erotic motive of Cosmos. Cosmos *is* desire. Desire *is* the nature of Reality. That's what evolution is: evolution is desire. Now, desire desires value. Value is clarified desire. Clarified desire desires to express itself as *value*.

At the fundamental levels of evolution, value is innate. When atoms are in a shared Field of Value, there is an impulse within them to become a molecule. Let's go back a little bit farther, about 380,000 years after the Big Bang, when there was an inherent desire in subatomic particles to create larger wholes. They shared this inherent desire for this larger value, and that value is called an atom. The desire of subatomic particles to become an atom is their core need because at that level, **at that fundamental level of Cosmos, there is no split between *need* and *desire*.**

Need and desire are the same.

Need and desire remain virtually isomorphic—virtually identical—throughout virtually every level of the world of matter, the *physiosphere*.

And then the world of matter triumphs in the Second Big Bang, which is the *biosphere*. In the biosphere, again, there is this desire for more value.

- More value means more *life*.
- More value means more *uniqueness*.
- More value means more *Eros*.
- More value means more *creativity*.
- More value means more *intimacy*.

Each one of those is a precise word that we've articulated in CosmoErotic Humanism, and we have formulated an interior science equation to talk about each one of those.

Again, need and desire are exactly the same at these levels of evolution. Now, at some point, we go through all the levels of the biosphere, and we get to the savanna and the human being, *Homo erectus*, gradually emerges. We are standing up straight. And at some point—and there is an argument among historians about when—between 75,000 and 400,000 years ago, two new dimensions emerge at virtually the same time: one is language, and the other is art, aesthetics. From those comes trade, and there's this new Third Big Bang, life triumphs in the depths of the self-reflective human mind and in *the noosphere*—to borrow a word from the Vladimir Vernadsky, the Russian cosmist—the world of culture, ideas, transmittable ideas. The next step emerges, which is allowed for through language, art, and through trade, but language is the core.

As the human emerges, there's an apparent split between need and desire. *My needs are what I really need, and desire is what I just desire.* **But that's only an apparent split—it disappears when I go deeper inside and clarify what I *truly* need and what I *truly* desire.**

Not *my surface desires, my pseudo-desires*, or—to use the language of CosmoErotic Humanism—*the pseudo-eros* that covers over my emptiness. But rather the question is: **what is the core Eros that expresses my core need and core desire?** Eros means desire. Eros is what Alfred North

Whitehead called the *appetition* of Cosmos. Cosmos has *appetite*, Cosmos has desire.

> *The desire of Cosmos, at the level of the self-reflective human, is able to enact a new possibility, which is a higher level, a deeper level of choice.*

I begin to choose, and I begin to be able to discern between my *pseudo-desire* and my *true* desire—what I called, together with my beloved evolutionary whole mate, Barbara Marx Hubbard—your *deepest heart's desire*.

Your deepest heart's desire is actually your *clarified* desire. It's the Dawn of Desire. **Your clarified desire is the realization that the evolutionary impulse, which is evolutionary desire, lives uniquely *in you, as you, and through you*.** You are, I am, we are clarified desire. I am no longer merely *Homo sapiens*, who is told by the religions:

> *Conquer your desire because we don't trust you to get your true desire.*
> *We are afraid of your pseudo-desires.*
> *We are going to tell you what you desire.*
> *You can't trust your body; we will tell you what your body can do.*
> *We will tell you what you're allowed to desire, and you are allowed to desire what we tell you is desirable.*

That's the beginning of oppression. It was perhaps, in part, a necessary stage in culture, but we now need to transcend that. We need to be at the dawn of a new age of desire, a new possibility of desire, in which the human being once again begins to realize the answer to this important question:

Who am I?

1. I am the CosmoErotic Universe in person.
2. I am evolutionary desire in person.
3. Evolution *is* desire.
4. Evolution lives uniquely in me, as me, and through me.
5. I am a unique incarnation of evolutionary desire.

I AM A UNIQUE FEATURE OF THE FIELD OF DESIRE

My desire is the desire of *She*. It is the desire of Cosmos. It is Goddess's desire. It's God's desire. It's Reality's desire. It is the *telos* of Reality itself, living both in me personally and in us collectively—in me as an irreducible Unique Self, and in us as Unique Selves coming together in Unique Self Symphony.

Unique Self is not merely *separate self*, a skin-encapsulated ego, who we can't rely on to trust their desire, lost in the optical delusion of separateness where *I see everything as rivalrous conflict governed by win/lose metrics, and my desire seems to be always at the expense of your desire, and I must be in competition with you because I'm trying to survive. It's me against you, a zero-sum competition.*

I've got to *trance-end* that—to *end* that *trance*, to realize I am True Self, *one* with the Field of Desire—and then **I've got to realize that the Field of Desire is *seamless* but not *featureless*, that I am Unique Self: I am that Field of Desire's unique feature.**

Who am I? I am a unique configuration of desire. That's who I am.

I am a unique configuration of desire, and my unique desire is needed by Cosmos.

At this level, need and desire come back together. **Just like for subatomic particles, need and desire are isomorphic, for the new human and new humanity**—the fulfillment of *Homo sapiens* as *Homo amor*, who understands him/herself as Unique Self, a unique expression of True Self, a unique expression of the Field of Desire, a unique configuration of desire, needed by All-That-Is—**clarified desire and clarified need are precisely the same**. Wow.

CLARIFIED DESIRE EQUALS VALUE, AND MY CLARIFIED DESIRE IS UNIQUE

I have to begin to trust my desire, to trust my body. I have to clarify my desire.

Clarified desire equals value. That's what value is. Desire is a desire for a new value, for a future that's not yet here. Can you feel that? That's what desire is. Do you get how gorgeous that is? **Clarified desire equals value, and my clarified desire is unique, and so I have a unique contribution to make to the shared Field of Value.**

THE DIGNITY OF DESIRE

We talked about Mahsa Amini who was brutally killed in Iran. She was an expression of *She*, of the Field of Desire, of the feminine. The feminine wants to take its scarf off. She wants to not just be seen through the scarf's slit.

The West is often the opposite, where there is a *degradation* of dress, without tastefulness, without holding the beauty and the subtlety of dress. That's a Western degradation, one of the shadows of Western freedom. But the other degradation of the world is the *covering up* of desire, and the degradation of *She*, the degradation of the divinity and dignity of desire. That's what Mahsa Amini stood for. She stood for the dignity of desire.

There is a song that's going around in Iran today, a year after Mahsa Amini passed. This is a song about the dignity of desire:

> *Take off your scarf, the sun is sinking!*
> *Take off your scarf, your pleasant perfume fills the air.*
> *Take off your scarf, let your hair flow!*

Don't be afraid, my love! Laugh, protest against tears!
Take off your scarf, let your hair flow!
Don't be afraid, my love! Laugh, protest against tears!
The dance of red tresses, the lump in my throat, all your hair.
My face gets wet, I get your wish.
Take off your scarf, make the air bright and fresh!
My love, don't be afraid, dance, boldly bend to kiss!
Take off your scarf, make the air bright and fresh!
My love, don't be afraid, dance, boldly bend to kiss!
Take off your scarf, the sun is sinking.
Woman, Life, Freedom
Woman, Life, Freedom

CLARIFYING OUR DESIRE IN RESPONSE TO THE META-CRISIS

The fourth response to the meta-crisis is to clarify our desire. Is it our clarified desire that we live lives filled with dread and emptiness? Is it our clarified desire that we cannot access our deepest heart's desire? Is it our clarified desire that we are alienated from our desire for community and communion? Is it our clarified desire that we cannot access our desire to be omni-responsible for the whole, to feel and care for past, present, and future, to love the unborn future generations? Is it our clarified desire that we cannot access our sacred will to create a world in which there's not two billion vulnerable people who are split-off from basic human dignity and human rights? Is our desire reducible to the lowest common denominator?

In order to feed that lowest common denominator frenzy of the hungry ghost—which needs to consume and consume and consume—**we develop an extraction model which extracts from planet Earth resources that took billions of years to create.**

This is an indication of a frenzy of pseudo-desire—driving exponential growth curves that ultimately are guaranteed to fall off—**that's the lowest common denominator,** *un-clarified* **desire.**

The response to the meta-crisis is to generate a new Story of Value in which we live. And a new Story of Value comes from only one place: clarified desire.

It's not denial. It's not doomer. It's not domination. It's the Dawn of Desire. **What's the Dawn of Desire?**

- It's the dawn of the *dignity* of desire.
- It's the dawn of *clarified* desire.
- It's the realization of the *divinity* of desire.
- It's our capacity to access our *deepest heart's desire*.
- It's the new story of CosmoErotic Humanism.

The new story of CosmoErotic Humanism is "*I become desire in person.*" *Homo amor* is the CosmoErotic Universe in person; *Homo amor* is evolutionary desire in person.

And I've got to be able to *trust* my desire:

- I trust my clarified desire.
- I trust my deepest heart's desire.
- I trust the deepest dignity of my desire, rooted as it is in the ultimate divinity of desire.

The fourth response to the meta-crisis is the recognition of our desire—clarified desire, our deepest heart's desire—as disclosing the true nature of value in Cosmos. The fourth response to the meta-crisis is to reclaim the dignity of desire in every unique human being. And from that shared Field of Desire, to create new intimate communions and new Unique Self

Symphonies: to create, to generate the new world for the new human and new humanity: *Homo sapiens* fulfilled as *Homo amor*.

Trusting, clarifying our deepest heart's desire, willing to go deep into our bodies, deep into our traumas, deep into our brokenness, and know that we can trace it back to its root—and find our goodness, our truth, and our beauty.

Knowing that the only recourse is not to *control* a human being because we falsely believe that they're empty of the Field of Desire and its dignities and its divinities—which is the doomer response, which is the domination response, and it's also part of the denial response. The denial response says, *I'm going to deny because there's nothing to do*. Yes, of course there's something to do. *Of course* there is something to do. What's there to do? Tell and *be* the new Story of Value. Move from unconscious to conscious evolution.

- I am done being just *Homo sapiens*.
- I am done being just a *separate self*.
- I am done with the *degradation* of my desires.
- I am going to begin to *trust* my somatic intelligence, to trust my deepest embodiment, my deepest ensoulment.
- I can trust that.
- I can trust the personal myth that has awakened alive in me. That personal myth that is me is not a myth in the small sense. It is my deepest heart's desire. It is a personal story of desire because my story is a story of desire.

That's what the new story is. It's the story of the *desire that we trust* and of our *collective desires that we trust*, which are not the short-term desires of the political structures and the economic structures that are built in rivalrous conflict, governed by win/lose metrics, that produce a world of brokenness.

DESIRE IS PRAYER, PRAYER IS DESIRE

Prayer is turning to the Field of Desire, to the Personhood and Infinity of Desire—to the Infinity of Intimacy, which is the Field of Desire—and saying:

> *Oh my God, help me, hold me.*
> *I hold You and I help You.*

We are partners with the infinite Field of Desire. **We are partners with the Goddess. We are partners with *She*.** I want to invite everyone to the Field of Desire and to pray by expressing your deepest heart's desire—for yourself, your life, your own humanity, for other people whose desires need fulfillment, and for the desire of humanity. I want to offer you a new way to pray, with your permission, so tenderly.

To say I desire is to say I pray.
To say I pray is to say I desire.

Do you see how that changes what we think about prayer and how we feel prayer? Prayer has become this outmoded structure to a homophobic, anti-body, ethnocentric God that is somehow alienated from Cosmos. No! The Field of *She* holds Cosmos and holds me. Every place I fall, I fall into *Her* arms. *She* knows my name.

She lives in me, as me, and through me, and I *participate* in *She* at the same time.

To pray means one thing: Prayer is *pallal*. *Pallal* means "to consider the nature of Reality."

And how do we consider the nature of Reality? I find my deepest heart's desire.

REALITY IS THE DESIRE FOR *EVER MORE* EROSVALUE

My deepest heart's desire always is value. Reality is the desire for ever more value. Evolution is the evolution of desire, which is the evolution of intimacy, which is the evolution of value. It's not that Eros *is* a value—it's *ErosValue*. Just like there is *LoveIntelligence*, and *LoveBeauty*, and *LoveDesire* (these are signatures of CosmoErotic Humanism), so there is *ErosValue*, there is *DesireValue*. It's one word.

Trust your deepest heart's desire. Find your deepest heart's desire. I find my deepest heart's desire. We collectively find our deepest heart's desire.

What's our deepest heart's desire? **We take the baton of the past, and we stand with every human being and with all of life in the present, and we hear the call of the unborn of the future.** We are in revolution and we are in *evolution*. We are evolution in person.

Desire rages in us—clarified desire. That's who we are. We are clarified desire. We are the dawn of the new desire.

We are at a moment of meta-crisis: The doomer response will destroy us. The denial response will destroy us. The domination response will destroy us.

We've got to go to a fourth response, which is a new decision we have to take. It's a decision about the Dignity and Divinity of Desire.

The Dawn of Desire: as you, as me, as *She*, as we.

CHAPTER SEVENTEEN

FROM CRISIS TO CROSSING: AVERTING EXISTENTIAL RISK OR PREPARING FOR "THE DAY AFTER"?

Episode 383 — February 11, 2024

LOVE OR DIE: CRISIS IS AN EVOLUTIONARY DRIVER

We are here in One Mountain, Many Paths. And I am excited. We are afraid to get excited, but I am filled with enthusiasm. We feel spirit moving through us. We are filled with "charism."

Charism is not a surface attractiveness. It's the allurement that we feel when we know:

- That *She* is moving through us
- *She* is speaking through us
- That there is something that wants to be painted—there is art that wants to emerge.

The artist is filled with charism. Something is moving through her that needs to be born.

We are here, standing on the abyss, on the edge, feeling *Her* voice moving through, like *She* has *always* moved through. That has always been the pulse, *the evolutionary impulse*—**the evolutionary impulse that in moments of crisis births a new Reality.**

That's the nature of how it unfolds. Crisis itself is an evolutionary driver. **The evolutionary impulse responds uniquely to the crisis in order to generate something new**—and that something new takes us to the next stage.

We are in One Mountain, Many Paths.

We are at this moment of meta-crisis.

We hear *Her* voice moving through us.

We feel charism moving through us. Charism is the charism of the community, which has come together in intimate communion.

A transpersonal community, honoring the irreducible dignity, autonomy, and power of all of its constituents, all of its players, and yet having a shared purpose. Not a separate-self community, which becomes a leveling of differences and a forum for egoic grandstanding. No, no, no, we are a Unique Self Symphony, with the irreducible uniqueness of all our holy players, with all of our holy instruments—and yet we are looking in a shared direction.

We are going somewhere.

Where are we going?

We are trying to respond to the meta-crisis.

We are trying to articulate, in response to the meta-crisis, a new language of value, a universal grammar of value, which is the ground of a new Story of Value that has the capacity to respond to the meta-crisis.

We understand that at this moment, at this juncture, we are faced with an ultimate choice.

> *The ultimate choice of this moment is: Love or die.*

It's a love or die moment. The next several decades are a love or die moment. We are talking about:

- Either **existential and catastrophic risk**, which is the potential death of humanity or the potential death of *our* humanity
- Or we actually **love this moment open into the fullness of its possibility** and generate a new Story of Value from which we create a new Reality.

ONLY A NEW STORY OF VALUE CAN CHANGE THE VECTOR OF HISTORY

In several of our conversations, we have focused on the details of the meta-crisis, which is extremely important to understand. The relationship between population growth, fossil fuels and climate change, methane gas under the tundra, the gap between have and have-nots, and money that's ungrounded from a universal objective standard of material value, and the collapse of value.

I'm not going to go into all that now. That's not generally what we are going to do on One Mountain.

We are going to try and look at what is the new Story of Value that allows us to engage, to approach, to transfigure, to transform in such a way that we can actually effectively engage the meta-crisis. That's what we are doing here.

In other words, One Mountain, Many Paths experiences itself—not in a grandiose way, in a humble way, but in an audacious way—as the heart of a revolution. **It's a revolution in human understanding.**

It's a revolution in *self*-understanding, and that revolution is an integral part of the movement of science—both the exterior sciences and the interior sciences, which are integrally related.

It is a constant series of movements of evolution and revolutions in self-understanding, both of the "I" and of the "We." The emergence of ever deeper self-understanding is the movement of evolution itself. That is the evolution of consciousness, which is the evolution of love.

At this moment of meta-crisis, taking the next step in that movement is the overwhelming moral imperative. We call it the new superstructure, the new Story of Value. We are placing it as being ultimately *the primary cause* that can allow us to avert the unimaginable suffering that the meta-crisis, in its full-blown form, will be:

- The suffering to *the present*
- The failure of *the past* to fulfill its destiny
- The stillborn *future* of trillions of lives

We take the meta-crisis seriously, but it doesn't move us into a doomer stance or a stance of denial. Rather, we view this as the place where we can articulate a new story that actually changes the vector of history, as new Stories of Value have *always* done.

New stories have always been the singular force that changes the vector of history.

WILL THE NEW STORY AVERT THE META-CRISIS, OR IS IT FOR THE DAY AFTER?

I want to try and address two questions today.

Question one: what is our intention in articulating this new Story of Value?

- Is it in order to *avert* the meta-crisis?
- Or is it for *the day after*?

I've taken contradictory positions on this, but the contradiction is, at its core, a paradox. Opposites are often joined at the hip.

Is it in order to avert the meta-crisis?

In other words, if we tell this new Story of Value, we can generate new structures of consciousness, which in turn generate the structures of economics and governance, which will allow the meta-crisis to be averted.

Or is there an inevitability of collapse, of the kind well-documented in the doomer literature?

The doomer literature is an enormously intelligent literature. Just read one book, *Overshoot*—it is a good place to start. You can read how Joanna Macy became a doomer. There are seven or eight serious thinkers and writers, who gathered an enormous amount of information and came to a doomer conclusion.

I think that conclusion is wrong, but it's a very well-reasoned and intelligent conclusion, hard to argue against based just on the material information and on the direction the vectors of the world are pointing today. To ignore it or dismiss it based on generalized inclinations or superficial observations that sound compelling but lack the depth of empirical data—both interior and exterior data—is a terrible mistake.

The doomer position is a real position that says that there is the inevitability of collapse. I don't think that position is true. I think that **there is a genuine possibility to evolve, to move from what we call *Homo sapiens*, the old human, to *Homo amor*, the new human and the new humanity**.

It is not a blissful idealism.

It's not unrealistic.

It's actually the nature of Reality.

It is the natural evolutionary movement:

- For *matter*—after the First Big Bang—to triumph, after all of its stages, in *life* (the Second Big Bang)
- For *life* to triumph, after all of its evolutionary stages, in *the depth of the human self-reflective mind* (the Third Big Bang)
- For the *human self-reflective mind* as it goes through all of its levels of evolution

But it doesn't go on in an *ad infinitum* loop. It is not only *circular*; it's also *directional*.

It's also going somewhere—it's pulled by the future.

The future places its attention on the present and calls it forward.

The depth of the self-reflective human mind, which we call *Homo sapiens*, the wisdom of *Homo sapiens*, actually can and will evolve and deepen— because that's the nature of evolution. **A new human actually can and *will* emerge.** This is the radical hope of the memory of the future.

It's a genuine possibility, but it's not an inevitability—just like the doomer position is not an inevitability, but a genuine possibility. It's real.

On some days, I am convinced that it's a genuine possibility. But on other days, my mood shifts. I've gathered an enormous amount of empirical data that point in a different direction, and on those other days, I think that we're preparing for the day after.

I don't mean *the day after* in a formal, precise way. I mean after the systems have either broken down, or we've had a near-extinction event, and we need to rebuild, or there has been a death of *our* humanity, and we need a rebellion, and we need to reclaim our humanity at the next level.

Whatever the day after looks like:

- We need the codes of the future.
- We need the sutras of the future.
- We need the new Story of Value that can hold us in the future.

So perhaps we are writing these codes for the day after.

Now, of course, it shouldn't be a sharp dichotomy—it's both to avert catastrophe and prepare for the day after.

And of course, mood *matters*. Part of what we're doing is changing the mood of the future. And we change the mood of the future by changing our own mood. Heidegger wasn't wrong when he said that mood is the fundamental constituent of Reality.

> *We change our mood by changing the way love moves in us, by changing our vision of Reality, and by changing the story from within which we generate consciousness.*

I remember years ago working with someone who was extremely depressed, and we finally explicated what the story was that he had been living within. And I said to him, "If I lived within that story, I'd be much more depressed than you are."

- What's the framework?
- What's the Story of Value?
- What's the grammar of value that forms my sentences and shapes my mood?

Both answers are true.

We hold the knowing that **the same evolutionary impulse that incepted Reality moves through us right now.** Evolution moved and transmuted, and the force of *She*, the force of Eros, and the force of value coded in

Cosmos sought its deeper and higher fulfillments. Those forces live in us. We are the evolutionary impulse in person.

We are value—coded in us, as us, and through us in person.

We are the Possibility of the Possibility of evolution.

That is absolutely true. We can do this. We are the evolution of love. We actually *can* be that *da Vinci force* in this time between worlds and time between stories and create a better world.

It's not inevitable, and it's not a Pollyannaish given, just like the doomer position is a real possibility, yet not inevitable. It depends on us.

It depends on us willing to go all the way, to stand all the way, and to be *Homo amor* all the way. This is absolutely worth doing. It's the most worthwhile thing we could possibly do.

Even if we knew we would fail at averting the meta-crisis, I would do the exact same thing. We would write a Great Library. We would download it into the source code of consciousness and culture.

We want to download the new Story of Value into the source code of culture, so that people who want to go *deep in* and actually become *part* of the new story—to become a unique, individuated, irreducibly gorgeous expressions of the One Love—can actually hear *the whole thing*.

We want to download a Great Library that source-codes the future—whether it averts the meta-crisis or codes the days, the years, and the centuries after.

THE ULTIMATE APPETITE OF THE UNIVERSE IS FOR ULTIMATE BEAUTY

Point two: There is an enormous amount of great and gorgeous things happening all over the world. That's really important to say. We are not simply at a place of breakdown.

I have said this many times before, but sometimes it gets lost.

There are several sentences that are incepting the vision of CosmoErotic Humanism, this new Story of Value we articulate in response to the meta-crisis.

The first sentence is: **We live in a world of outrageous pain, and the only response to the outrageous pain is Outrageous Love.**

We refuse to look away from the outrageous pain. We refuse to give Pollyannaish responses to the outrageous pain—whether they are classical spiritual responses or the New-Age responses:

- The classical spiritual responses say the outrageous pain is ultimately only an illusion. If I rest in eternity, there is no suffering. Although there *is* a deep truth to that, it's ultimately a Pollyannaish response, which violates the integrity and dignity of humanity. It's a non-humanistic response, which goes against CosmoErotic Humanism, a non-dual humanism that honors the irreducible dignity of *every* human being—and that includes *the dignity of suffering*.
- The New Age response is: *You created it*. This is all your creation. If you just shift your attitude, it'll disappear. Not true.

You *do* need to shift your attitude.

We need to transform.

We need to change our mood, and we need to evolve our consciousness—*and* suffering is real.

We don't turn away from suffering, and we don't allow either a fundamentalist mystical or a fundamentalist New Age Pollyannaish response to degrade the dignity of suffering. We take it seriously. We live in a world of outrageous pain. We refuse to let *theo-logic* of any form allow us to turn away from that suffering.

The only response to outrageous pain is Outrageous Love. Outrageous Love is not ordinary love. It's not love as a social construction. It's the force of Eros that moves through Reality. It's not mere human sentiment; it's the heart of existence itself.

That force of Eros that moves through Reality is not just Eros. It's ErosValue.

It's ErosValue. There is no split between Eros and value, so we have coined a new term, we call it *ErosValue*.

Value is *valentia* in Latin, which means "worth." Meaning we are *worthy*. It is related to the word *valid*, as in *I validate*, or *valor*: the hero aligns with value in Reality.

It is also related to the word *valence*. The valence of an atom is its combinatorial power. The movement of Eros of the atom, the movement to combine elements into something new. *Covalence* refers to shared electrons between atoms. Valence is the Eros of Reality, which is the movement towards deeper contact, and greater wholes.

Valence is the poetry of Reality, the poetry of the sciences. It's the nature of Reality itself.

There is an ErosValue in Reality, and there is an *ErosValence* in Reality, which moves towards *ever deeper* gorgeousness, *ever deeper* goodness, truth, and beauty.

And that has not stopped.

It's not just that we live in a world of outrageous pain, and the only response is Outrageous Love.

We live in a world of outrageous *beauty*, and the only response is Outrageous Love.

By beauty, I don't just mean *aesthetic* beauty, although aesthetic beauty is a form of Reality that reminds us of Reality's goodness. I look at the depth of aesthetic beauty, the depth of the color blue, and I feel Reality embracing me with aesthetic pleasure. All forms of aesthetic pleasure in their depth remind us of the sanity of Reality.

By beauty, I mean the way the interior sciences of Hebrew wisdom use the word to mean that which embraces all value. **Beauty is the place where all contradictions of value become paradoxes, and they all have a place.**

Whitehead says, *the ultimate appetite of the Universe is for ultimate beauty*. He's speaking in a way that's similar to the interior sciences of the wisdom of Solomon. The Universe moves towards more beauty, which is more value, and that's happening all over the place. The world is filled with outrageous beauty, and technology is filled with outrageous potential for new potency.

BETWEEN DYSTOPIA AND UTOPIA

The planetary stack could come alive—what Benjamin Bratton describes as the technologically wired Reality we all live inside, encircling the planet in a kind of temple.

Will it be a temple of Solomon or a temple of doom?

That is what we mean when we say we are poised between utopia and dystopia.

We are literally inside of that planetary stack.

It means that we are not just poised before *dystopia*—we are poised before potential *utopia*. However, and this is the big however, **the planetary stack will be animated by the simple first principles and rules that govern it**. The way the technology goes will not be determined by people declaring techno-optimist manifestos, by people who call themselves *effective* *accelerationists*, or by those who talk about the inevitability of technological progress.

That will get us nowhere.

You have to look at what are the simple First Principles and First Values that animate the temple: Is the direction they take us in—their plotline—*collapse*? Or is there a plotline of *emergence*?

Does the plotline lead to catastrophic and existential risk?

That's currently the major plotline. The major plotline right now, based on the simple First Principles and First Values that govern public culture and private culture in most of the world is leading us towards dystopia and breakdown:

- whether it's degraded forms of fundamentalism of the religious kind
- or degraded forms of reductive materialism of the scientific kind

But it's not that there isn't outrageous beauty happening all the time—*there is*!

- There are billions of people doing beautiful things.
- There are mothers holding children and children holding fathers.
- There are people working for peace.
- There are people taking care of each other.
- There are people pouring goodness into each other all the time.

Don't allow legacy media governed by win/lose metrics to hijack your view of Reality!

Just as an example, take the legacy media of the United States of America. In 2016, the entire liberal legacy media hated Donald Trump, and yet they helped elect him because every single individual legacy media company was in the red at the beginning of the 2016 presidential election in the United States. Donald Trump brought in ratings. He was the ultimate clickbait. He put all those companies in the black, so they covered him in a disproportionate way, which helped him to get elected.

Their claimed values were that Donald Trump is the Antichrist, and yet they helped him because what actually governed their behavior was rivalrous conflict governed by win/lose metrics:

- Both *personally*, in terms of each person keeping their own positions as CEO, vice president, senior executive, etc.
- And in terms of the win/lose metrics of *the companies* vying for market share with each other, which corrupted and destroyed their values.

But of course, since they didn't believe that value was real anyway, the only value that *actually* drove them was this rivalrous conflict governed by win/lose metrics, which leads to negative outcomes. It's a big deal. We are poised between utopia and dystopia.

However, the way it's going to go is a dystopia, unless we change the Story of Value and recognize that there actually are plotlines of Reality that are not contrived or socially constructed. There *is* actually intrinsic value in the Universe. **Value is backed by the Universe, and therefore, we can be heroes.** To be a hero is to align with the value of the Universe.

GREAT THINGS ARE HAPPENING ALL OVER THE PLACE

To sum up:

- The first question was, *are we articulating the new story for the day after, or are we trying to avert the meta-crisis?*
- Then we brought back online three core statements: We

live in a world of outrageous pain. The only response to outrageous pain is Outrageous Love. We live in a world of outrageous beauty—and the only response to outrageous beauty is Outrageous Love.

- That leads us to part three, which we've already expressed: **Outrageous beauty is happening all the time.** We are *not* (just) in a place of breakdown. We are in a place of radical emergence and breakthroughs of all kinds all over the place.

Part of social synergy is to be able to connect that which is already working, which has already broken through. We need to create new modalities of social synergy.

This was one of Barbara's dreams—my beloved evolutionary whole mate, Barbara Marx Hubbard. One of her dreams and one of my dreams is what she called a *Social Synergy Engine* to connect what's working worldwide. I called it a *Unique Self Facebook*. It could actually change the very structure of Reality. The problem is to do it right costs between five and ten million dollars—but that's not an insurmountable problem at all. We can create a Social Synergy Engine in which we generate relationships between the different sectors of co-creation.

Barbara created what she called "The Wheel of Co-Creation." Before Barbara died, we created what we called Wheel of Co-Creation 2.0, and the idea was to identify the most successful breakthroughs and then create social synergy between the different sectors of the wheel—economics, politics, education, etc. It was a great social experiment that never got implemented. Barbara and I spent the last few years of Barbara's life talking about what it would mean to implement it.

But put that aside for a second. The truth is there are great things happening all over the place. And as I said, don't allow the legacy media to hijack your view of Reality.

Reality is *not* a bunch of corrupt people running around who are all degraded and satanic. That is not the nature of Reality. No, the nature of Reality is gorgeous, stunning, beautiful, unimaginable people—men, women, children, white, brown, black, old, and young of all types, and all forms, and all shapes—who are actually *living* in the Field of Value because they feel it inside of them, even if they can't articulate it. They are desperate for an articulation of the new story, but they are already living it in some way.

It's gorgeous. People are gorgeous all over the place.

This is why I am filled with hope.

And yet—we also need to articulate a new story that people can live in, that people can come *together* in.

We need to articulate a vision, a strange attractor that calls us to the future.

We need to move beyond closed societies and open societies and integrate the best of both:

- The best of closed societies that have *organizing principles*
- The best of open societies that are *fully free and individuated*

In other words, we need to create a new way, a new attractor into the future, which is the emergence of **a new Story of Value as a context for our diversity**.

We're focusing on creating a shared Story of Value because that drives everything else, and a shared Story of Value emerges from the establishment of First Principles and First Values. We just published a book, our first attempt to articulate First Principles and First Values.

It's not Marc Gafni's name up there, and it's not Zak Stein's, and it's not Ken Wilber's. We wrote it under the name of David J. Temple because at key moments in history, as Pitrim Sorokin at Harvard pointed out, we move to transcend the win/lose metrics, to transcend the egoic posturing of authors, and to create something new.

Let's create a new angel.

Let's create a new voice in history.

- That's what the sutras were.
- That's what the Vedas were.
- That's what the Bible was.
- That's what the Zohar was.
- Perhaps that's what Shakespeare was.

Let's create David J. Temple, this new figure. By the way, I don't know if David is a girl's name or a boy's name. Not clear. Maybe David's trans; I'm not sure. But in any case, David J. Temple is writing First Principles and First Values.

That's what we are here to do.

WE NEED TO CROSS TO THE OTHER SIDE

Let me see if I can phrase it in another way.

We need to respond to crisis by *crossing*. It's *The Crossing* that responds to the crisis, and that's always been true in history. It always means to cross from one side to the other side.

Ibrahim is the father of the Islamic world, the father of the Judeo-Christian world in many lineage traditions, and a primary player in the world of the East, of Buddhism and Kashmir Shaivism. There's a story of Ibrahim sending messengers to the east. This mythical historical figure experiences that the whole world is on one side, *ever echad* in Hebrew, where the word *side* also means "past." The world is locked in cycles of prior causation. It cannot break out of the patterns of the past. And so, Ibrahim says:

> I'm going to cross to the other side. I'm going to become the new human. I'm going to introduce, through my very being, through my Unique Self, a new Story of Value, a new story of what it means to be a human being.

This births an explosion of *ethos* in the world:

- The explosion of what we call history
- The seeds of universal human rights
- The seeds of the emergence of the feminine
- This new Story of Value
- This crossing to the other side

The great artists and scientists of the Renaissance—artists and scientists always need to be together, as they are inter-included with each other—also came together, in that time between worlds and that time between stories after the Black Death had destroyed Europe and the old order was breaking down, as unimaginable suffering with no known cause was plaguing bodies and hearts, and destroying the fabric of much of civilized humanity.

Da Vinci, Marsilio Ficino, and others—artists and scientists—came together and told a new Story of Value. They crossed to the other side. They went from *crisis* to *crossing*, and their success in telling a new Story of Value birthed the plotlines of value, which—to the extent they were accurate—birthed the *dignities* of modernity. But to the extent that the plotlines were corrupt and missed essential dimensions, they birthed the *disasters* of modernity and brought us to the meta-crisis.

And now we are again at this time between worlds and time between stories. But this time, exponential technologies have the capacity to do what bows and arrows couldn't quite do. We now have thirteen or fourteen vectors of meta-crisis that have the capacity to actually destroy humanity—or to destroy *our* humanity.

So what do we need to do?

- We need to engage in *The Crossing*.
- We need to cross to the other side.
- We need to *not* look away.

We don't need another meditation event or another psychology event, although those all have enormous value, and they have their place. We *do* need them in terms of their right place in the architecture of Reality, but we don't need them to respond to the meta-crisis. They won't respond to the meta-crisis.

We need to articulate a new blueprint, a new Story of Value, the next level of human evolution, which is what Reality always does. It's the most realistic thing to do.

We need, at this moment, to cross to the other side, to move from crisis to crossing, from *Homo sapiens* to *Homo amor*, to actually become the new human and become the new humanity.

That is the invitation of this moment in time.

It's the most electrifying; it's that which causes the most trembling, the most celebratory, filled with quaking terror, and yet depths of joy and artistic, creative, Eros and possibility, filled with the Possibility of Possibility. That's *The Crossing*. We've created an event in Europe called *The Crossing*.

The Crossing is an expression of this new Story of Value that I've been working to articulate for the last thirty years. I've invited many wondrous, gorgeous people to participate in those conversations, and I've drawn from many conversations and many people around the world:

- One Mountain, Many Paths, founded with Barbara Marx Hubbard
- The Center for World Philosophy and Religion (formerly Center for Integral Wisdom), founded with Ken Wilber and Sally Kempton
- The Great Library, which is co-emerging from joining with Zak Stein

There are dozens of names that I could mention who have taken a critical and crucial role.

At a certain point, I called my dear friend James Bampfield, who came to study this teaching, this *dharma* in 2015, and was with us for five, six, seven festivals, dove in deeply, and read deeply. James is an excellent facilitator. I called him and invited him to join me in enacting The Crossing, to bring his skill of facilitation and his skill of convening. He has stepped in as a partner on the facilitative, operational, and convening dimension. And I am holding the Story of Value, the *dharma*, if you will, this vision that we have been in for all these years. We are coming together to enact this crossing.

The Crossing happens inside of each of us.

That's how The Crossing happens.

- We *decide* we are going to cross over, and we decide we are going to *take a risk*.
- We *decide* we are going to be the new human.
- We *decide* we're going to be the new humanity.

MOTIVATIONAL ARCHITECTURE FOR CHANGE

We come together every week to be in an intimate communion with each other.

We come together to hold hands.

We come together to practice.

Why would we say "I love you" if we already know that we love each other? We say "I love you" because when we say "I love you," a *new* love is born, a new *intimacy* is born.

We place our attention. **We come together to place our attention on the evolution of consciousness, which is the evolution of love.**

We come together to place our attention on what it means for us to move from *Homo sapiens* to *Homo amor*.

We come together to love this moment in history open and take our places at the table of history.

We come together to actually cross over to the other side. We come together every week to do *The Crossing*.

That's what it's about. We are practicing. We are meditating. We are in the deep space of the Field of Value, which is who we are.

That's our true selves. And then we experience our unique individuation in that field. Then we play our instruments in the Unique Self Symphony. But we do it every week because we are polishing the stone of the new human that lives in us.

> *The Crossing means that I actually place crossing to the other side at the center of my consciousness.*

It's not a hobby. It's not something I do once a week for an hour and give another couple hours and give some resources to but am basically otherwise living my life. That's *Homo sapiens*. That's *Homo sapiens* with a hobby, which is great. But to be *Homo amor* means that I'm actually willing to take the unique risk to step out as the new human and the new humanity.

A colleague of mine wrote a bunch of points about the meta-crisis. His main point is: "We could solve this, but we're not going to." He writes,

> Could we invent our way into abundance? Could we heal our planet, feed the world? Could we usher in the next chapter of a joyful human renaissance? Could we invent our way into abundance, govern ourselves to peace and equity? Could we not just maintain, but even increase our prosperity and standard of living for ten billion souls on this earth? Yeah, we could. It's a major lift, but not impossible, but we're not going to.

So why? What he basically says is that we're just not going to change. There is no motivational architecture to change. But that's not exactly right—it's exactly wrong.

There *is* a motivational architecture to change.

There is a motivational architecture to *The Crossing*.

That motivational architecture is the erotic motive of Cosmos itself. It is the ErosValue of Reality. It is the valences of Cosmos moving towards the evolution of consciousness, which is the evolution of love, the evolution of value.

It's the ability to take a stand, make distinctions, and know that ErosValue lives in me and calls me forward and that I shouldn't spend my whole life reorganizing the memories of my past.

Yes, we need to recover our past memories, stabilize, and allow ourselves to find our ways through the traumas of yesterday. But that won't take us home. I won't even be able to find my way through the recovered traumas of yesterday, through the memories of yesterday, unless **I am pulled forward by a memory of the future, in which I'm in the unique Eros of my life, giving my unique gift, taking my unique risk, and going all the way in this lifetime.**

If you want to know how to deal with the fear of death, you cannot deal with the fear of death just by making it benign, sweet, nice, and lovely, or even exhilarating and ecstatic.

Those are all beautiful things to do, and they should be done, but **you can really only deal with the fear of death by living life to its absolute fullest *now*.**

To live life to its absolute fullest now is not about *The Bucket List* movie, with all due respect. It's not about your bucket list, which is about the separate self.

The real bucket list is: What are the ten unique risks that I need to take with my time, my heart, my money, my creativity, my attention, my Eros, my intimacy, my forgiveness, my discernment, my effort, my commitment, my steadiness?

Unique risk doesn't mean to be foolhardy.

It means moving from *Homo sapiens* to *Homo amor*.

TAKING UNIQUE RISK

The reason I'm hopeful is because I believe in people.

And the reason my mood changes is that I'm sometimes devastated by people not being who they should be. Sometimes I am devastated by myself.

- Why am I not trying harder?
- Why am I not working harder?
- Why am I not more focused?
- Why am I not placing more attention?

But it's in joy. It's in celebration.

We can do this. And there is *a joy in the demand*. It's not an anxiety demand. It's not like, "Oh my God, here's another schoolmaster. Here's another reprimand. Here's another controller from the outside." No, none of that.

My unique risk is to do what love demands of me for the sake of my highest fulfillment and my highest transformation, which—if I'm awake and feeling the whole—is also the highest fulfillment and highest transformation of the whole.

But it's a risk. And it has to be outrageous. You've got to be outrageous.

> *We live in a world of outrageous pain.*
> *Our response to outrageous pain is Outrageous Love.*
> *We live in a world of outrageous beauty.*

> *The only response to outrageous beauty is Outrageous Love.*

So, we've got to step forward and say, "I'm crossing over." I'm not worried if it's going to be unpopular to three or four people. I'm not worried because I got some critique. I'm not worried about what they're going to say about me. I'm going to lead.

To be a leader means I'm going to step out in front. I'm going to trust my body, and I'm going to trust *Homo amor* emerging in me.

- I'm going to trust my capacity.
- I'm going to trust my unique gift.
- I'm going to trust my irreducible, unique pleasure.

The greatest pleasure is the pleasure of power—not *power over*, but the evolutionary impulse, the power of Cosmos moving in me that can actually impact and transform the whole. That's the pleasure of power. **We don't think we have power, but we do**—when I step up, when I take my unique risk, when I go all the way, when I'm willing to have that clash with this person or that person, or with this or that split-off part of myself.

I'm willing to have the hard conversations, I'm willing to actually be unpopular in order to be popular with my own highest self.

That's a unique risk.

That's The Crossing.

That's to cross over to the other side.

At the moment of my death, the only way to be in full joy is to know that I've lived all the way, that I've crossed to the other side, that I haven't died as *Homo sapiens*, that I haven't died as *Homo armor*.

- I've taken my armor off.
- My heart is naked.
- I am *Homo amor*. I am the new human. I am the new

humanity.

It's that consciousness of *Homo amor*, which is my continuity of consciousness, which will take me into the next life and the next dimension and the next possibility.

PASSION IS THE ONLY TRUTH

I apologize if I am a little too passionate about all this. But this is a bit of an insincere apology.

Passion is the only truth.

Not *unclarified* passion. Unclarified passion is not passion. It's pathetic. And pathetic is okay—we've all been pathetic. Who hasn't been pathetic?

But unclarified passion is the *pathetic* that covers over the failure of potency.

The true passion—the throbbing, tumescent Cosmos that lives uniquely in me, as me, and through me, that's telling this new Story of Value—is taking my unique risk. That's crossing to the other side.

That's leading fearlessly.

That's not afraid of being unpopular.

That's telling a new Story of Value.

That's not being worried about, "What are my friends going to think?"

No, no, no...

- What am *I* going to feel?
- What am *I* going to think?
- Let me be in my wisdom and my feelings because I'll recognize this; I'll know it's true inside of me.
- I'm going to master this.
- I'm going to understand this.

- I'm going to place my attention and become a master of my attention.
- And I'm going to cross the other side.

So, my friends, who's willing to cross over? I'm going to cross to the other side—and then we are going to link hands together.

We *should* be ecstatic about it. We should not let cracked fundamentalisms seize ecstasy and hijack it as their property. We should be ecstatic.

- We should be *beside ourselves*, which is what *ecstasy* means—beside our separate selves and in our Unique Selves.
- We should be beside our *Homo sapiens* self and in our *Homo amor* self.
- We should feel the ecstatic urgency, and we should celebrate. It's a celebration.

It's only radical joy that's going to take us to the other side. And radical joy is often cracked with pain.

I am heartbroken most of the time. I am heartbroken most of the time for a thousand reasons. And my heart is ripped open with joy all the time for a billion reasons.

We have to put our hearts together. We hold hands together. We are "the ones we've been waiting for." Bono got it right. This is what's true. And we have to be willing to pour our hearts in, to pour everything in, but not because anybody told us to. No, no, no, because it wells up inside of us and it gives us more joy and more pleasure than anything else could possibly give us. Is that crazy? No—it's the only sanity.

Thank you. Thank you. Thank you.

CHAPTER EIGHTEEN

TOWARDS THE POST-TRAGIC HERO, PART 1

Episode 388 — March 17, 2024

I CANNOT BE WELCOME IN THE UNIVERSE UNLESS I AM A HERO

This is a very important week—in this time between worlds, this time between stories. We are going to talk about the hero today (we are using the word *hero* to refer to both male and female hero, in the same way as we use the word *poet*). It's one of our most important weeks. We're going to talk about the hero, and *be* the hero, and *become* the hero—because there's no way to respond to the meta-crisis without the emergence of a new Story of Value.

A new Story of Value answers three questions:

- **Where?**—Where am I?
- **Who?**—Who am I?
- **What?**—What ought to be done?

We call these the three great questions of CosmoErotic Humanism, the new Story of Value in response to the meta-crisis.

We are here to be heroes for Her Majesty, the Queen of the Universe.

Do you remember the Three Musketeers? *One for all, and all for one, and all for France.* To be a hero for Her Majesty Queen of the Universe—*Malchut*. An old friend of mine likes to talk about being *secret agents* for Her Majesty, the Queen of the Universe. It's beautiful.

To do that, we need to begin to understand what it means *to be the hero*—because to be the hero means something *new*. It's not the old version of the hero. To be a hero for Her Majesty Queen of the Universe—along with the King of the Universe, in *hieros gamos*, with line and circle together—we need to *participate* in royalty.

We are not only the hero *for the sake* of royalty—for the sake of the vision. **We *become* the vision**. We *become* the royalty. I actually become the queen; I become the king.

We want to talk about how to evolve the source code and elicit the new hero.

I cannot be welcome in the universe unless I am a hero.

It's okay—and sometimes beautiful and necessary—to critique each other. But we can never critique each other in a way that undermines our ability to evoke the hero in you. I want you to get this distinction. It's so precise and so beautiful.

There's a certain kind of critique that we can hold: You are giving me an important critique to help me become better.

But there is another critique that has a withering effect. It's the silent assassin of the anti-hero. "There are no heroes. You're not a hero. I'm not a hero. There's no *Her Majesty*. There's no Field of Eros." And I critique you in a way that undermines your capacity to be a hero. Sometimes friends do that to each other. Sometimes parents do that to their children. Sometimes children do it to their parents. Sometimes a teacher does it to their students, or students do it to their teacher. All of that is off-limits. *None* of that is okay.

All critique has to be in the context of *welcome*—and I can only welcome you if I can *see* you, if I can *love* you madly.

To love is to see with God's eyes.

To be a lover is to see with God's eyes.

To see with God's eyes is to see that my significant other—whoever that significant other is—as a hero. My beloved—whoever that beloved is in my circle of intimacy—is a hero. When someone sees me as a hero—and not in a bypass-y way, not in a superficial way. No, *you are a hero*—I am actually being seen with God's eyes.

Very few people know how to see us as a hero.

DEMOCRATIZATION OF THE HERO

"I took a New Age seminar, and I studied Joseph Campbell, and I'm on the hero's journey." This kind of language has been a bit overused. It's stopped meaning anything. But in fact: **Hero is the fundamental category of Reality itself. I am not I, unless I am a hero.**

Does that make sense? There's no *I* without being a hero. Who I am, in the most fundamental way, is a hero. The emergence of the new human and the new humanity, which emerges in this new Story of Value as a response to the meta-crisis—that's *Homo amor*:

- The human being who incarnates uniquely the Eros of the Universe,
- The human being who is giving their unique gifts and living

their unique presence, which itself becomes a gift as an expression—an irreducibly unique expression—of the Field of ErosValue.

That's a hero.

Homo amor is about the democratization of the hero.

It used to be that there were only a few heroes in service of Her Majesty Queen of the Universe, a mixture of public and private heroes: A few 007s, private heroes, and some Walter Scott public heroes and some Musketeers (from Dumas's novel). But in order to respond to the meta-crisis, we have to do the only thing that ever changes history—we have to tell a new Story of Value, in which *each one of us is a hero*, and we all have different roles. We have different instruments to play in the Unique Self Symphony—and we are *all* heroes, and then together, we form the Unique Self Symphony, which is the ultimate hero.

We have a name for the Unique Self Symphony. We have named the hero. **We have named the hero David J. Temple.** There is a book by David J. Temple, which is a pseudo-anonymous name, and it's the Unique Self Symphony itself, the hero.

I am only welcome in the universe if I am a hero.

I love feedback. Feedback is important. One of the things I've actually said in the Unique Self Symphony is that—and I function in many roles, but one of them is a teacher role—I want feedback always. But there is a distinction between two different kinds of feedback. I give feedback and sometimes sharp feedback. And I always want to hold that distinction on my side as well, which is I always want to give feedback that makes you *more* of a hero.

We recognize each other as heroes.

THE GLIMMERINGS OF THE HERO

Let me share with you how you can be more of a hero.

TOWARDS THE POST-TRAGIC HERO

I cannot be welcome in the universe unless I experience Reality profoundly *needing* me. I am needed to save the day.

Sometimes, I am actually a secret agent. 007 never gets disclosed. 007 is always operating behind the scenes. Sometimes, I am in the 007 mode. James Bond or Jane Bond—James's sister. She doesn't just have to be James's love interest. She can be Jane Bond. We like her.

And sometimes my job is to be the Three Musketeers, to be a public hero. It depends on what part of the incarnation and which incarnation. But it's all about being a hero.

Fundamentally, the people who love me know that I'm a hero. Now I've got to actually *be* that. That's what it means to become *Homo amor*.

We're going to be doing an event in a few weeks called *The Crossing*. I named it The Crossing after a hero named Ibrahim, Abraham. Abraham crosses over to the other side. He becomes the ultimate antecedent founder of Islam, Christianity, and Hebrew wisdom. He moves to the East as well. **He's a hero *because* he crosses to the other side.**

So let's cross to the other side.

The way I cross the other side is: I begin to *experience myself* as a hero. Can we hold that? It's so crazy deep. Let's go deep into the hero, but the beginning is a re-visioning of the self, but not an intellectual, cognitive restructuring. It is about how I actually experience myself: *I literally experience myself as a hero.*

I want you to notice the reaction to that. Our first reaction to that—even if we love each other, and I'm home, and I hope you love me, and I love you, and we love each other—nonetheless, our first reaction to that is psychological. "Huh! I wish he could do some psychological work to deal with that grandiosity." Otto Rank, one of the inner players in Freud's inner circle, talks about this. No! Wrong! **You cannot reduce the grandness of the hero to a superficial, reductive materialist grandiosity.**

The artist experiences his or herself as a hero: I've got to paint this canvas, I've got to write this verse—wherever the tapestry of my artistry might be and whatever form it might take. **When I experience myself as an artist, I experience myself as a hero.**

I experience the urgency of my creativity.

I experience that it's ultimately valuable, that it matters, that I stand for it with everything that I have, that I lay down my heart, body, and soul for it—and I have this sense of ecstatic urgency.

The artist is the hero. The hero is the foreshadowing of *Homo amor*. It's one of the reasons why in modernity and late modernity, and then in postmodernity, when the human being thought that he and she were stepping out of the Field of Value, they continued to revere art—not just love art, but *revere* art—because the artist is still the hero.

Or we revere sports figures as heroes. And then there were comic book heroes. It started with Superman with a bunch of kids doing the Superman thing in Cleveland, Ohio, in the 1930s. That was still the era of modernity, but then even as postmodernity exploded in the mid-1990s, it's still there. There is this glimmering of the hero.

But when you step out of the Field of Value, you go to *destroy* the hero. That's why postmodernity said there are no heroes. Postmodernity is the great destruction of the hero. Postmodernity problematized—in many ways correctly—the premodern and modern hero and then said there are no heroes. That heroism is a problem. That is fundamentalists blowing themselves up as suicide bombers. Yes, yes, of course, there is a problematized hero. Of course, we need to move from the pre-tragic hero to the tragic and recognize the potential tragic in the hero, but then we move to the post-tragic and reclaim the hero.

That's *Homo amor*.

That's the democratization of the hero. And literally the first spiritual practice before any other spiritual practice, number one—it's not two, it's not three, it's not four, it's number one—the very first and primary spiritual practice is: **I have to experience myself, accurately, as a hero**.

I commit to being a hero. That's The Crossing. That's crossing to the other side. I'm a hero. Not a *grandiose* hero but a hero, a *grand* hero.

It's only in the true grandness, which is the truest index of my real situation, that I begin to feel welcome in the universe.

EVOLUTIONARY LOVE CODE: HOMO AMOR IS THE POST-TRAGIC HERO

> There is no way to be filled with joy unless you are a hero. Heroes are real.
>
> Postmodernity problematized the hero. Postmodernity mocked the hero. Postmodernity said the hero is dangerous; let's do away with the hero.
>
> Postmodernity was not entirely wrong. Heroes were dying for the wrong things. Heroes were covering up their vulnerability, which was far greater than mere kryptonite.
>
> We *needed* to complexify the hero. But now that we've complexified the hero, we have to *reclaim* the hero. In CosmoErotic Humanism, we call this *the post-tragic hero*.
>
> *Homo amor* is the post-tragic hero.

BARAYE—FOR THE SAKE OF THE WHOLE

Shervin wrote a very beautiful song called "Baraye." He was sentenced to several years in prison for this song. It was in response to the terrible murder of a wonderful young woman, Mahsa Amini, in Iran, which set off this explosion of brutality, in which young boys and many young girls (meaning high-school age) were taken out, beaten, killed, abused for opposing the fundamentalist version of the hero, the premodern hero:

- who was the hero who had to deny their essential nature,
- who had to deny their participation in the Field of Value,
- who was the hero because they submitted to a larger field that wasn't *truly* a larger field.

It was a larger field that contradicted the language of their body, the language of the heart, and the language of their soul. But in submission to that, they were thought to be a hero. It's a desecration of the hero.

And so, Shervin writes a song. We are going to play the original version of the song with his words. He is going to prison. I want to really just honor him and be with him. And I want to find a way to actually make contact with him. He is a gorgeous man, and he is a hero. He is going to prison for standing against the old version of the hero. He actually incarnates the hero.

I want to just take a moment to honor the hero together and just hear that song. And see the words. And feel it together.

He is going to jail for several years for that song. May he be able to leave jail alive, whole, and healthy—which is not obvious.

We are here not in wisdo-tainment, not in entertainment. We are coming together as a Unique Self Symphony. In order to bring down this next chapter in the Story of Value, we want to become the hero.

I want to invite you to actually, in this moment—not later, not tomorrow, not in twenty minutes from now, but literally now—to make the transition. The transition is: *I am a hero*.

WHEN I AM AROUSED, I AM THE HERO: REALITY IS MAKING LOVE

Imagine what that means, to actually *be* a hero—then everything changes, doesn't it?

Everything changes—how I hold my anxiety and how I hold my pain. Isn't that true? This is *The Crossing*. The Crossing is right now. We are crossing to the other side. I am going to change the fundamental experience of who I am—not to a diluted grandiosity, but to an accurate grandeur, to knowing my true nature.

My true nature is I am *not* merely separate from the whole. The experience of being separate from the whole is an "optical delusion of consciousness." Albert Einstein got that one right. I am actually inseparable from the Field. The Field of the Whole is seamless. Everything is connected to everything. There is no separate self.

There is nothing that's separate.

But that Field is not merely a Field of *Awareness*. It's a Field of *Wholeness*. Can you feel that? Read David Bohm's later writings on the wholeness that Reality moves towards. One of the core qualities of Eros is the yearning for wholeness.

The field is not merely a Field of Awareness. Awareness is but one predicate of the field—the field is actually a Field of Wholeness. It's a Field of Eros.

One of the four core qualities of Eros, its primary quality, is wholeness—nothing is separate from anything. But it's a quivering, trembling, infinite, tender wholeness of which I am an irreducibly unique, gorgeous expression.

- I am a part of the whole that makes the whole more whole.
- I am a whole emergent from the whole that makes the whole more whole.
- I am a whole who is part of the larger whole.
- I participate in a larger whole.
- In realizing my own irreducibly unique wholeness, the Field of the Whole becomes more whole.

That's a hero. That's *Homo amor*!

Baraye means *for the sake of.* Isn't that gorgeous? *For the sake of.* I am a hero. I experience myself as the hero—and then my wholeness makes it all more whole.

The original lineage word for hero is *gibbor*. It has two meanings: it means *hero,* and it also means *arousal*. It's a particular quality. It is the line quality of arousal that lives in all men and all women. This line quality of arousal—because **when I am aroused, I am the hero**.

It's why lovemaking means arousal—whether you are kissing your partner's shoulder or just looking into their eyes across the room. Or it's with a friend or beloved... There are many ways to make love.

We've exiled lovemaking to a very narrow field.

***Reality* is making love.**

When I am making love, I am aroused—and when I am aroused, I am a hero. I actually get that what I'm doing is ultimately significant. I could be making love as I paint, as I write, as I search for a document, as I organize a piece, or as I'm writing an outrageously beautiful note to the milkman.

I'm telling them I am going to be away for a few days, so don't leave any milk. But then I add something to that note that makes it an Outrageous Love Letter—and the person feels recognized and seen. It is an Outrageous Love Letter.

It's the experience of being aroused. And **when I am aroused, I am in the field.**

See, there is no local arousal.

> *There is no local desire. It doesn't exist. All desire is non-local. I am participating in the Field of Desire.*

Even if it's completely unconscious, I am experiencing the whole moving through me. And I experience the ultimate significance of my actions, of my engagement.

Do you know why people kill and destroy each other—for the sake of passion, for the sake of relationships made and relationships broken?

Because they are disconnected and alienated from the Field of the Whole.

Because they don't feel like heroes at any place in their lives.

The only place where they feel a glimmering of the aliveness of being a hero is in that one relationship—and if you don't relate to me in the way I want to relate to you forever, and then I feel that I've lost access to the Field and to being a hero, I am going to kill you to cover up the emptiness. I am going to explode murderously to murder your Eros because I've lost access to mine.

No, no, no, no, no. The word *hero* and the word *arousal* are the same because the hero is omni-considerate for the sake of the whole. The whole lives in the hero. *Baraye*—for the sake of the whole.

We are going to play the song again, Shervin's song. Let's just be in it.

We are in practice. We are in mad, holy practice around the world.

We are the hero. We are coming together. We are linking hands. Heroes for Her Majesty. Shervin is a hero for Her Majesty Queen of the Universe.

Baraye means *for, for the sake of.* It changes everything. It is not a psychological strategy. It's *dharma. dharma* means the nature of Reality, the best integration of First Principles and First Values.

YOU KNOW AND I KNOW THAT YOU ARE A HERO

We just did the Academy Awards in the United States, in the year 2024, in the month of March. And Ryan Gosling did a rendition of "I'm Just Ken," which was the great Ken song in *Barbie*, which brought the house down at the Oscars. What a tragic moment! The entire point of the song is: I'm just Ken; I'm not really a hero.

When you read the text of the song, you realize that Ken is actually looking for the hero. He looks to his arousal, which is dismissed. He looks to his desire to love, which is dismissed. And then he just falls back into singing "I'm Just Ken," which is understood as a silly song. Why did this bring the house down? It was of course a beautiful moment. It was done well, aesthetically, artistically, at least from a performance perspective. It was actually a tragic moment because everyone got together around the silliness of it all. *I'm Just Ken.*

But I'm not just "Ken." I'm a fucking hero—Ken is a hero, and Barbie is a hero.

The universe desperately needs my service. I am the unique hero of Her Majesty Queen of the Universe. It's one for all and all for one.

I feel the whole pulsing in me, trembling in my body, I hear the voices of the trillions of unborn who look to our generation to be heroes.

That's why we're doing *The Crossing* in Europe. That's why we're doing the Mystery School. That's why there is a Center. That's why there's One Mountain—to be heroes. We are the heroes of the future.

And my friends—Romans, countrymen—lend me your ears just for a moment. We have to get over the fear of our grandiosity in order to be grand. This is the secret. It's the furtive secret that lurks deep within.

You know and I know that **you are a hero**. You know and I know that that's actually your true nature.

You know and I know that **your life *matters* insanely**.

You know and I know that **you were intended**. You didn't just appear; you were intended by All-That-Is. You are completely a radical surprise, and yet you were intended by All-That-Is.

You know and I know that **you are the chosen one**, that you are the one—that you are Paul Atreides, that you are Messiah, that you are the hero.

You know and I know that **you are recognized by All-That-Is**—recognized, seen. All of Reality is a stage and you are center stage. You are the hero.

You know and I know that **you are madly adored**. You're not just loved. You're adored by All-That-Is.

You know and I know that only a series of explosions of desire could have brought you into existence—unique meetings of desire. You know and I know that you're both contingent, **radical surprise** and an expression of the deepest, most stunning **design**. You are desired by All-That-Is.

And finally, you know and I know that **you are needed by All-That-Is**.

What are you needed for?

You are needed to be your unique transformation. Your transformation, my transformation. When I speak to you, I'm speaking to *me* and to *we*. A mirror in front of me, speaking out loud to you. **Your trajectory of transformation is heroic and unique—and from that place, you give your unique gift, which is desperately needed by All-That-Is.**

Sometimes you'll do it as a secret agent of Her Majesty Queen of the Universe. You're going to be her hero. Sometimes you'll do it publicly, but sometimes you'll do it as one of the Three Musketeers. But that's who you are. It's who I am. It's who we all are. We are a league of superheroes.

That's who we are but not fancifully, not as an interesting motivational talk. No.

It's the true nature of who we are.

INDEX

2001: A Space Odyssey (movie) 215

Abhinavagupta 160
Abraham 365
addiction 10, 212
Akiva 170
Alexanderi, Said R. 297
All-That-Is xxx, 13, 27, 30, 88, 105, 330, 372, 373
Amorous Cosmos 34, 268
Anthro-Ontology xii, xxxi, 32, 253, 254
Anthropocene 168
Ark of the Covenant 102
artificial intelligence xi, xii, xxxvi, 56, 154, 155, 175, 191, 192, 205, 206, 210, 211, 212, 213, 214, 215, 216, 217, 218, 219, 220, 221, 222, 223, 314, 315, 322
Auschwitz 14, 15, 16, 187

Baal Shem Tov 167
"Baraye" xv, 367, 370, 371
Barbie (movie) 371, 372
Beckett, Samuel 188
Being and Nothingness (Sartre) 139
Big Bang xi, 72, 116, 194, 202, 268, 321, 326, 327, 341
biosphere 9, 116, 123, 125, 217, 283, 327
Blessing of the Father 138
Blessing of the Mother 137, 138
Bloom, Howard 164
Bohm, David 369
Book of Psalms 119, 250
Bostrom, Nick 48, 51, 55

Campbell, Joseph 363
Carlebach, Shlomo 13
Center for World Philosophy and Religion iv
chanting 1, 22, 23, 24, 36, 37, 44, 64, 181
chaos theory xxi, 32, 170
Chapman, Gary 127
China 31, 49, 54, 55, 56, 57, 58, 61, 115, 133, 221, 249
Christ Consciousness 193, 260
codependency 76, 109, 132
Cohen, Leonard 8, 62, 63, 64, 119, 298
Confucianism 49
continuity of consciousness xxxi, 17, 25, 32, 103, 117, 118, 121, 359
CosmoErotic Humanism x, xvi, xx, xxi, xxiv, xxx, xxxviii, xl, xli, 24, 71, 79, 80, 87, 88, 96, 99, 153, 170, 183, 190, 207, 222, 267, 320, 324, 325, 327, 332, 335, 344, 361, 367
Covid pandemic xxxiii, 1, 2, 3, 4, 10
crisis of imagination 217, 222, 223, 224
crisis of intimacy xxxviii, 29, 81, 87, 93, 122, 124, 125, 130, 133, 135, 143, 151, 152, 175, 176, 222, 223, 247
curiosity 269

da Vinci, Leonardo xxvi, xxxiv, 22, 41, 89, 343
Dawn of Desire xiv, 319, 323, 324, 328, 335
death xxxi, xxxii, xxxiii, xxxviii, 1,

INDEX

13, 14, 15, 16, 17, 25, 26, 27, 32, 42, 48, 56, 57, 60, 95, 104, 109, 114, 115, 117, 118, 130, 137, 142, 154, 166, 177, 179, 206, 207, 221, 223, 263, 302, 307, 320, 322, 323, 338, 341, 356, 358

Debt (Graeber) 231

deepest heart's desire 28, 30, 59, 195, 196, 264, 294, 328, 331, 332, 333, 334, 335

democracy 43, 137, 219, 226, 232, 235, 243

Denial Response xiv, 319

depression 2, 275, 290, 300

dharma xvii, 12, 17, 36, 181

dignity 91, 109, 142, 143, 145, 149, 150, 166, 208, 237, 250, 263, 271, 272, 273, 274, 275, 277, 284, 291, 292, 293, 294, 320, 330, 331, 332, 337, 344

DiPerna, Dustin 185

Divine Field 312

Divinity viii, 75, 77, 80, 99, 103, 193, 335

dogma xvii, xviii, 7, 61

Domination Response xiv, 319

Doomer Response xiv, 319

Dostoevsky, Fyodor 139

Dowd, Michael 320, 321

Eastern Enlightenment 5

engagement 212, 214, 371

Eros of Cosmos 33

ErosValue xiv, xviii, 200, 254, 320, 335, 345, 356, 364

Evolutionary Love vi, vii, viii, ix, x, xi, xii, xiii, xiv, xv, xvii, xxiii, 6, 7, 33, 95, 96, 98, 101, 155, 172, 208, 303

Evolutionary Unique Self 31, 124, 148

Existential Psychotherapy (Yalom) 139

existential risk i, iii, xxvii, xxxi, xxxii, xxxv, xxxvi, xxxvii, xxxviii, xxxix, xl, 4, 12, 18, 21, 25, 26, 27, 48, 57, 60, 136, 155, 191, 205, 206, 207, 208, 209, 220, 223, 227, 249, 252, 263, 264, 301, 311, 315, 320, 321, 322, 323, 347

Eye of Consciousness 184

Eye of Desire 184

Eye of Value vii, 22, 23, 184

Farrell, Warren 137

Father xxiv, 137, 138, 140, 143

Feynman, Richard 116, 160, 181

Ficino, Marsilio xxxiv, 41, 352

Field of Desire xiv, 98, 265, 266, 281, 329, 330, 332, 333, 334, 370

Field of Eros 98, 265, 266, 268, 282, 302, 362, 369

Field of Intimacy 265, 266

Field of Outrageous Love 69, 97, 98

First Principles and First Values vi, xviii, xix, xx, xxiv, xxvi, xxvii, xxx, xxxi, xxxiii, xxxvi, xl, 1, 2, 12, 15, 17, 19, 20, 21, 22, 31, 36, 37, 42, 43, 44, 51, 52, 53, 55, 58, 59, 68, 94, 142, 155, 181, 183, 190, 206, 207, 249, 254, 302, 317, 320, 324, 347, 350, 351, 371

first shock of existence xxxi, xxxii, 25, 26, 27, 32, 33, 114, 177

Floyd, George 213

freedom 116, 146, 149, 150, 330

Freud, Sigmund 365

Getting the Love You Want (Hendricks) 127

global intimacy disorder xiv, xxxviii, 122

God
 as Infinity of Power xxiv, 63, 74, 77, 78, 99, 187, 193, 197, 204, 261
 as Infinity of Intimacy vii, xxiv, 8,

24, 77, 99, 181, 272, 334
Goddess viii, 22, 23, 65, 67, 68, 74, 78, 80, 82, 87, 88, 93, 94, 99, 101, 102, 113, 160, 162, 171, 174, 181, 231, 259, 260, 261, 287, 288, 300, 325, 329, 334
Gödel 20
Gordis, Daniel 238
Graeber, David 231
Gray, John 127
Great Library xx, xxii, 187, 207, 303, 343, 353

Habermas, Jürgen xxxiv, 41
Harari, Yuval 19, 140, 143, 209
Harris, Marvin 19, 43
Harris, Sam 23, 143
Hasidism 269, 270, 271, 290, 291
heartbreak 39, 81, 82, 199, 263, 269, 271, 273, 274, 275, 276, 277, 278, 279, 280, 283, 284, 285, 286, 287, 288, 289, 290, 291, 292, 296, 297, 298, 299, 300
Heidegger, Martin 139, 140, 151, 342
Hendricks, Harville 127
hero 373
Hinduism 22, 182
Hubbard, Barbara Marx xvi, 31, 32, 50, 115, 120, 121, 224, 247, 302, 309, 328, 349, 353
Hume, David 312, 313
hunchback 14, 15, 16

immortality 103, 104
Infinity of Intimacy vii, xxiv, 8, 24, 77, 99, 181, 272, 334
Integral Theory 185
interdependency 76
interior sciences xviii, xxx, xxxi, xl, xli, 20, 27, 37, 71, 72, 78, 79, 80, 81, 93, 96, 99, 102, 107, 160, 162, 170, 179, 184, 185, 259, 268, 269, 271, 325, 339, 346

Intimate Universe xiii, xxxviii, 24, 34, 65, 68, 93, 112, 151, 253, 262, 267, 268, 288, 297
Isaac of Vorki 269
I-Thou 62

Kahneman, Daniel 192
Kalman, Kalonymus 13, 14
Kant, Immanuel 313
Kashmir Shaivism xxi, 22, 160, 351
Kauffman, Stuart 116, 160, 283
Kincaid, Kristina xvi, xx, 267, 281

Laszlo, Ervin 177
Levi Yitzchok of Berditchev 8
Lewis, C.S. xi, 54, 207, 208, 209, 213
Lifton, Robert J. 321
LoveDesire xxviii, 13, 27, 200, 335
LoveIntelligence xxviii, 13, 27, 28, 31, 58, 62, 200, 250, 335
Lovejoy, Arthur 72
Luria, Isaac 170, 171

MacAskill, Will 48, 49, 51, 53, 54, 55, 248
Macy, Joanna 320, 340
Marshall, Perry 228, 283
Maslova-Levin, Elena xxiii, 229, 230
Mead, Margaret 138, 182
meditation 7, 353
Menachem Mendel 288
Men Are from Mars, Women Are from Venus (Gray) 127
Messiah 188, 373
Meta-crisis vii, 18, 207
Metzinger, Thomas 49
MIT Media Lab 143, 210, 223
Mizmor Shir 22
modernity xxxiv, 41, 44, 114, 115, 154, 163, 227, 264, 313, 352, 366
Mother xxiv, 79, 137, 138

neuro-cultural plasticity viii, 36

INDEX

nihilism 53, 55, 58
Noble, Denis 228
Nussbaum, Martha 270

Ord, Toby 48, 51, 55, 248
Outrageous Acts of Love ix, 28, 66, 67, 68, 69, 70, 71, 74, 75, 77, 78, 86, 87, 91, 92, 93, 97, 98, 99, 101, 103, 104, 105, 106, 112, 113, 250, 286

Parfit, Derek 48, 51, 54, 55, 248
Peirce, C.S. 96
Pentland, Alex 143, 192, 210, 211
Personhood vii, xxiv, 24, 63, 160, 181, 334
pleasure 2, 9, 52, 89, 112, 187, 201, 202, 203, 273, 276, 346, 358, 360
pleasure of transformation 9
Plotinus 79
pornography 195, 196, 203
postmodernity xxvii, 19, 21, 42, 44, 51, 313, 366
post-tragic xvii, 145, 150, 206, 290, 291, 366, 367
prayer vi, xiii, xiv, xxiii, xxiv, 7, 8, 62, 63, 64, 181, 245, 271, 272, 294, 309, 315, 316, 334
premodernity 40, 311, 312, 313, 317, 318
propaganda 218, 242
pseudo-eros xxi, 10, 11, 202, 203, 279, 311, 327

Rabin, Yitzhak 243
Rank, Otto 365
Reality is Eros xxx, 39, 269
Reality is relationship 62, 132
Reality needs your service 85
Reich, Wilhelm 54, 281
Reznikoff, Charles 163
Rodgers, Aaron 304, 305, 306, 309, 316, 317

role mate 122, 125, 126, 127, 128, 129, 132, 135, 143, 144, 145, 146, 147, 151, 257

sacred autobiography 34, 172, 197
Sartre, J.-P. 139
Schleiermacher, Friedrich 78, 79
second person of God xxiv, 8, 62, 160, 161
second shock of existence. xxxiii, 26, 114, 122, 177, 183, 190
second simplicity xvii, 27, 229, 290
sexual models Eros 102, 150
Shakespeare, William 284, 351
Shakti 23, 250
shame 97, 198, 239, 251, 291
Shapiro, James 117, 228
shevirat ha-kelim (the shattering of the vessels) 79, 80, 268
Simcha Bunim of Peshischa 299
Singer, Peter 248
Skinner, B.F. 209, 210, 211, 218, 219, 223, 320
Skinner box 209, 210, 218, 223, 320
social media 191, 192, 206, 210, 211, 214, 215, 217, 218, 224, 349
Social Physics (Pentland) xi, 192, 210
Solomon xxi, 95, 102, 161, 170, 260, 261, 268, 271, 272, 297, 346
Song of Songs 95
Sorokin, Pitrim 350
soul mate 122, 125, 127, 128, 129, 130, 131, 132, 133, 134, 135, 143, 144, 145, 146, 147, 151, 172, 257
Soul Prints (Gafni) 162, 176
source code of consciousness and culture xxi, xxv, xxvii, 2, 12, 24, 79, 95, 106, 118, 151, 152, 154, 157, 166, 189, 206, 247, 249, 262, 263, 311, 343, 362
Star Wars 25, 160
Stein, Zak xi, xvi, xx, xxiii, xxxi, 6,

31, 96, 177, 205, 213, 214, 222, 223, 224, 253, 350, 353
Story of Value vii, xi, xii, xiv, xv, xvi, xvii, xviii, xix, xx, xxiii, xxv, xxvi, xxvii, xxix, xxxiii, xxxiv, xxxvi, xxxix, xl, xli, 20, 21, 22, 41, 42, 44, 51, 52, 58, 59, 61, 66, 67, 68, 71, 80, 94, 95, 96, 99, 110, 115, 118, 119, 120, 121, 122, 124, 142, 143, 144, 153, 154, 155, 156, 157, 158, 160, 166, 168, 170, 174, 178, 180, 181, 183, 190, 191, 192, 206, 222, 249, 264, 265, 266, 267, 302, 303, 310, 311, 317, 320, 324, 325, 332, 333, 337, 338, 339, 340, 342, 343, 344, 348, 350, 351, 352, 353, 354, 359, 361, 363, 364, 368
suicide 2, 15, 58, 366
superstructure 19, 42, 43, 57, 68, 155, 192, 324, 339

Taoism 49, 208
Tao, the xviii, 54, 55, 82, 208, 209, 318
TechnoFeudalism 213, 214, 320
Thank God for Evolution (Dowd) 320, 321
The Abandonment of the Jews (Wyman) 187
The Age of Surveillance Capitalism (Zuboff) 212
The Book of Creation 162
the erotic and the holy are one 150
The Five Love Languages (Chapman) 127
The Holy Fire (Kalman) 13
The Language of Emotions (Nussbaum) 270
The Lord of the Rings 207
The Matrix (movie) 307
The Universe: A Love Story xxxviii, 33, 117, 177

third person of God xxiv, 62, 160, 161
tikkun 81, 82, 298
time between stories xvii, xxvii, xxxiii, 40, 49, 50, 51, 53, 58, 59, 173, 175, 183, 190, 247, 248, 302, 343, 352, 361
Tolkien, J.R.R. 207
Toward a Psychology of Awakening (Welwood) 5
trauma 38, 96, 97, 101, 110, 111, 112, 127, 129, 144
Trilling, Lionel 171
True Self 5, 6, 31, 96, 97, 98, 101, 112, 124, 148, 152, 198, 329
tzadik 80
tzimtzum 80

Ukraine 59, 229, 230, 231, 233, 236, 243, 245, 248
unique gift 28, 30, 62, 224, 266, 356, 358, 373
unique risk 85, 86, 87, 103, 104, 105, 106, 112, 201, 355, 356, 357, 358, 359
Unique Self vii, ix, x, xvii, xx, xxii, 6, 11, 18, 22, 24, 25, 26, 27, 28, 29, 30, 31, 32, 33, 35, 55, 57, 61, 62, 67, 68, 74, 84, 86, 87, 88, 92, 94, 97, 100, 101, 102, 103, 104, 105, 106, 112, 124, 148, 152, 157, 158, 164, 167, 172, 173, 177, 180, 185, 189, 197, 198, 201, 203, 223, 224, 250, 266, 275, 295, 319, 322, 329, 332, 337, 349, 351, 355, 364, 368
Unique Self Symphony vii, xvii, xxii, 6, 22, 25, 27, 28, 29, 30, 31, 32, 35, 57, 61, 62, 86, 88, 94, 101, 103, 105, 106, 148, 158, 173, 180, 189, 201, 224, 250, 266, 329, 332, 337, 355, 364, 368
Up from Eden (Wilber) 7

Waiting for Godot (Beckett) 188
Weir, Andy 45
Welwood, John 5
What We Owe The Future (MacAskill) 49
Wheeler, John Archibald 9, 266
Whitehead, Alfred North 39, 67, 96, 328, 346
whole mate 119, 122, 131, 132, 133, 134, 135, 143, 144, 145, 148, 151, 152, 257, 302, 328, 349
Wilber, Ken xvi, xx, 5, 7, 185, 350, 353
Wyman, David 187

Yab-Yum 102
Yalom, Irvin 139, 140, 143, 151

Zohar 85, 160, 170, 351
Zuboff, Shoshana 211, 212, 213, 216

Volume 23 — Existential Risk and the Evolution of Love

LIST OF EPISODES

1. Episode 201 — August 16, 2020
2. Episode 279 — February 13, 2022
3. Episode 315 — October 23, 2022
4. Episode 334 — March 5, 2023
5. Episode 335 — March 12, 2023
6. Episode 340 — April 16, 2023
7. Episode 341 — April 23, 2023
8. Episode 347 — June 4, 2023
9. Episode 348 — June 11, 2023
10. Episode 349 — June 18, 2023
11. Episode 351 — July 2, 2023
12. Episode 352 — July 9, 2023
13. Episode 353 — July 16, 2023
14. Episode 354 — July 23, 2023
15. Episode 360 — September 3, 2023
16. Episode 362 — September 17, 2023
17. Episode 383 — February 11, 2024
18. Episode 388 — March 17, 2024

www.ingramcontent.com/pod-product-compliance
Lightning Source LLC
Chambersburg PA
CBHW032029150426
43194CB00006B/206